Introducing Marketing

Gordon Wills is Principal and Professor of Customer Policy of the International Management Centre from Buckingham. He has held professorial appointments at Cranfield and Bradford, taught extensively in Australia, Canada and the United States and lectured throughout Europe, Asia and Central America. A prolific writer on marketing, he is co-author of *Effective Distribution Management*, also published by Pan.

John Cheese is Assistant Director of the Centre for Bank Marketing and Fellow of the International Management Centre from Buckingham.

Sherril Kennedy combines chairmanship of an electronics company with the post of Professor of Marketing Communications at the International Management Centre from Buckingham.

Angela Rushton has her own business called Time-Share Marketing, which provides marketing services for small businesses. She was formerly Director of the Centre for Small Business Development at the International Management Centre from Buckingham. She is co-author of the Pan book *Effective Distribution Management*.

Gordon Wills   John Cheese
Sherril Kennedy   Angela Rushton

Introducing Marketing

revised edition

Pan Books   London and Sydney

First published 1975 by MCB Publications Ltd, Bradford
Published 1980 by Pan Books Ltd
This new and revised edition published 1983
by MCB University Press Ltd, Bradford
Published 1984 by Pan Books Ltd,
Cavaye Place, London SW10 9PG
9 8 7 6 5 4 3 2
© Gordon Wills, John Cheese, Sherril Kennedy, Angela Rushton 1984
ISBN 0 330 28380 4
Phototypeset by Input Typesetting Ltd, London
Printed and bound in Great Britain by
Cox & Wyman Ltd, Reading

Contents

Preface

Introducing Marketing is a practical textbook on marketing. It will be of primary interest and value to those managers who have an interest but no formal training in marketing and who have neither the time nor the inclination to decipher jargon-ridden specialist volumes where theory seems to have totally usurped practice. A concern to see marketing in its total business context does not, of course, apply solely to non-marketers and we anticipate that both marketing practitioners and marketing students will find the book useful for their different purposes.

In earlier editions, with the titles *Effective Marketing Management* and *Introduction to Marketing*, the book has proved successful both as a background text for training programmes and as an aid to individual learning. The text has its origins in our experience of teaching marketing to post-graduate students at University Business School level. The first edition of the text had as a co-author Dr David Walters who is now at the Oxford Management Centre. Subsequent editions prior to this major re-write were co-authored with Professor Martin Christopher and Dr Malcolm McDonald at Cranfield School of Management.

This new edition introduces a wider range of practical examples of different marketing situations from organisations operating both at home and abroad in industrial, consumer and service markets. In the chapters of the text which discuss the detail of marketing's four 'P's – product, place, price and promotion – we have also introduced 'action points' which offer practical guidelines to the marketer.

One of the features which readers found particularly useful in the earlier editions was the structuring of the text round a series of questions which are commonly asked about marketing. This feature we have retained but in a revised form which allows for a greater ease of reference and which points up the need for all marketing activity to culminate in a successful sales effort. By posing 'application questions' at the end of each chapter, the book also continues to encourage readers to relate what they have learned to the activities of their own organisations.

Many colleagues contributed to the text in its final form. In particular, William Giles offered many insights on the subject of marketing planning; and Paul Fifield devoted much time and care to the chapter on international marketing.

Abby Day, Gillian E. Hanscombe and Marsaili Cameron gave valuable editorial help. We are also extremely grateful to Maryanne Mills, David Seekings and Derry Young for their hard work, skill and patience during the production of the book.

JC SHK AR GSCW
October 1983
IMCB, the International Management Centre from Buckingham, Castle Street, Buckingham, Buckinghamshire, England

1   What is marketing?

Overview

The focal point of an organisation's activities should be the wants of its customers. Marketing provides the match between the organisation's human, financial and physical resources and these wants. It must do this against a background of the dynamic characteristics of the environment in which the matching takes place. This includes direct and indirect competition, economic uncertainties, legal and political constraints, cultural and social trends, technological change and institutional patterns.

The matching is typically undertaken for an organisation by a formalised department headed by a senior executive at board level. He plans, coordinates, and controls the product *or service offered, the* price *that is charged, the style of* promotion *and the* place *where it is to be made available. In doing so, he is concerned with not only the separate effects of these four 'P's, but also their interactive effects. This blend of the four 'P's is known as the marketing mix.*

Meeting customers' wants

Marketing is the way in which an organisation matches its own human, financial and physical resources with the wants of its customers. Since many organisations continue in business over relatively long periods of time, it is necessary for them to plan both the particular human, financial and physical resources they offer and the particular customer wants they wish to serve. The need to look ahead and to develop products, services and groups of customers normally requires all medium or large organisations to formalise marketing as a specific activity if the matching process is to be successfully accomplished. Whether or not a formalised activity is present, the matching inevitably proceeds. Unless its causes are speedily detected, any mis-match leads to failure because customers will simply refrain from acquiring the product or service offered. The customer is also undertaking a continuous process of matching his or her wants with the offerings of the competing organisations.

In the simplest market place the customer and the marketer meet personally. The customer can respond directly to the product or service offered and, if any mis-match is present, inform the marketer in order that the offering can be adjusted to conform accurately to what the customer wants. Regrettably, few organisations work today in such a simple situation. A successful UK manufacturer of industrial metal bearings has some 6,000 customers throughout Europe and a further 4,000 in North America and Australasia. He offers a full range of products together with maintenance servicing, as well as financial support for the purchase of specific items. He deploys technical sales representatives travelling to meet his major customers once or twice a year, but in many countries he deals through agents rather than directly. His marketing activity is complex but its success is also dependent on matching his organisation's resources with the wants of its customers. And he will continue to succeed only if he gleans regular information about what customers want in the future as well as how they are reacting to his present range of products or services.

Lest any metal bearing manufacturer should be daunted in his task, however, let him count his blessings when he compares his marketing challenge with that faced by a food manufacturer who sells his produce throughout the EEC. Whilst the preferences for metal bearing technology the world over have some striking similarities, the diets of fellow Europeans in Denmark, Holland and the UK, to cite but three, differ distinctly. Just observe the Dutch preference for cheese at breakfast time in contrast to the tastes of the UK population; or consider that while the Danes like to eat crispbread for breakfast, the British have an observable preference for toast. Then recall that there are just short of 300 million customers in the EEC for breakfast most days and some 85 million housewives doing their shopping from something in excess of one million retail stores. As one can well imagine, it takes a great deal of planning to meet the varied needs of so many folk successfully. Yet in the pan-European food manufacturing companies like Unilever, that's exactly the measure of the marketing task they face. The principle that guides this task is the basic marketing concept that the focal point of the organisation's activities is the wants of its customers.

Fortunately, the task is not as daunting as it can sound. Even large organisations have neither the ability nor the desire to enter such vast markets in one step. They add to their resources and knowledge of customer wants as they go. The organisation itself and its employees become a bank of information and knowledge about what customers want. This bank of information means that most established organisations know in rough and ready terms what customers will want in the immediate future. All too frequently, however, much of that information is lost, either by inadequate analysis or codification, and lessons have to be learned again at the expense both of customers and organisations.

The marketing environment

A variety of environmental factors beyond the control of any one organisation affects the attainment of marketing objectives. Domestic and international competition are continually becoming more vigorous. The state of the economy – in terms of changes in levels of income and employment, inflation and foreign

Figure 1

exchange rates – affects the level of consumption and the standard of living.

The legal environment is becoming more complicated and restrictive; while even governments with a strong belief in the unfettered operation of market forces still have a prominent role to play as participants, regulators and manipulators. Changes in birth rates and marriage patterns and increases in the number of women entering the workforce indicate social trends to which marketing activities must respond. Rapid changes in technology make today's product innovation tomorrow's antique. The evolution of retail, wholesale, and other distributive institutions takes place over a time span that often limits the marketer's ability to change in the short term. As Figure 1 illustrates, all these environmental variables need to be considered in planning marketing activities.

Direct and indirect competition

Few organisations are left alone in our world to match their human, financial and physical resources with their customers' wants. The matching process goes on in an open environment with varying degrees of competition either from similar or identical products or from quite different opportunities for customers to spend their limited financial resources.

In the short-term savings market, for example, the banks compete not only with building societies but also with alternative uses of the available funds, such as a long holiday, redecorating the outside of the home, or a pony tethered in a paddock for the children. There is a great deal of competition for these short-term savings, and the building societies have done particularly well, increasing their share of this segment of the savings market from 24% to 41% during the 1970s. The building societies have more than tripled the number of branches in recent years and therefore can offer convenience as an important service to customers. In addition, societies are open on Saturday mornings while most banks are not. More importantly, a share account in a building society earns a high rate of interest while a current account in a bank does not. The ease of withdrawal and attractive interest rates provide competitive advantages for the building societies which serve to intensify the competition in the short-term savings market place.

Economic uncertainties

In times of economic uncertainty, people may postpone purchasing certain products or services which do not seem immediately essential, while at the same time they may maintain or increase expenditures in other areas.

With the recession and high unemployment of recent years, for example, the demand for holidays abroad fell, but in other ways people seemed determined to behave as though times were more prosperous, with the traditional Christmas peak in spending reaching record levels.

Not that the travel industry took this pattern of behaviour as inevitable. On the contrary, their highly successful marketing response was to offer tempting discounts and special offers, such as family holidays with no charge for children, and extra weeks beyond the usual fortnight offered at rock bottom prices.

The status of the economy has also affected the growth of the do-it-yourself market which tends to expand when the economy turns down. Consumer expenditure in the UK on repairs and maintenance has quadrupled in the last decade. Black and Decker reorganised their industrial orientation to take advantage of this consumer opportunity whilst continuing to serve their traditional industrial markets.

Economic uncertainty reduced capital investment in new equipment and plant during periods of very rapid European inflation, often accompanied by high interest rates. When the cost of labour is increasing relatively much more rapidly, substitution of capital goods for labour should logically occur. The movement towards more capital-intensive activities occasioned by these changes in the respective productivity of labour and of capital does occur, but with a lagged time effect.

Legal and political constraints

The environment in which the organisation's marketer operates also includes legal and political facets. Within the EEC there are Community Laws and Regulations, made as a consequence of the terms of the Treaty of Rome, which govern numerous aspects of trade, from transport and distribution to the description and packaging of products.

Each nation within the EEC has its own laws in addition, such as the UK's Fair Trading Act or Supply of Goods Act. Outside the EEC, each and every country will have further laws and regulations governing export/import activities and trading terms. Many countries, for instance, require that products sold within their borders must be partly or wholly manufactured or assembled there, regardless of whether this is in the best economic interests of either an organisation or its specific customers in any particular transaction.

Legal issues of this kind merge into political issues very easily. The long-term boycott of South African or Israeli goods by individuals or countries, the USA's sanctions against suppliers and contractors involved in the construction of a Soviet oil pipeline, and international financial and trade pressures against Argentina during the Falklands conflict – all are outstanding instances of international political environmental factors. Less obvious examples, but nonetheless just as effective in distorting a simple organisation to customer matching process, are quota schemes between countries, or barter deals such as have been widely concluded between Comecon countries and Western nations for the past two decades and more.

In recent years there has been a shift of emphasis away from government controls over economic activity. Restrictions on consumer credit have been relaxed, for example, so that it is now no longer a legal requirement for any one buying a new car to pay a substantial deposit. Instead, 100 per cent hire purchase terms are available. Foreign exchange control has also been abandoned.

On the other hand, even governments with a dislike in principle for restrictive legislation find that there are particular instances where they feel that on balance it is desirable. The present government, for instance, is committed to introduce lead-free petrol by the 1990s (or, rather, to ban the use of petrol containing lead). This will in due course exercise massive constraints on marketing in the whole automobile industry. Not only is the price of new cars likely to rise, reflecting the higher cost of producing cars adapted to lead-free petrol, but the pump price of the petrol itself is also likely to be higher. The second-hand price of cars not adapted to the new petrol, by contrast, could well fall drastically.

Government regulation of the economy, via taxation, monetary controls and public expenditure policy, also continues to exert a massive influence on the entire economic climate, and hence on the conditions faced by marketers. Tight government control of the money supply in recent years, for instance, has been accompanied by widespread cash flow problems. One solution for many companies has been to shed labour, with a consequent national rise in unemployment and a correspondingly depressed consumer market. Marketers have also found themselves thwarted in the development of products and their markets by such cash flow difficulties.

Cultural and social trends

Across the EEC the different cultures reflect the different behaviour patterns of each nation's society. A variety of ethnic groups comprises the market place within each nation as well. Britain today is a multi-racial society; the coloured segment of the UK market is of sufficient size, over 1½ million, to present a marketing opportunity. For example, the Asian religious aversion to animal fat provided Blue Band, a vegetable oil margarine, with a marketing opportunity to promote the product to the Asian market as a valuable source of vitamin D.

Regional tastes in food suggest different marketing efforts in certain parts of the country. The people of the West Midlands and Wales consume 40% more bacon and ham than do the Scots. And the Welsh have taken over from the East Midlanders as the nation's biggest butter eaters with a 40% greater consumption than the people of Yorkshire and Humberside.

Trends in population growth, such as births, deaths and migrations, exert great pressure on the future plans of marketers and influence how they approach a market. The advent of the Pill, women's lib, working wives and the fashion for smaller families have turned the baby boom into a slump. Between 1971 and 1977 the baby food market dropped by 50%. The startling decline of the baby market means that manufacturers have had to adapt their marketing strategies. In the mid 1960s, when the birth rate started to fall, Johnson & Johnson began to promote the use of its baby-care items, like baby powder, shampoo and lotion, to adults. Now a mere 30% of its volume is used on babies and the company's turnover has increased four times in the last decade.

The toy industry is faced not only with the steady decline in the number of children but also with the fact that children are maturing faster. At the age of twelve a child is no longer interested in toys, but in cassette players, clothes and cosmetics. No longer interested, that is, in toys which would merely identify them as immature. On the other hand, there has been a phenomenal growth of interest among children and teenagers in 'toys' that enable them to upgrade their social status. Rubik's Cube, in the early 1980s, enabled millions of children to outwit their parents, and the advent of personal computers on a wide scale now enables youngsters to project themselves gleefully as masters of the future world.

The very large number of working housewives has led to many changes in family lifestyles: for instance, the amount of family income has increased, the housewife has less time to spend on family chores, and the housewife's expectations about the quality of life are different. For a growing number of working wives, time really means money. Thus, convenience products have shown considerable growth. But the growth of convenience foods has been moderated by the belief that convenience foods contain too many artificial ingredients. One manifestation of this is the increasing ownership of home freezers. The desire to return to more natural ways of living juxtaposed with the time constraints of working women has produced a boom in home freezing – a process which is believed to offer a nutritional or health advantage over convenience foods.

Technological change

Rapid product obsolescence due to changing technology is the rule rather than the exception in modern industry. Today the advent of microelectronics is the second version of the industrial revolution. On a broad scale it has accelerated the pattern of transfer of jobs from the manufacturing to the service sector. Specifically, the microprocessor has changed the fabric of many industries. Microprocessors have allowed the introduction of small, low-cost micro-computers that have household applications for monitoring weather conditions and adjusting room temperatures as well as home record keeping and budgeting. Motor car manufacturers are using microprocessors to control the operation of the car engine by matching speed, petrol, air flow and ignition timing. Microchip voice simulations are used to give warning of low oil pressure or petrol level, and there are even systems to keep drivers on course for a particular destination across the most complex and unfamiliar cross-city routes.

The arrival of video recording has likewise revolutionised the entertainment industry, from films available on video cassettes at High Street shops, to the home recording of television programmes, to pop music videos. Even before the implications of this new technology have been fully explored, cable television looks set to provide not only a new aspect of entertainment, but also the communications infrastructure to 'computerise' homes and offices throughout the country, with boundless marketing potential in as yet unexplored fields, not just of the consumer sector, but also services and industrial goods.

In many markets consumers have rapidly accepted microelectronics. Traditional companies have suffered because they were tied to their existing technologies. Consider this quote from a Swiss watch manufacturer: 'The major slice of the market will remain with the traditional watch manufacturers because we have the distribution, the style and the brand name. Our policy on watch design for the next five years is to concentrate on the production of the mechanical watch for the middle and upper end of the market.' But the market didn't remain loyal to traditional, mechanical watches. Today electronic watches are distributed not only through jewellers but also through chemists, camera dealers, electronics shops and even petrol stations, and are manufactured by large, reputable electronics companies, new to the watch business but not new to the arena of a competitive market place.

Institutional patterns

Another aspect of the marketing environment is the pattern of institutions bequeathed to contemporary marketers by years of trading activity. Until the late 1960s, the major pattern of food distribution throughout Europe consisted of relatively small grocers or multiple chain stores operating through local retail outlets. The advent of mass car ownership has transformed this pattern in two decades to one of hypermarkets, supermarkets, and shopping centres in almost every EEC country. Along with this development, several other traditional retail institutions have decreased in numbers – the pharmacist, the butcher, the greengrocer, the fishmonger, the dairy, and even the baker.

The roots of modern franchising stem from the eighteenth century British brewers. This early form of franchising tied economically beleaguered public houses to a particular brewer, requiring pubs to serve only that particular brewer's beer, in return for a capital investment from the brewer. The agreement precluded the distribution of any other brewer's products through a tied public house. This form of exclusive agreement is common to all forms of franchising. The current generation of franchises includes Budget Rent-A-Car, Dyno-Rod, Prontaprint, ServiceMaster, Wimpy and Ziebart, to name a few. In effect, wholesaler-retailer agreements, such as Spar and VG in food distribution, are forms of franchising.

Franchising seems likely to grow in Britain in the next decade and manufacturers who fail to take note may find their distribution options quite limited. These instances of change demonstrate the need for the marketer to identify the pace at which customers are willing and able to respond to new institutional patterns.

Because of increasing difficulties in world money markets, bartering has partially replaced the traditional exchange of goods for money as a method of payment for goods amongst companies involved in world trade. This calls for change in the attitudes, skills and organisation structure within companies.

The organisation must respond to the changes in the marketing environment as they happen in the short and medium term. The long-term changes in the environment are beyond the planning horizon for most organisations. Besides, in the words of the well known economist, John Maynard Keynes, 'In the long run, we are all dead.' This is the dynamic backcloth against which, and the milieu within which, the matching of organisational resources and customer wants must take place.

The marketing activity

Formalised marketing activity in an organisation is concerned with analysis, planning and control of the process of matching human, financial and physical resources with customer wants. It has already been demonstrated how vital it is to have a flow of evaluative and behavioural information back from the customer in the market place. This, plus accumulated learning about the markets served, provides the effective basis on which marketing plans can be prepared, put into effect and subsequent performance assessed and controlled.

Successful matching depends on customers being aware of the products or services on offer, finding them conveniently available and judging the products' or services' attributes, in terms of both price and performance, to be capable of satisfying the customers' needs and wants. This satisfactory state of affairs is best accomplished by attention to what are often termed the four 'P's –

product, price, promotion and place. As will be demonstrated in some detail later each 'P' is a continuing problem to the marketer. It must be both attended to separately and as it interacts with the other elements in what is termed the *marketing mix* (see Figure 2). A satisfactory solution one year may well expect to be challenged in the next. Products or services will be introduced, improved upon, and made obsolete. Prices may be undercut. Promotions can be upstaged by competitive campaigns. The place where customers buy can change at any time as alternative retail shopping opportunities emerge or distribution develops.

And these comments all assume that a sufficiently robust solution has been identified in the first place, which will take account not only of the separate importance of each of the four 'P's to the customer, but of their interactive impact as well. For example, to what extent can a higher price with more effective promotion improve the overall profitability of a branded herbal soap, rather than some other combination of strategies?

Figure 2

A company producing household goods may be finding it difficult to obtain shelf space in retail outlets at a time when competitors' product ranges are on the increase. An immediate but expensive solution would be to buy the space by offering attractive terms to retailers. Instead of increasing distribution costs in this way, however, an alternative would be to go for direct mail rather than High Street stores. This implies a fresh approach to promotion as well as place; and pricing strategy would certainly need to be reconsidered as well, as part of the firm's bid to reach its customers more profitably. These are marketing mix problems.

To wrestle with such mixing problems, and to plan for and to implement solutions, most medium and large organisations establish a marketing department and charge one of their senior executives to co-ordinate all such activities at director or boardroom level. This, along with the activities discussed above, comprises the marketing function. Its aim is to produce the *marketing plan* for the organisation. This plan will be discussed in Chapters 3 and 26.

Application questions

1.1 *What major types of external factors, beyond your control, influence your organisation and its marketing effort? What important changes have taken place in these factors in the last ten years? Is the marketing effort of your organisation co-ordinated so that it can:*

(a) maximise opportunities presented by a changing environment?
(b) minimise potential losses due to changes in the environment?

What precautions is the organisation taking to manage future changes in the environment?

1.2 *Compare a selection of your own recent purchases, such as a house, a tube of toothpaste, a newspaper, an insurance policy and an electric appliance. In each decision, what was the relative importance of the product itself, its price, the place where you could get it and the way it was promoted?.*

1.3 *Think of some recent purchases made by your organisation. In each decision, what was the relative importance of the product itself, its price, the place where it was available and the way in which it was promoted? Identify any ways in which your purchasing behaviour as a private individual differs from your behaviour at work. Can you explain any of these differences?*

2 What is the difference between marketing and selling?

Overview

Selling is simply that part of marketing concerned with persuading customers to acquire the product or service which best matches an organisation's human, financial and physical resources with its customers' wants. If the marketing job has been well done, such selling may still be tough, but it will be effective. If not, salesmen all too often find themselves trying to sell what the producing organisation wants the customer to want.

Selling frequently takes place through intermediate organisations, engaged either in undertaking manufacture or in assisting distribution, as well as direct to the customer. It can also be undertaken at a personal level with face-to-face contact, or impersonally, as via the telephone.

Sellers need marketers

Marketing has been described in Chapter 1 as the matching of an organisation's human, financial and physical resources with the wants of its customers. It has also been indicated that the matching is achieved by an organisation's careful integration of the four 'P's – product, price, promotion and place – into the marketing mix. *Selling* is one aspect of promotion. It is quite specifically intended to clinch a transaction, to persuade a customer to agree to acquire the product or service offered at the prevailing price. As such, it should represent the consummation of marketing's efforts to match what the organisation is offering with what the customer wants. Figure 3 illustrates this concept.

If the marketing process as a whole has been done badly, even highly persuasive sales staff, or advertising, will be of no avail. Consider, for instance, the case of a large brewer in Britain who distributed his draught beers through a limited number of public houses. Most of these were in the South, although some were located in other areas of the country. In order to promote his product, the brewer initiated a national television advertising campaign. An extremely high recall of the product and the message was achieved but, since the beer was only available in limited areas, much of this investment and awareness was wasted. The inadequately thought-out campaign (which we shall examine again in a different context in Chapter 22) also damaged the brewer's long-term opportunity to influence potential customers.

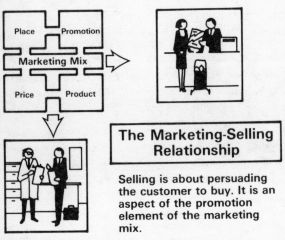

The Marketing-Selling Relationship

Selling is about persuading the customer to buy. It is an aspect of the promotion element of the marketing mix.

Figure 3

In the brewery case, bad marketing can be identified in the brewer's failure to plan the co-ordination of price and place. By contrast, the evidence suggests that the task of persuading customers to buy had been well done, in this instance by means of advertising, rather than through the personal selling method of promotion.

In industrial and service markets too, effective selling outside a carefully planned marketing framework may even be counter-productive for overall company objectives. Take, for example, the case of a sales force which habitually sells only those products which are 'easy' to sell and puts little effort behind 'difficult' products. These products may be 'difficult' for a number of reasons, which may include the fact that they are new to the product range or new to the customer. It may well be, however, that increased take-up of the 'difficult' products is essential for the fulfilment of the organisation's marketing objectives and that the success of the sales force with other product lines is in danger of jeopardising overall corporate plans.

It sometimes happens, as well, that short-term promotional activity can be extremely successful, but without the backing of a sound marketing strategy to anticipate a host of threats and opportunities that lie just around the corner, the situation can go badly awry.

This may happen quite suddenly if, for instance, a company is taken unawares by a rival's new product development or shift in pricing tactics. In the medium to longer term, good marketing will ensure that a weather eye is kept on such factors as shifts in consumer preference and advances in technology that give rise to new product possibilities, so that sales staff are not left high and dry with unsaleable products on their hands.

A mining engineering company in Cornwall is the subsidiary of a large mining concern based there. This subsidiary has an impressive record both of producing a wide range of tools for use by the parent company, and selling such tools on the open market. Company management are aware, however, that the continued success of their selling effort depends on careful planning for the future. They anticipate that the parent company will be moving more and more of its extraction activity overseas. As a result, the pumping equipment that the engineering firm traditionally services is also going overseas, and so a large part of their business is likely to disappear from under their feet. They know that in an area like Cornwall, where industrial customers are not in great abundance, they will have to think hard about new products and new customers if they are to survive.

Market or product orientated?

If the marketing process has been well done, then selling may be difficult, but it will not be impossible. If little or no planning of the marketing mix has been undertaken, all but the lucky must expect to fail. Unless the item just happens to be one which the customer really needs and for which there is no viable alternative, only good marketing can sell a product or service twice to a customer.

Selling any product or service to a customer for the first time round is a somewhat different matter. Half truths or exaggerated claims for efficacy can often persuade folk to acquire a product or make use of a service that is subsequently found wanting. No further sales follow and few organisations face a situation where they can make an adequate profit from single purchases by subsequently dissatisfied customers. Naturally, in any circumstances, some who buy once will fall by the wayside later, but the selling effort of the well planned marketing mix gives rise to only a small proportion of dissatisfied customers. Furthermore, information feedback from the market place alerts the organisation to the main reasons why customers fail to buy again. If necessary, this then becomes the basis for improving or modifying the product, service, or any element of the marketing mix.

Selling is not about half truths or exaggerated claims for what is on offer. These practices are folly because they reflect a poor image of the organisation and, as a result, they are counterproductive. Their occurrence is overestimated because the news media report them with a frequency disproportionate to the number of actual incidents.

When it is part of a carefully thought out marketing activity, a well planned sales effort is about persuasion. The sales representative or the direct mail leaflet or the industrial/technical advisory service, depending on the organisation's chosen mode of selling, seeks to persuade the customer to take the leap from *wanting* to *acquiring* the product or service. The more the organisation knows about the customer's wants before the salesmen make the effort, the greater is the probability of success. The salesman should not discover that he has a product or service in search of a customer. This cannot happen in a market orientated organisation. Where it does occur, the phenomenon is normally described as product orientation. In other words, the organisation has developed a product or service that the organisation wants the customer to want. The organisation relies on its salesmen to persuade customers to buy, come hell or high water. If the salesmen fail, they tend to get the blame, rather than the organisation's overall stance towards its customers. Chapter 22 describes persuasion in the context of a marketing approach.

In the 1960s, before the first oil crisis, a modest sized European engineering firm developed a splendid idea into a viable technology. It harnessed the heat from factory chimneys, diesel exhausts and other industrial processes, thereby recycling energy. The inventors believed in their process, but fifteen years ago, well before the first oil crisis, potential customers, even when assailed by salesmen, did not want it and they did not buy it. Only today, with the massive escalation in world energy costs, has a viable market emerged for the long viable technology. Its savings are now sufficiently attractive to command attention. The inventors have been one of the few organisations lucky enough to benefit from the OPEC cartel's activities. But their product development, no matter how clever, could have been their downfall. The premature timing of the introduction wasted the cost of introducing this product fifteen years ago. The firm incurred the additional cost of reintroducing the product once the market was more inclined to buy. Few organisations have the cash reserves to survive too many poorly timed introductions.

In contrast is the marketing orientation of a large French printing engineering company which was established by an electronic engineer and a salesman from one of the more traditional industries. The salesman's frequent visits to printers had given him a clear understanding of the bottle-necks in production, especially the problem of maintaining a correct 'register' for long print runs. An automatic electronic process was perfected, specifically for printing, which, although primitive in the sophisticated world of space electronics, exactly met a readily perceived need with printers across the world. Furthermore, it was engineered to give value in the context in which it was expected to operate. Its price was seen as realistic in terms of the savings it afforded on the more traditional processes of human adjustment. Technical selling of the electronic registration device was still needed, but it was undertaken on fertile, marketing-prepared soil in some 84 countries throughout the world by the mid-seventies.

Different levels of selling

There are two levels of selling, *direct to the customer* and *indirect through intermediaries*. The latter can be divided into two types. Figure 4 illustrates the pattern of the relationships.

Indirect selling
There are two types of indirect selling. One is to intermediate manufacturers who use materials or semi-finished components in producing end products or services. This type of indirect selling is often co-ordinated with direct selling to stimulate end-user

The Different Levels of Selling

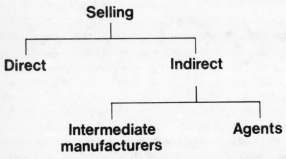

Figure 4

demand. The second type is where the agent or broker offers service availability or stocks on a localised and more convenient basis for the customer. Any particular organisation can have either of the two types, both, or neither. It depends on the resources of the organisation and the wants of customers, and how the organisation chooses to meet them.

Examples of markets which use the first type of indirect selling, through intermediate manufacturers, are those where customers are purchasing low value items on a frequent basis, such as consumable household items, or where customers for industrial items are geographically widely spread. In such situations, the organisation making the product or service needs first to sell to the intermediary, and then to assist the intermediary to sell to the eventual customer on his behalf. This is the way in which Svenska Cellulosa sell their pulp, paper fibres and newsprint to European industry and Courtaulds sell their synthetic fibres to cloth manufacturers or carpet producers throughout Comecon, EEC countries, and the rest of the world. In circumstances such as these, both the producer and the intermediary must of necessity sell to their eventual customer, the newspaper readers or the consumers of clothing, furnishing fabrics, carpets and the like. Their sales activities must be based on a careful analysis and understanding of the role which the newsprint or the fibre used plays in the satisfaction the customer wants. This is the way most retailing has worked since the start of the twentieth century, although in recent years the growth throughout Europe of 'own label products' has somewhat reduced its role in food distribution.

Different forms of selling

All the levels of selling mentioned above can be accomplished in a variety of ways by an organisation, but they can all be characterised as either *personal* or *impersonal* selling. A clear example of personal selling is the use of representatives to visit the customer's premises. Impersonal selling can be illustrated by the use of advertising designed to elicit a direct response.

Personal selling

The most obvious example of personal selling is the call of a representative at a customer's premises. Knowing whether this is the most fruitful form of selling and, if so, how frequently to visit and how long to spend on each visit, are problems which call for careful analysis. Quite obviously, the nature of the product or service will influence the requirements. Selling a complex technical product or service may well only be achieved after the most complex series of discussions and negotiations between teams of individuals. In industrial markets a myriad of individuals may influence the sales outcome within a customer organisation, and some will play a more significant role at certain stages in the process.

However, once a customer has become familiar with an organisation's offering, a representative's call can often become almost a matter of courtesy or public relations, provided always that such a pattern does not indicate complacency in an ever-changing marketing environment. It will be supplemented on occasion by telephone selling or follow-up calls; this pattern is common, for example, amongst routine, frequently ordered industrial components.

Exhibitions, where customers come to meet salesmen and technical advisers, are an interesting variant of direct calling by a representative on a customer. In certain industries, and especially in Eastern Europe, exhibitions are a widespread selling technique. The method is most widely used at the introductory stages of new products where sufficient curiosity exists to persuade potential customers to travel at their own expense. The data-processing industries and camping and caravan manufacturers have, for instance, used this method regularly. It has the disadvantage for any sales organisation that many of the competitors' products are arranged alongside one's own, but this can rebound to one's advantage when there is a clear product or service superiority.

Impersonal selling

Impersonal selling has grown massively in popularity throughout Europe in the past half century. Most typically, it takes the form of orders placed as a direct result of promotion either in the mass media or on the telephone. By offering a 'no questions asked' refund service, organisations have been able to persuade customers to acquire products or services simply on the basis of descriptions and/or pictures. In European retailing alone, mail order is estimated at somewhere in the region of 6 to 10% of all selling activity today, although there are distinct differences in levels between EEC member states. Chapter 21 will consider the levels and the forms of selling as part of the communications mix.

Selling and buying

If a producer has sold something, then a customer must have bought it. Throughout this text, the terms 'acquire', 'buy', 'lease', and 'hire' will be used interchangeably to mean any method by which moneys pass from the customer to the producer or interme-diary in return for goods and services.

Application questions

2.1   *How might the impact of an imaginative advertising campaign, or a skilled and energetic sales team, be thwarted by poor marketing?*

2.2   *Who 'sells' and who 'markets' in your organisation? How do their jobs and objectives differ? In what ways are they co-ordinated?*

2.3   *Compare the roles of the sales representatives employed by the manufacturer of the steel used in your car, the manufacturer of the car itself and the dealer from whom you bought the car. To whom were they actually selling in each case?*

2.4   *What type of product or service would you be prepared to buy:*

(a) *by mail as a result of reading a catalogue or other advertisement?*
(b) *after discussion with a sales representative?*

What are the common characteristics of products or services which are sold in these two different ways? Which of your organisation's products and services could be sold by indirect means and which need a personal selling approach? Are both means of selling employed by your organisation?

3   What is our marketing plan?

Overview

Marketing planning is the systematic application of marketing resources to achieve marketing objectives. It is the means by which an organisation seeks to monitor and control the hundreds of external and internal influences on its ability to achieve profitable sales. Marketing planning also provides an understanding throughout the organisation of the particular competitive stance that an organisation intends to take to achieve its objectives. This helps managers of different functions to work together rather than to pursue their own functional objectives in isolation.

A marketing plan will contain a review of the marketing environment, assumptions, overall objectives and strategies, and more detailed programmes concerning responsibilities, timing, and costs. The degree of formalisation of the planning process will depend on the size and diversity of the organisation, although the planning process itself is universally applicable. This chapter describes the general issues considered in a marketing plan. Chapter 26 explains the detailed development of the marketing plan.

Is marketing planning essential?

There can be little doubt that marketing planning is essential when we consider the increasingly competitive and dynamic environment in which organisations operate. Most managers accept that some kind of formalised procedure for marketing planning helps to reduce the complexity of business operations and adds a dimension of realism to the organisation's hopes for the future. Without some planning procedures there is a danger that the organisation will exhaust much of its energies in internecine disputes, whilst its marketing may become little more than an uncoordinated mixture of interesting bits and pieces.

Consider for a moment the four typical objectives which organisations set, of maximising revenue, maximising profits, maximising return on investment, and minimising costs. Each one of these has its own special appeal to different managers within the organisation, depending on the nature of their particular function. In reality, the best that can ever be achieved is a kind of 'optimum compromise', because the different objectives often seem to demand conflicting courses of action. Managers must understand how all the variables interact. They also need to *plan* their business decisions, no matter how important the contribution of intuition, feel and experience are in this process.

A recent study of the marketing planning practices of leading European industrial goods companies has shown that:

– most companies understand the importance of, and the need for, formalised marketing planning procedures;
– only 15% of the companies have any such procedures other than forecasting and budgeting;
– this results in grave operational difficulties;
– in spite of this, companies do not institutionalise marketing planning procedures because they do not know how to design and introduce planning systems which will help them to reduce their operational problems.

The challenge of marketing planning

The organisation needs an institutionalised planning process, one designed to work out and write down the plan of the organisation's particular competitive stance. The marketing function must find a systematic way of identifying a range of options, choose one or more of them, and then schedule and cost out what needs to be done in order to achieve the objectives. This plan should be communicated throughout the organisation so that everyone knows what is necessary to take the organisation towards its objectives. This whole process can be defined as *marketing planning*, which is the systematic application of marketing resources to achieve marketing objectives.

Whilst it is easy to understand the marketing planning process in principle, in practice it is the most difficult of all marketing tasks to accomplish successfully. There are several reasons for this.

One reason is that it involves bringing together into one

coherent plan the four 'P's discussed in Chapter 1. In order to do this, institutional procedures must be introduced, and it is this formalisation which seems to be so difficult for organisations. One difficulty arises from the fact that there is little guidance available to management on how the planning process itself might be managed. It proceeds from reviews to objectives, strategies, programmes, budgets and back again, until some kind of acceptable compromise is reached between what is desirable and what is practicable, within the organisation's operating constraints.

Another reason is that, although a planning system itself is little more than a structured approach to the process just described, the varying size, complexity, character, and diversity of commercial operations means that there can be no such thing as an 'off the peg' system that can be implemented without some fundamental amendments to suit the particular requirements of each organisation. Also, the elements of the marketing environment – competitive, economic, legal, political, cultural, social, technological and institutional – differ sufficiently from organisation to organisation to require an individual marketing planning process.

A further reason for the difficulty which organisations experience in drawing up a marketing plan is that the degree to which any organisation can develop an integrated, consistent plan depends on a deep understanding of the marketing planning process as a means of clarifying the objectives of all levels of marketing management within an organisation.

The marketing planning process

The study mentioned above also showed that a marketing plan should contain:

– a summary of all the principal internal and external factors which affected the company's marketing performance during the previous year, together with a statement of the company's internal strengths and weaknesses *vis-à-vis* the competition;
– some assumptions about the key determinants of marketing success and failure;
– overall marketing objectives and strategies;
– programmes containing details of timing, responsibilities and costs.

These elements are the substance of the marketing plan. At the very heart of successful marketing management is a conceptually simple marketing planning process which consists of the following steps:

1 Gathering relevant information about the external environment and about the organisation's internal resources (that is, carrying out a marketing audit).

2 Identifying the organisation's internal Strengths and Weaknesses *vis-à-vis* the external market Opportunities and competitive Threats facing the organisation (this is generally done by means of a SWOT analysis, discussed further in Chapters 14 and 26).

3 Formulating some basic assumptions about the future.

4 Laying down the marketing objectives of the organisation, based on the results of the first three steps.

5 Laying down strategies for achieving the objectives.

6 Laying down programmes for implementing the strategies to include timing, responsibilities and costs.

7 Measuring the progress towards achievement of the objectives, reviewing and amending the plan as necessary.

These steps are summarised in Figure 5.

Figure 5

In principle, the marketing concept, which states that the focus of the organisation's activities is the wants of its customers, is very easy to understand. But, in practice, the marketing concept is sometimes difficult to implement because marketing management does not know how to focus on its customers' wants. Likewise, the marketing planning process is also very easy to understand in principle. In practice, the problem is also implementation. Institutionalised procedures are necessary in order to implement the marketing planning process. It is these procedures which cause so much practical difficulty.

Formalised planning procedures

Although research has shown that these marketing planning steps are universally applicable, the degree to which each of the separate steps in the diagram needs to be formalised depends to a large extent on the size and nature of the organisation. For example, an *undiversified* organisation, one with only one product line, generally uses less formalised procedures, since top management tends to have greater functional knowledge and expertise than subordinates, and because the lack of diversity of operations enables direct control to be exercised over most of the key determinants of success. Thus, marketing audits, the setting of marketing objectives, and so on, are not always made explicit in writing, although these steps still have to be carried out.

In contrast, in a *diversified* organisation with many different product lines, it is usually not possible for top management to have greater functional knowledge and expertise than subordinate management. Thus, the whole planning process tends to be formalised in order to provide a consistent discipline for those who have to make the decisions throughout the organisation. There is a substantial body of evidence to show that formalised marketing planning procedures generally result in greater profitability and stability in the long term and also help to reduce friction and operational difficulties within organisations.

Common planning failures

Where marketing planning has failed, it has generally done so because organisations have placed too much emphasis on the procedures themselves and the resulting paperwork, rather than on generating useful and comprehensible information for management. Also, where organisations relegate marketing planning to someone called a 'Planner', the planning invariably fails for the simple reason that planning for line management cannot be delegated to a third party. The real role of the 'Planner' should be to help those responsible for implementation to draft the plan. Failure to recognise this simple fact can be disastrous.

Planning failures often result from organisations trying to do too much too quickly, using staff untrained in the new procedures. One UK metal bearings company tried three times without success to introduce a marketing planning system. It failed each time because managers throughout the organisation were confused by what was being asked of them. Also, not only did they fail to understand the need for the new systems, but they were not provided with the necessary resources to make the system work effectively. Management training and careful thought about resource requirements finally overcame this company's planning problems.

In contrast, a UK soap company lost profits and ran into grave operational difficulties through not having an effective marketing planning system. Over a three-year period they introduced a system that provided adequate resources and a training programme about the use of the new procedures, thus making them work effectively. This company is now firmly in control of its diverse activities and has recovered its confidence and its profitability.

We shall consider the marketing planning process in more detail in Chapters 25 to 28.

Application questions
3.1   *Does your organisation develop an annual marketing plan? If so, what are seen as the advantages of having such a plan? Do you consider that your organisation does in fact gain these advantages? If your organisation does not develop an annual marketing plan, what reasons are given for the decision? Are they really justified?*

3.2   *Who is, or should be, responsible for producing a marketing plan in your organisation? How do, or should, they produce it? To whom is the plan made available? Is it used in the most effective way possible?*

3.3   *During the last five years what problems have been avoided by your organisation's use of a marketing plan? Were there instances where the plan should have forewarned you of problems but did not? Why was this? Where no plan existed, were problems encountered which could have been avoided by the use of a plan?*

4 What are the differences between consumer, industrial and services marketing?

Overview

On the face of it, there are many differences between marketing to industrial customers and to household consumer markets. Likewise, the marketing of physical goods would appear to call for a different approach to that used in the case of intangible services. However, upon closer examination many of these differences are more apparent than real.

The successful marketing of services depends partly on a clear understanding of the two basic types of service that can be offered. The 'service product' is marketed purely as a service (as, for example, banking, insurance and hotels) and offers the customer an intangible series of benefits. The 'product service' is offered along with industrial or consumer goods and is often an inseparable part of a package (as, for example, computer installation and maintenance).

An analysis of all marketing situations will reveal that the principles are constant but that it is in the application of those principles to different types of market that differences often arise. In practice, the observable distinction lies in the particular blend given to the marketing mix.

Marketing principles

Any company wishing to achieve a profitable and durable penetration of a market must base its marketing strategy upon a thorough understanding of customer needs and wants. It must also make itself thoroughly familiar with the buying process utilised by the customer and the factors that influence the customer in his or her choice. This requirement holds for all companies, whether their products are aimed at the consumer, industrial or service markets. (The word 'product' is used throughout this book to include services as well as consumer and industrial goods.)

One of the universal factors influencing choice, and one that cannot be overstressed, is that customers do not buy products. Rather, they buy the benefits that those products provide. This is not just a semantic point; it is an important distinction which can be vital to the long-term survival of the firm. There are many examples of companies that have taken a narrow view of their business and defined it purely in terms of the products that they provide; as a result, they were forced out of business when competitive products were introduced which provided the same benefits but in a more cost-effective way. (The distinction between products and benefits and its implications for marketing practice are discussed in detail in Chapter 12.)

When it comes to devising a marketing strategy, the same factors need to be considered by all firms, whether they provide services or physical goods and whether they are aiming at consumer or industrial markets. A close examination of apparently very different forms of marketing activity reveals the need to relate all such activities to the fundamental principles of marketing.

What are the differences between services, consumer and industrial products?

A useful definition of industrial products might be those that are sold to industrial, institutional or government buyers to be incorporated into their own products, resold or used by them within their own organisations.

But does this really make such products fundamentally different to consumer goods or services? Clearly, it does not, because in many instances the same good or service can be classified as either an industrial or a consumer product.

An example of this is the electronic calculator. If it were sold to a business firm, it would be classified as an industrial good; if it were sold to a student, it would be considered to be a consumer good. There are many other examples. The same model of motor car is sold both as a representative's car to a business firm and as a family saloon.

Similarly services, which may be defined as intangible products, can be marketed in either an industrial or consumer context. Insurance against fire or theft, for example, is a service used by industrial and consumer customers alike. And the fact that a service is intangible, whether it be hairdressing, a train journey, or a businessman's intensive course in Arabic, makes no essential difference to the fact that it is a marketable product, subject to the same four 'P's of marketing that apply to other types of product.

If the product type cannot be used to differentiate marketing types, can the method of production be used to make a distinction? A power station, aircraft or ocean liner is usually custom built, on a one-off basis. The marketer is involved in developing the product with his customer for a period which could extend over a few months or over a number of years. But much the same could be said in the consumer field for a bespoke tailored suit; or in the service field for a management consultancy contract.

Thus, developing a clear distinction between services and goods, and between consumer and industrial products is not easy. What can be shown is that the approach to their marketing follows common basic principles.

Industrial and consumer buyer behaviour

It is sometimes suggested that a major difference between industrial and consumer marketing lies in the behaviour of buyers. Industrial buyers, it is often presumed, tend to be 'rational' in their decision making whilst consumer buyers are open to influence from a whole range of sources such as media, merchandising, packaging, word-of-mouth and even impulse. Yet, if we look more carefully at industrial buyers, we find that they are influenced by much the same factors.

The many studies which have been conducted of the industrial buyer all suggest that the buying process is highly complex and that non-price factors tend to predominate in the purchase decision. Thus, the marketer of industrial goods needs to pay careful attention to the nature of the buying process and to adapt the marketing mix accordingly.

Service products and product services

In order to compare the marketing of services with that of physical goods, we first need to understand the difference between 'service products' and 'product services'. The *service product* is marketed purely as a service (as, for example, banking, insurance and hotels). *Product services*, on the other hand, are offered along with industrial or consumer goods and are often an inseparable part of a package (as, for example, computer installation and maintenance).

Service products
Service products (see Figure 6) are those products which produce a series of benefits which cannot be stored. They must be consumed at the moment of manufacture. If we consider this aspect for a moment, we can see that a railway seat or a hotel room cannot be stored for later use. If it is not available when it is required, or not used when it is available, the opportunity for raising revenue is lost. The same seat or room may be required on an alternative day but it cannot be put into store on one day and sold on another. This attribute does not mean that the marketing of service products presents insurmountable difficulties. Rather, it means that the marketing mix elements must be combined in a suitable manner.

Consider, for instance, the problems of SNCF (the national railway system of France) or British Rail. Many of the services to and from Paris or London are stretched to their limits for only a few hours each day while commuters are travelling to and from work. For the remainder of the day their trains travel far from full. To utilise this wasted capacity and to obtain a contribution towards profits, SNCF and British Rail both offer lower-priced off-peak facilities.

In this example, as in the case of many other service products, commercial success can be measured conventionally in terms of profitability. Clearly, the lack of profit from a service product raises the same questions as does the lack of profit from either consumer or industrial goods. Is the service right? Am I promoting it in the appropriate way? Is the price too high or low? Is it being sold in the right places? In some service sectors, these questions are more easily posed than answered. Professional services in medicine, dentistry, accountancy, architecture and management consultancy are of this type. For service products of this kind, constraints are imposed in terms of promotion and pricing. Advertising a particular expertise is often forbidden, and prices may not be freely set. Nevertheless, they can and do compete with each other by innovating within the marketing mix structure, through their choice of place of business, for example, or in the mix of services that they provide.

Figure 6

Let us consider those service products for which profitability cannot be used as an efficiency measure. Primarily, these are service products in the social or welfare field. For example, the motor car has brought untold benefits to society. It has also given rise to many serious problems, amongst them the dangerous combination of drinking and driving. Can marketing help to reduce the incidence of drunken driving?

The principles of marketing can be applied to such problems by identifying the 'consumers' and their needs. Commercial organisations attempt to make a profit and satisfy customer needs by means of a profit objective. Reaching this objective or failing to do so is in fact the measure of their efficiency. Relating this to the social/welfare context, we can use as a measure of efficiency the success or failure in reducing social problems. Thus, fewer road deaths at hours notorious for drinking and driving can be used as a measure of success. It is by no means perfect. There can be many extraneous influences at work as well but, despite this, it is better than no measure at all.

In addition to both commercial and social/welfare service products, there is often a dimension of service in connection with physical products. Many companies engaged in the marketing of physical products have found that they can develop profitable diversification spin-offs by marketing their 'know-how'. Thus, a Dutch company engaged in the production of dyestuffs found that there was a small but highly profitable market for the production knowledge and application techniques that they had acquired over the years. A separate company was set up to exploit these skills – a service product spun-off from an industrial product. Similarly, British Rail have established a successful consultancy company which advises other countries on how to develop rail services.

Product services

We must also consider our second major aspect of service (see Figure 7). Many consumer and industrial goods are sold on the basis of service either before the sale is made, or after the sale, or indeed both. A British minicomputer manufacturer's sales staff spent a considerable amount of time with prospective customers determining their specific needs before attempting to sell them any particular computer. Highly trained systems analysts studied the prospective company in terms of the tasks done by company employees. In this way, they traced the flow of information, decisions, organisation inputs and outputs. Using these studies, the manufacturing company made recommendations not only for the applications of its products, but also for improvements in the

Figure 7

client company's operations. Following the sale, and depending upon the size of the computer and its type of application, the company provided maintenance engineers to service the equipment. This detailed attention to product services built them a most successful business in a highly competitive market.

Consumer goods can also be subject to both before- and after-sales service facilities. Indeed, for Germany's VW/Audi, the reduced after-sales service requirement has been made a major sales feature. VW promote computerised servicing diagnosis, and Audi prolonged servicing intervals. Washing machine manufacturers offer service insurance packages to consumers across Europe whereby, for an annual payment, the appliance will be serviced regularly and replacement parts supplied without charge.

A major Norwegian house builder has been developing a before-sales service which extends well beyond a choice of sanitary ware and paint colour finishes. Within the constraints of local authority planning permission, and customers' budgets, a complete design service is offered to purchasers once a building site has been purchased. The customer can specify the number and size of rooms and, to a degree, their location. Sales have boomed.

Difference in emphasis

The concept of the marketing mix has already been introduced in Chapter 1 in the context of the four 'P's. We have found so far in this chapter that such distinctions as we can draw between industrial and consumer marketing, and between the marketing of goods and services (whether service products or product services) do not alter the fact that in all cases marketers will be seeking a satisfactory mix of the four 'P's.

The questions that need to be asked in each case are the same. Who are the customers? What are their needs? What benefits do they seek? How sensitive are they to the various elements of the marketing mix? While the questions are the same, the answers can be expected to vary. That is to say, different emphases within the marketing mix will often, though by no means always, be appropriate in the different fields of marketing.

Promotion in the different types of market

The means of promotion, for instance, can be expected to vary from one market type to another. Advertising in industrial marketing, for example, fulfils a rather different function from advertising in other sectors. Unlike consumer goods, where many sales are made on a daily or weekly basis, the sales of many capital goods may occur only once in the life of a firm. This suggests that, for many industrial goods, advertising is often viewed primarily as a source of information for industrial buyers, sometimes detailed technical information which may be put on file and not acted upon for some considerable time. Clearly, most consumer advertising is aimed at generating more immediate sales.

So far as the salesman's work is concerned, some of the more complex and expensive service products, such as life insurance, have traditionally involved lengthy face-to-face discussions with individual customers backed by extensive sales literature – a style in these two respects, if in no other, more akin to that normally used in industrial selling than in the consumer field.

There are few eternal truths as to how a marketing activity should best be conducted, however, and a recent development has been for insurance companies to question the need for person-to-person selling. These companies, just like a consumer goods firm selling such everyday products as a range of saucepans, have been opting for direct mail. The customer simply reads a brief description of the policy and its benefits in a newspaper advertise-ment, fills in a cut-out coupon with his or her name and address, and sends a cheque for the life insurance, the subscription based on a simple scale according to age.

Direct mail advertising, such as personal postal advertising aimed at named prospective customers, is usually thought of as being of greatest advantage in industrial markets, because the range of potential customers is normally very clearly defined. Although the sophistication of the computer enables direct mail to be applied to consumer markets, success rates are generally lower than in industrial marketing. This is partly because of the difficulty in consumer markets of identifying the prime target audience and partly because costs continue to escalate, making direct mail techniques non-viable for low value items.

Again, however, this is not an eternal truth. The cost of printing and mailing a 600-page catalogue is formidable, but the same does not apply to video tapes, and still less to video discs, which are now being used to provide home customers with comparable information.

A questioning approach to the marketing mix

More and more, it seems, marketing management is willing to re-assess the traditional marketing mix in industrial, consumer and service sectors. New technical possibilities and other market factors make such re-assessment desirable; and so too do successful pioneering practices in apparently dissimilar markets.

Lloyds Bank, for instance, now promotes commercial services to farmers by means of television advertisements that have much in common with those aimed at non-commercial customers. Similarly, as we have seen, even an expensive and sophisticated service product, like life insurance, can be sold as you might sell saucepans.

Differences of marketing mix emphasis in the various kinds of market can be expected to remain, insofar as they truly reflect different market needs and sensitivities. The criteria determining how to handle the mix, though, should not be sought in the distinctions between goods and services, or between consumer and industrial products. These lines are far too crudely drawn, and obscure the more important specifics of each particular market.

Application questions
4.1 *What do you see as the differences between marketing in industrial, consumer and service markets? Relate your answers to the four 'P's. Are there fundamental differences or are they differences of degree?*

4.2 *Does the product range offered by your organisation present any opportunity for you to develop a 'product service'? How could new forms of 'product service' be initiated? Who should assume responsibility for this?*

4.3 *If your organisation offers a 'service product', how do you market it? Are there particular difficulties associated with marketing a 'service product'? How could these difficulties be minimised or eradicated? How could your present marketing strategy be extended?*

4.4 *What scope is there for your organisation to make greater use of approaches usually associated with types of market other than its own? For example, if yours is an industrial market, could you make good use of some consumer marketing methods? If your product is a service, could you market it as you might do certain physical goods?*

5   What challenges does international marketing pose?

Overview

International marketing is the performance of the marketing task across national boundaries. The basic principles of marketing hold good, although the environment in which international marketing takes place is different from the domestic environment; customer needs and wants are often different; and there is a difference in the degree of control which can be exercised over the four 'P's.

The most critical determinant of the way an organisation markets abroad is the method chosen to enter a foreign market.

The key questions in international marketing are concerned with whether to market internationally, which markets to enter, how to enter the foreign market(s) and, finally, how to operate and grow there.

Marketing principles

Perhaps the best way of beginning to answer this question is to remind ourselves that marketing is the way in which an organisation matches its resources with the wants of its customers against the background of a changing environment. International marketing is simply the performance of that marketing task across national boundaries. All the different activities involved in the marketing task still have to be undertaken. Marketing research has to be carried out. Appropriate products must be developed and realistic pricing, packaging and branding policies adopted. Sales forecasts must be made and effective communication with customers established. Distribution policies have to ensure that the product gets to the right place at the right time.

So, in principle, international marketing is no different from domestic marketing.

Yet, in practice, many organisations with an impeccable

marketing record in their domestic market encounter immense difficulties when marketing internationally. The experienced international marketer can take nothing for granted when operating in foreign markets and concentrates on differences rather than similarities in market conditions as a means of improving performance.

As illustrated in Figure 8, international marketing has four unique elements:

– the differences in the international environment;
– the control which it is possible to exercise over the four 'P's;
– the marketing mix appropriate for the international environment;
– the nature of international information requirements.

Let us consider each of these unique features in more detail to see how they affect the organisation's marketing activities.

The international environment

Organisations operating internationally must analyse the environment in which they will be operating. The environment will largely determine the actions they can take and the kinds of adaptations they must make.

The cultural environment

When a marketing operation extends beyond its own domestic frontiers, there are always problems related to differences in customs and habits. While operating in its domestic market, the organisation has the advantage of being a part of the dominant culture and understanding it completely. Internationally, there is no such advantage and misunderstanding or ignorance of cultural differences can lead to the most elementary and expensive marketing mistakes.

Seven elements of culture which need careful attention can be readily identified.

Material culture is represented in a society by its tools, artifacts and technology. The 'technology gap' between North and South represents a difference in material culture between the two hemispheres, the effects of which are readily apparent. For 40 years Volkswagen marketed the 'Beetle' car in Europe with great success, but by the 1970s a new range of cars was needed to

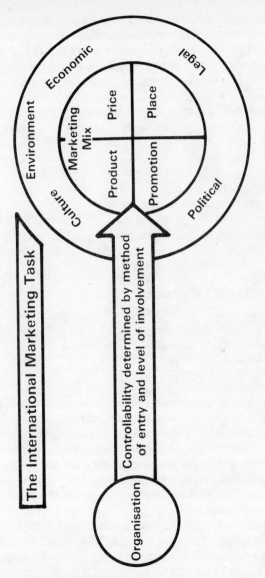

Figure 8

satisfy contemporary consumer demand for changed standards of performance and style. Production of the Beetle moved to Brazil, where the different material culture placed more emphasis on owning a car that was rugged, reliable and able to withstand the rigours of the local road system.

Material culture clearly determines marketing possibilities. Video recorders may find a ready market in Europe and North America; but they will not do so in countries where there is no television, or where disposable income is so low as to be spent exclusively on necessities such as food, clothing and shelter.

Language is often the most obvious differentiating feature; it is also a critical one since it constitutes the principal vehicle for carrying cultural ideas. Language is especially important when considering brand names and communicating ideas, as the Parker pen company found out when translating 'Save embarrassment . . . use Quink'. In Spanish this idiomatically became 'Avoid pregnancy . . . use Quink'.

Special attention must be given to the numerous multi-lingual markets and even to 'translating' from English to American, or from French to French-Canadian. Americans, for instance, use 'washing-up' products in the bathroom shower, not the kitchen sink. A company marketing detergents in French Canada used the French for 'the really dirty parts (of the wash')', and came up with a phrase which meant 'private parts' to the local French Canadian.

Aesthetics involves such considerations as colour, design, music, brand names, and so on. This is another area where embarrassing and costly mistakes can be made. For example, any company marketing baby clothes in Europe should beware: in the UK it is customary to buy blue for a boy and pink for a girl – in the Netherlands the colours are reversed.

Education, in the sense of the degree of literacy in a market, will determine how products are branded and promoted. Products with complex written instructions may need to be modified to meet educational and skill levels of the market. For example, if the organisation wished to make an appreciable impact on the Turkish market, which has a literacy rate of approximately 25%, radio advertising would have to make up a significant part of the promotional mix.

Religion has an immense impact on the everyday life of a society. This is sometimes to be seen in taboos on certain types of food and drink, and often affects the role of women, the raising of children and birth control. The subservient role of women in some Middle Eastern cultures necessitates interesting changes in the promotion of sewing machines, which are purchased by the male head of the household.

Attitudes and values are fundamental to determining how the customer decides what is right or wrong, what is important and what is desirable. Attitudes to risk taking will influence the likelihood that a customer will try a new product. Attitudes to change are important. In our society, promotion often emphasises that a product is 'new', but this may be a disincentive in markets which are more tradition orientated. Early convenience packaged soups introduced into Italy met with little success, being considered inferior to the traditional home-made variety.

Social organisation relates to the way that people group together, and is important at two levels. Firstly, as a possible method of segmentation with social groups such as teenagers, pensioners, and caste or class groupings. Secondly, the size of the family unit often differs widely, from the small nuclear units in the West to large extended family groups elsewhere. Imagine the changes in approach required by Land Rover when selling a vehicle which is purchased not by an individual but by a whole African village, to be held in common possession.

The economic organisation

Import controls set by the foreign government in terms of tariffs or quotas are intended either to protect home industries or earn revenue. They affect either the price or quantity available of the imported goods, making them uncompetitive against locally produced goods.

Export controls are set by the domestic government to control the exit of products considered sensitive, such as high technology (USA) and armaments (UK and others).

Non-tariff barriers have an equally dramatic effect on sales by making import difficult with regulations on packaging, transportation, testing and complicated documentation.

Exchange controls are restrictions placed on the movement of currency. It is important to the organisation to know of any restrictions that may be imposed on the repatriation of eventual profits from an overseas market.

Regional economic groupings such as the EEC, EFTA, LAFTA

work on the basis of reducing tariff barriers between member states while maintaining common tariffs to outsiders. For those companies who can manufacture within the group the advantages of a large protected market are obvious.

Inflation can vary from 3% to 200% per annum across markets and can seriously affect both revenue and costs of raw materials as well as international pricing policies.

The political/legal environment

The role of the government in the economy differs from country to country, from relative freedom of operation to complete state control of all business, including all distribution channels.

Political stability is very important if the company is considering any sizeable investment in a foreign market. It needs to know that it will be able to stay long enough to cover and make a return on the investment without the danger of expropriation or nationalisation.

Tax treaties are agreements between governments to avoid double taxation of profits by the foreign and the domestic governments.

Patents and trademarks law offer protection on the investment made by the company in developing its products. It is important that protection be secured for every country where the product might eventually be marketed.

Foreign laws often restrict the company's freedom to promote or even market certain products.

Methods of entering foreign markets

Often the most critical decision facing the organisation is the way in which the foreign market should be entered. The chosen method of entry will determine the organisation's level of involvement in international marketing and as such will define, at least initially, the amount of control that can be exercised over the marketing mix in any given market. There are seven broad methods of foreign market entry.

Indirect export takes place when a company's products are sold in a foreign market but no special export activity is carried on by the company itself. The actual exporting can be done by a specialised export house, by a special buying group working on behalf of overseas clients or by 'piggyback' exporting where another, often larger, company includes the product alongside its own and exports actively.

Direct export takes place when the company becomes actively involved in the process of exporting products to foreign markets. Typically, the export manager takes on the tasks of documentation, shipping, pricing and selecting agents or representatives.

The decision to establish a *marketing subsidiary* will be taken when a market shows sufficient potential. The subsidiary operates under the company's direct control within the market in question. A marketing subsidiary still receives product from outside the market but can operate as effectively as the local companies, perhaps with its own sales force, advertising, after-sales service and full facilities.

Establishing a *marketing subsidiary plus local assembly* means continuing to make the product's components at home, while assembling them abroad into the final product. This method is used extensively by the motor industry and Coca-Cola. It is economical on transport costs, often avoids some of the tariff barriers and tends to make the final product more price competitive in the local market.

Licensing enables the company to obtain local manufacture without a capital investment on its part. In a licensing agreement the licensor (international company) will normally receive royalties of sales of the product and the licensee (local company) normally receives either the patent rights, the trademark rights, copyrights or the technical know-how, together with the right to produce and market the licensor's product in a pre-determined market.

Joint venture is similar to the licensing agreement but in this case the international company takes an equity stake and a management responsibility in the foreign firm.

Wholly owned operation represents the greatest commitment to foreign markets by the international company and may be achieved by acquisition of an existing local firm as well as starting a subsidiary from scratch. In some countries such ownership is against the law and joint ventures operate instead, with the majority shareholding in local hands.

ICI gave the following reasons for beginning production on the European continent:

1 You are more credible to your customers if they know your plant is close.
2 You are more acceptable to local authorities and have more influence on them.
3 Britain is an island and is especially vulnerable to interruption of supplies.
4 Perhaps most important, the possession of a local plant means that you force your own company to commit itself to the market.

It can be seen clearly that the method of entry defines the degree of control which the company can impose on the four 'P's. With indirect export, for example, there is no control over any of the elements; with a wholly owned operation, the organisation's control over all of the four 'P's is complete.

The international marketing mix

It is worthwhile at this stage to consider briefly the special complexities brought to the management of the four 'P's by marketing internationally. No matter what sort of product or service the organisation markets, once the move is made into foreign markets, one or all of the four 'P's is almost certain to require modification from the domestic mix.

International product policy

Despite the undeniable attractions of a standardised international product offering, the market pressures are such that some adaptation usually has to be made. Often there are differing use conditions in the foreign market, tastes and habits may be different, or government regulations (for example, on voltage or safety requirements) may necessitate adaptation.

Other areas of the product mix may also be subject to change, such as packaging (customer tastes, different retailing and distribution systems and transportation), labelling (language and multilingual markets, literacy, differing information needs and different government requirements as to what information must be included), brands and trademarks, warranty and after-sales service (different market requirements at different costs).

It is not always appropriate for the international organisation to match perfectly its product to customer needs in each market, since the cost of maintaining an adapted product range is so high. Internationally, the costs of foregoing some sales must always be balanced against the economies of scale in producing and marketing a more limited range of products. Nevertheless, the costs of assuming that differences do not exist can be high, as one British exporter found when his large consignment of toilet seats were all returned from West Germany as being too small.

International pricing policy
The exporter should first look at two major areas.

Export credit and payment   In this area, the government can be of some help in reducing the risk involved in dealing with overseas customers.

The currency of quotation   Decisions in this area are difficult to make in an environment of fluctuating exchange rates. However, it is important that well-informed decisions are made – particularly in the market of industrial goods when there is often a considerable delay between signing and completing a contract. Whether the contract is quoted in sterling or another currency, the organisation is advised to cover itself against adverse exchange rate movements.

When considering the right price to set in the foreign markets, the organisation is advised to look firstly at differences in market conditions. Inflation causes prices to rise at varying rates; each market has its own distinct demand curve; government policy (involving tariffs, retail price maintenance, VAT, and so on) has an important influence; and competition will differ from market to market. With all these factors it is not possible for the same price to be fixed in each separate market – nor is it desirable. Rather, the organisation should aim for a uniform pricing strategy which ensures that the product occupies the same relative price position in each market.

International place policy
Some organisations whose products sell in foreign markets do not have to face the task of managing distribution within those markets. For them this question was resolved, for better or for worse, when they decided on their level of involvement in foreign markets. Indirect exporters, and to a lesser extent licensors, must accept the distribution offered by the chosen intermediaries.

For the rest, a number of uncontrollable market factors will affect the organisation's distribution strategy, including, notably, the size, number and efficiency of existing intermediaries, such as wholesalers, importers and agents. The availability and level of service which the intermediary can offer will vary greatly from market to market. For some products, such as washing machines or motor cars, it is essential to have a reliable after-sales service; if no suitable intermediary exists in the foreign market, the organisation may have to set up its own network or not enter the market at all.

For consumer products, the retail system is also important. Here, differences are even more pronounced since retailing closely reflects the economic and cultural life of the nation. Retailing can differ in size of outlet, the type of service to the consumer (for example, self-service or served), and also the type of service which is offered to the producer, such as product display, promotion, carrying stock and extending credit.

With such differences it is unlikely that an organisation will be able to operate the same distribution system in all its foreign markets. Even Proctor & Gamble, a mass merchandising pioneer in America and Europe, sells soap and other products via door-to-door salesmen in the Philippines and other developing countries.

International promotional policy

Promotion is the most visible as well as the most culture-bound of the organisation's marketing activities. Promotion is normally aimed at enhancing the image of the company, its product and its brands. We have already seen, however, that the situation of the company, in terms of product line and brand names, is often not the same from one market to another. As a result the promotional task will probably also differ from market to market.

Certain constraints must always be considered when decisions on *advertising* are made.

Language   In the few cases where the product and its advertising appeal are universal, the languages will probably be different.

Media availability   In many markets, media are simply not available for advertising because of government restrictions or the local communications system. This can affect television, radio, press, posters, cinema, direct mail and so on.

Competition   The style and intensity of competition will vary from market to market. This will affect the selection of a sound promotional strategy since competitive reactions will be different.

Agency availability   The number of agencies and the quality of their service will also vary. Many markets only offer one good agency if the market is small or the *per capita* income is low. The question is often asked, 'How far can an advertising campaign be standardised through foreign markets?' As we have seen in the matter of product standardisation, there is no easy answer. Essentially, the response must be, 'How similar are the buying motives from market to market?'

Evaluating advertising effectiveness in foreign markets is as critical as in the domestic market. It is more difficult to achieve such evaluation internationally for two reasons: the budgets allocated are often smaller, and foreign markets often have less experience of conducting the more advanced forms of market research that may be required. Personal selling is often more important in foreign markets than in the domestic market because of the restrictions placed on alternative kinds of promotional media. Local wage rates are also probably lower, allowing for recruitment of a larger sales force.

Sales promotion methods have proved very effective in many markets, although the organisation is almost certain to find more restrictions placed on promotional activity in foreign markets than is normal in the home market. Local laws cannot be ignored and will very clearly limit the types of actions that can be considered.

A brief look at some of the restrictions which exist will demonstrate the complexity of the international promotional task. In Germany, for example, it is against the law to use any form of comparative terminology. It is therefore not possible to mention a competitor's products by way of unfavourable comparison, or to make a general claim that one's own product is the best on the market. In Italy, many common words such as deodorant and perspiration are banned from television. In Kuwait, television advertising is limited to 32 minutes per day, all in the evening and a number of products cannot be advertised at all, such as pharmaceuticals, airlines, alcohol and chocolate. In Austria, children must not be portrayed in advertising and midgets are used instead.

International marketing information

The amount of information required by the organisation will depend on its level of involvement in international marketing. This, in turn, is largely determined by the chosen level of foreign market entry.

In addition to the kinds of information required for normal domestic marketing operations, the organisation must also pay special attention to local culture and habits, the availability of distribution channels, media, raw materials and finance and so on, as well as the present and likely future movements of exchange rates, foreign taxes, domestic controls and foreign political and economic situations.

Since all this must be ascertained for each market, it is clear that internationally the problem is one of breadth of information. The only way such an amount of information can be processed effectively is within an informational system which reduces the problem of 'information overkill'. The organisation should therefore ask itself:

1   Who makes the international decisions?
2   What decisions do they make?
3   What information is needed for those decisions?

Application questions
5.1   *What existing arrangements does your organisation have for reaching international markets? What are the advantages and disadvantages of these arrangements? What alternative arrangements could be explored?*

5.2   *What additional markets is your organisation moving into? On what criteria should the organisation decide to go into a new market, and how should it approach the task?*

5.3   *What is the justification for your organisation restricting its activities to the home market? Should other markets be considered?*

5.4   *Explain how the cultural and environmental differences of other countries are taken into account in your marketing efforts overseas. Is this provision adequate? What problems have been encountered because insufficient attention was paid to these factors? What could your marketing department do to reduce the risk of marketing overseas?*

6   How do marketing ideas
work for smaller organisations?

Overview

*The principles of marketing are just as relevant to small businesses
as they are to large organisations. However, it is usually appropriate
for small concerns to implement marketing ideas in rather different
ways from larger organisations.*

*Few small organisations have a senior manager concerned solely
with marketing matters. This means that owners and managers must
find time to do their own marketing thinking. Either through desk
research or direct contact with the market place, they must acquire
relevant and reliable information on their customers. They must
assess the degree of control they have over the variables in their
marketing mix and exercise that control in a way appropriate to a
customer-orientated organisation. Many small businesses find that
they can exercise most control over the promotion element of the
mix.*

*Systematic marketing planning enables small businesses to make
the most of their limited resources and to exploit the best market
opportunities. Such planning need not be complicated and time-
consuming.*

The relevance of marketing

Marketing activity is often most visible in large organisations –
but this does not mean that marketing is either more important
or more relevant for them than it is for smaller organisations.
In fact, the marketing approach is just as relevant for smaller
organisations, since the small concern has an equal, even a
greater, need to keep abreast of its customers' requirements and
to gear its resources towards matching them.
   The need for small businesses to adopt a marketing approach
is underlined by the large numbers of businesses that fail every

year for reasons that can be traced back to shortcomings in marketing. Small businesses need to take this aspect of their business seriously and to devote the necessary resources, especially managerial time, to it.

Small businesses operate quite differently from larger businesses. This means that whilst the principles of marketing apply to all sizes of enterprise, the most relevant and effective marketing activities for small concerns are very often different in substance to those used by larger ones. Furthermore, the practical means of implementing marketing ideas are likely to be different. A small business is not just a 'little big business' – it is more than that.

The marketing concept

As we saw in Chapter 1, sensitivity to the needs of customers lies at the very heart of the marketing concept. Quite simply, the marketing concept, or the marketing approach to business, is one of *customer orientation*, which means focusing on the requirements of customers and then organising the business to meet these requirements.

Owners and managers of small businesses are usually in close contact with their customers and hence very well placed for finding out what their customers want and for keeping abreast of changes in these requirements. Even so, it is quite easy for owners or managers to develop a fixed impression of what their customers want – particularly when there are so many other demands on their time and attention. However, since continuing sales depend on providing continued customer satisfaction, a constant concern with, and awareness of, customer demands are vitally important.

Those who think in terms of customer orientation will usually be more outward-looking than other businessmen and, therefore, better able to spot opportunities that arise in the ever-changing market place. A commercial contract cleaning company based in England's home counties, for example, identified a market opportunity in cleaning private homes. They discovered that domestic cleaners in their area are in very short supply, relative to demand, and that, for reasons of privacy, many people do not like the idea of someone local in their home when they are out. A 'professional' home cleaning service was launched and promoted by leaflets through letterboxes in target areas. The venture has been a great success.

Acceptance of the marketing approach to business also opens the door for the better application of marketing tools. Promotion and publicity, for instance, can be developed without a sound knowledge of customer needs, but such promotion is unlikely to be used as successfully. Selecting the best method of promotion depends on having a clear idea of who the customers and potential customers are and what they want from the product. The ability to build up this picture comes, in turn, from being well informed about, and sensitive to, customer wants and needs.

Using marketing ideas

The first step then in using marketing ideas effectively is *believing* in the marketing concept and, therefore, in making customer satisfaction the focus and aim of the business. It involves consciously and actively accepting the notion that long-term survival (and even profitable growth) is only possible by identifying, anticipating and meeting customer requirements.

How might the smaller organisation implement the marketing concept and conduct its marketing activities? What marketing tools can be used, and how? Obviously, this short chapter cannot provide comprehensive answers to these questions – but it can illustrate some ways in which small firms, or more accurately their owners and managers, can and do use marketing to good purpose.

Whether a one-man greengrocery or, say, an engineering firm with a dozen or so employees, the management of small firms is usually general rather than specialist. Where managers in large organisations tend to have clearly defined specialist roles, managers in small firms will usually do some – or all – of everything. Few small organisations will have a senior manager concerned solely with marketing matters. This means that every owner or manager has to do his own marketing thinking – to keep, so to speak, a marketing department in his own head.

This is no bad thing. Marketing is too important to leave solely to the marketing man – it needs to involve everyone, especially the top management, in a company. When small businesses do turn to marketing, such involvement is virtually automatic. This can provide a distinct advantage over larger competitors who are frequently fighting against specialism becoming compartmentalism and thus marketing becoming no more than 'what the marketing department does'.

But being a one-man marketing department does have its problems. Finding the time to do marketing is one. Finding out what has to be done and how to do it is another.

Marketing information

Owners and managers of small businesses will always have to make decisions about marketing, and their businesses generally, with less information than they would ideally like to have. There will always be some areas of uncertainty. What is important is that there are not more areas of uncertainty than there need be. The collection, understanding and use of marketing information cannot replace marketing decision making any more than it can replace managerial judgement, intuition and sound commonsense. But gathering such information can reduce the uncertainty and risk surrounding marketing decisions by enabling them to be based on facts and a fuller appreciation of circumstances.

The different types of marketing information and methods of collecting this information are discussed in Chapter 25. For the moment, it is enough to note that there are two main types of data, primary data and secondary data. *Primary* data is information collected directly from the market place through the use of such tools as observation, questionnaire surveys and interviews. Its purpose is to obtain information that is not already available from published sources. *Secondary* data is the term that refers to the information that already exists and which can be brought together by working from a desk – in other words, by desk research. The value of secondary data should never be underestimated.

A small company engaged in moving and installing heavy industrial machinery, for example, was in business for nearly a hundred years before management adopted a systematic marketing programme – whereupon sales doubled in two years. The foundation stone of this marketing programme was a change in the method of collecting information on potential customers.

The firm had always relied on secondary sources of marketing information, principally business magazines. To gather the necessary information, business magazines were painstakingly read for leads on plans for building new plants or expanding existing ones. These leads enabled the firm to contact the companies controlling the projects with relevant information about the services that could be provided. But the firm became increasingly aware that reports in the business press often came too late. Because of this, the firm decided to subscribe to fortnightly construction industry reports that give notice of new projects. These reports mean that prospective customers are now nearly always contacted during the critical early planning period.

But what happens in cases where the information required by the firm does not already exist, where it still has to be collected? The collection of primary data does not have to be either complex or expensive. What the owner or manager of a small business needs is relevant and reliable data – and this is not necessarily, nor indeed usually, the same as statistical results from a large scale survey conducted by a trained market researcher.

Looking, listening and asking questions are particularly useful ways in which small businesses can collect information about their market – especially a geographically compact and physically easily accessible market. A small egg producing and packing firm serving an area with a radius of about ten miles used this approach to obtain information about its market that just was not available elsewhere. One of the partners in the firm made deliveries personally over a period of three weeks. This allowed him to talk with existing customers and, while in a particular town or village, to visit other likely shops to see which were selling eggs and whose eggs they were selling. He could also ask the shop managers how they felt about the eggs and the service they were getting. Over the weeks, the partner was able to build up a clear picture of the major competitors in the area, what retailers were looking for in an egg supplier and which types of retailers would be most susceptible to sales efforts.

Of course, there will be occasions when a smaller business may need to employ more extensive marketing research, possibly using the expertise of a professional market researcher. It should always be borne in mind, however, that the object of the exercise is to clarify a situation and to give ideas – not to collect information for its own sake. All information gathering has a cost attached to it; and for small organisations with limited resources, it is particularly important that these resources are not wasted on collecting information that only serves to complicate matters, or even to confuse.

The marketing mix

As we have seen, the marketing mix refers to those variables – the four 'P's – over which the firm has control and which can be put together to respond to customer requirements.

The elements of the marketing mix can be varied to suit the needs of customers and the aims and resources of the firm. To do this, decisions must be made and implemented on the products to be sold, the price at which they are to be sold, the promotional support to be given and the distribution systems to be used. As with other aspects of marketing, the approach to each of the four 'P's and their mix will tend to be different in smaller firms than in large firms, and this different approach will be reflected in the emphasis given to each element of the marketing mix.

The managerial discretion exercised by small firms in developing product, pricing and distribution strategies tends to be limited. Most small firms have a restricted product line which is fixed over fairly long periods of time. This means that few options are open for manipulating the product element of the marketing mix. With pricing, small firms tend to be 'price takers' rather than 'price setters' (a subject discussed in detail in Chapter 18) and as such they usually react to competitor pricing rather than set price norms for the market. Furthermore, cost considerations are often a bigger constraint on pricing for smaller businesses than they are, or should be allowed to be, for large businesses. In the case of distribution, small firms are frequently in the position of being chosen rather than choosing, and of having to accept the conditions of those with whom they trade rather than determine what these conditions are.

It is in the field of promotion that most choice is open to the smaller business. Brochures, posters, trade fairs and exhibitions, point-of-sale display material, coupons, demonstrations, free samples, yellow pages, press and cinema advertising are just some of the promotional methods available to the smaller business. Once again, the focus of the promotional activity undertaken by smaller firms will normally differ from that of larger ones. In part, this is due to differences in the funds available for promotion, but it is also due to smaller firms having different promotional requirements.

This is probably best illustrated by considering a small furniture manufacturer making high quality sofas, chairs and foot stools.

This manufacturer first promoted its products through the use of a high-quality, full-colour brochure, a display case in an enclosed shopping centre and classified advertisements in glossy magazines such as *Ideal Home*, *House and Garden* and *Homes*. The themes of the promotion were exclusivity and personal service, both of which accurately reflected what the firm did in fact offer the customer.

These promotional methods attracted the first customers. Today, these promotional methods reinforce the most powerful tool of all in gaining new business for the small firm – recommendation by satisfied customers.

Admittedly, the limited resources of this furniture manufacturer precluded the use of full-page colour advertisements in glossy magazines and the national press, but in any case such promotional activity would have been inappropriate. The manufacturer was not going for the mass furniture market but that part of the furniture market comprising people who want high-quality, custom-built furniture of individual design. A large furniture manufacturer such as G Plan, in contrast, can afford extensive press advertising and, because the company aims to appeal to the mass market, such coverage is needed.

Marketing planning

As we saw in Chapter 3, to be really effective marketing activities need to be integrated and co-ordinated – and this requires planning. The need for systematic planning applies to all organisations, regardless of size.

Owners and managers of small businesses are often tempted to introduce *ad hoc* marketing measures. Whilst taken individually these measures might be sound, very often taken as a whole they do nothing to reinforce each other; and they may even be inconsistent and incompatible. Planning discourages such wasteful use of resources.

Another temptation for small but ambitious businesses is to spread marketing resources and effort too thinly, with the net result of failing to exploit fully the best opportunities. A planning approach used properly can counter this temptation because, by its very nature, it encourages the concentration of marketing effort into the most promising areas.

Planning the marketing effort does not have to be a complicated affair involving the production of a lengthy document. As indicated in Chapter 3, the essence of marketing planning lies in working through a series of steps that order and focus ideas so that, by the end of the process, the owner or manager of a small business should know where the business is now, where it is aiming to get and how it intends to get there. In a very small business with only one or two products serving one or two markets, there is unlikely to be any need to formalise the planning into a written marketing plan. Only as the firm becomes larger and the products and markets more diverse, do formal planning procedures, including the production of a detailed written marketing plan, become necessary.

The practical value of marketing planning for a small business can be seen in the fall and rise of a traditional nursery in England's Midlands. The management had never given any thought to the possibility of a change in attitude towards gardening and the purchase of gardening supplies. The owner of the nursery loved plants and knew he sold the best quality plants in the district at very reasonable prices so he did not worry when a garden centre opened a couple of miles away. Yet the beautifully tended and stocked greenhouses lost more and more trade to the garden centre which sold not just plants, but tools, fertilisers and lawn mowers – everything, in fact, that the gardener could need, and all set out in an attractive self-serve display.

At this time, a younger nephew came into partnership and decided the nursery needed to change. The layout was changed, a full range of garden supplies stocked and a service not available at the garden centre introduced – a gardening advisory and planning service which capitalised on the expertise and love of plants of the original owner. The nursery is again a commercial success – but a planned forward-looking marketing approach would have avoided the need for an eleventh-hour rescue.

Application questions
Note: If you are not the owner/manager of a smaller business, try to answer the following questions from the perspective of a smaller business which you know well.

6.1 *Would you say that your business was genuinely customer-orientated? If so, what evidence do you have of customer orientation? If not, why is this? How might you become more customer-orientated?*

6.2   *What information do you collect about your customers, competitors and other important market factors? How do you use this information in your marketing effort? How might you make better use of the information?*

6.3   *Briefly describe your product(s), price(s), method(s) of distribution and the promotional activities you undertake. Do they all 'fit together'? What changes do you think should be made?*

6.4   *Do you plan your marketing effort? If so, how? If not, why is this? How would your business benefit from more marketing planning?*

7 Who precisely are our customers?

Overview

The first stage in planning and implementing an effective marketing strategy is to define in precise terms, on which it is possible to take action, just who the organisation's customers are or could be. Knowing where sales are coming from, and the source of profits, is the key to understanding current market positions and to assessing the potential for the future.

A number of questions immediately present themselves. For example, are the customer and the consumer the same? What measures can be used to define a market? Who actually makes the decision to buy and on what basis? The answers to such questions are vital to a rich and full understanding of the organisation's markets.

The nature of our market

We have seen how marketing can be defined as the matching of the organisation's resources with the needs of the customer. This presupposes both the identification of those *needs* (a subject to be considered in the next chapter) and the identification of the *customers*. The nature and identity of the organisation's customers is not always given the attention that it deserves. Some indication of the importance of this knowledge can be gained from the following data, taken from a UK company's survey of the soap market:

– 24% of the customers of its best selling product accounted for over 82% of its sales;
– 61% of the sales of the product were to women up to the age of 35;
– the sales of the company's product accounted for 18% of the total industry sales.

The company management felt that this survey data could provide some useful cues for marketing action. Clearly, the data had to be interpreted. Only a small percentage of customers, for example, accounted for a majority of sales, and most of these customers were under the age of 35. The reasons for this pattern of purchasing – why some people bought in great quantity and others not at all – still had to be explored. (The 'why' of customers' behaviour is examined in Chapter 9). But the initial identification of customers provided the basis for future investigation and action.

Customers and consumers

First, we should distinguish between *customers* and *consumers*. This difference is more than semantic. In many cases, the customer is acting as an intermediary or an agent for the final user of the product.

Consider the case of the industrial purchasing officer buying raw materials, such as wool tops, for conversion into semi-finished cloth. This cloth is then sold to other companies for incorporation into the final product, say a suit or dress, for sale in consumer markets. Here we can see that the requirements of these various intermediaries and the end-user himself must be translated into the specifications of the purchasing officer to the raw materials manufacturer. Consequently, the market needs that this manufacturing company is attempting to satisfy must in the last analysis be defined in terms of the requirements of the ultimate user, the consumer – even though the direct customer is quite clearly the purchasing officer.

A similar situation exists with the housewife who in her weekly shopping trip is acting as an agent on behalf of her household. She is the customer, her family are the consumers. Her motivations and her actions, like the purchasing officer's, can be explained, partly at least, by her perceptions of the needs of the consumers on whose behalf she is acting.

The distinction between customers and consumers can also be seen operating in the service sector, as when a conference organiser acts on behalf of an organisation in setting up the venue for an internal conference, arranging speakers and so on. Here the organiser is the customer for the different promotional and administrative services needed; the organisation is the consumer.

Given that we can distinguish between customers and

consumers, the next questions to be faced are: who are our potential customers (as distinct from our actual customers) and who are our 'lost' customers? The answers to such questions can often provide an organisation with more valuable insights for marketing strategy than a simple analysis of existing customers alone. Being able to identify potential customers is the first stage in converting them to actual customers. A definition of the potential market for any product or service must be grounded upon a clear view of what basic customer needs the product meets or is intended to meet. Do these people use alternative products or do their needs go unsatisfied?

It is common practice in marketing to refer to the market share that a product or brand currently holds. This is essentially a measure of the proportion of the total sales of similar types of products that the product accounts for. Thus, Gerber babyfoods could be described as having a percentage share of the Belgian or British market. This share could be expressed either in terms of the value of the market, often called the 'sterling' share, or it could be expressed in terms of units sold. Either way, it is a measure of actual sales as a proportion of actual market rather than as a measure of the potential market. The difference between these two measures gives some indication of the scope for extending the market penetration of a product.

Past or lost customers are equally difficult to identify but, like potential customers, a knowledge of who they are could be invaluable in increasing an organisation's marketing effectiveness. When, in Chapter 25, we discuss the methods of marketing research, we will see that there are ways in which both potential and past customers can be identified. Investigation can then be made into the reasons for their behaviour in relation to the company's product.

Describing the customer

Knowing who our customers are implies an ability to describe them in terms appropriate for marketing action. Depending on the nature of our business, we might usefully describe industrial customers in terms of their level of purchases from us, the size of their total turnover, or the sort of business that they are in. For consumer markets, geographical location, age, occupation, education, marital status or income are typical measures of markets.

Such measures are termed *demographic characteristics*. One of the benefits of demographic characteristics is that they are commonly used bases for the majority of data collection exercises such as censuses. They have the additional advantage of being relatively straightforward to measure. However, convenience should not be allowed to obscure the possible irrelevance of demographic measures to specific market circumstances. This is a point which we will develop in the next chapter.

It is essential to be able to describe the organisation's markets in terms which will act as guidelines for marketing strategy. Knowing the precise ages of the customers in a market, for example, is of no use to the organisation if it is unable to capitalise upon this fact in terms of advertising or distribution strategies. Nevertheless, basic demographic data can provide a valuable source of initial market information, even though the company may then wish to look beyond that data.

The problem of identifying our customers is complicated by the scale of the markets in which the organisation operates. Philips of Eindhoven, for example, have a pretty clear idea of who their customers are for heavy electrical equipment stations. On the other hand, the same company faces greater problems in defining their market for domestic electric light bulbs. A market which can be measured in terms of tens of customers is generally easier to define than one measured in terms of tens of millions of customers.

The decision to buy

Having identified characteristics of our customers on which marketing attention can be concentrated, it is vital to ensure that this attention is directed towards individuals who are actually involved in the decision to purchase. This may well be more than one person. It could be several people or indeed a whole committee, especially in the case of industrial buying, and different marketing messages may need to be communicated to each member of this Decision-Making Unit (DMU).

Identifying just who it is within an organisation who has the power to make or influence the buying decision is often difficult, and is complicated by the fact that some members of a DMU may have positive attitudes towards a selling company's product, while others have negative views.

Let us, for a moment, put ourselves in the shoes of an industrial salesman who is intent on identifying the decision makers within an industrial company which has professed some interest in the machinery he has to sell. Experience tells him that it is rare for a single person to be responsible for such a purchasing decision. This responsibility is usually shared by several people who work together as a formal or informal purchasing committee. This purchasing committee usually consists of the following members:

– the works manager, who wants reliable, functionally superior products;
– the user, who wants a product that is simple to use;
– a buyer, who wants the cheapest product;
– a finance director, who wants the product that will deliver the best return on capital.

Potential conflicts of interest between the members of this purchasing committee have to be taken into account and different promotional messages must be devised which will be consistent with each individual's interest.

The industrial DMU is not always a formal, extensive group; and in the consumer field a DMU may consist of a husband and wife. While such a unit is relatively simple, there may still be differences of interest to watch out for. Husbands questioned in a market research exercise as to what is important when buying a washing machine, for instance, gave significantly different answers from their wives. The women were more concerned with the machine's functional attributes, such as load capacity and programme flexibility, while the men thought in terms of quiet running and ease of installation.

Those with overall marketing responsibility should co-operate with sales staff – through research, conversation, and so on – to identify which individuals comprise the DMU and, when appropriate, who is likely to make the final decision whether or not to close the deal. With this background knowledge, the salesman will be able to tailor his messages to suit the information requirements of the different people involved. Without such background knowledge, he is likely to end up wasting time and effort in telling the wrong things to the wrong people.

In industrial situations, in particular, he would be well advised to be sceptical of claims to all-embracing authority on the part of one, possibly junior, member of the management team; few organisations allow such concentration of buying power.

Frequently, in the case of large financial decisions, it may be necessary to understand the status of the company in question. To a bank manager who is seeking to offer financial services to a company, for instance, it is important to know if the company is a subsidiary of a larger organisation. If this is the case, then the management team is unlikely to have the authority to make the final decision on a major financial undertaking.

The 80/20 rule

As a market increases in size, there is almost always encountered a phenomenon known as the '80/20 rule' or the 'Pareto effect'. This simply means that it is usual for a small number of customers to account for the largest part of the business. It may not be 80/20, it could be 82/18, but there is rarely a proportional balance between the customers and the purchases they make from the organisation.

In many manufacturing companies, this relationship can be used as the basis for describing a large market in terms of the importance to the business of individual customers. If we draw a graph to show the proportion of customers that account for a certain proportion of sales, then we might expect to find a relationship of the kind shown in Figure 9.

In this diagram, an organisation's customers have been categorised simply as 'A', 'B' or 'C' customers according to the proportion of total sales that they account for. The 'A' customers, perhaps 25% of the total, account for 80% of the sales; the 'B' customers, say 55% of the total, account for 15% of total sales; and 'C' customers, 20% of the total, account for the remaining 5% of sales. This type of classification can be extremely useful when it comes to developing a strategy for taking particular products to particular markets.

It can also be of great practical use in dealing with existing customers. The branch manager of a bank, for instance, could make good use of the information if he is uncertain how much attention to give to individual customers, whether corporate or personal. A careful analysis of the range of his customers may well show him that the greater part of his business – and profits

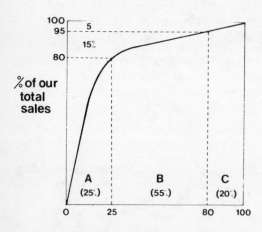

Figure 9

– actually comes not from, say, several very large companies, but from a number of small to medium size businesses. These may have been somewhat neglected over the years on the assumption that very large and very small businesses were more deserving of time and attention.

The same phenomenon can often be found if we plot the proportion of our products that provide a given proportion of profits (to be discussed in Chapters 12 and 13).

The Pareto effect is found in almost all markets from industrial compressors to banking, postal services or dog food. The marketing man in consumer markets will frequently concentrate his efforts on the 'heavy half' because a small percentage of committed users of the product account for a large percentage of sales. In the direct mail business, for example, it is an accepted principle that customers who have bought a product, any product, through direct mail in the past are the prime market for selling additional, even different, products to in the future.

Knowing the customer sounds easy enough. However, detailed analysis of exactly who he or she might be is vitally necessary if effective matching of company resources with customers' needs is to be accomplished.

Application questions

7.1   *Who are your organisation's customers, and who are its consumers? What needs do these two groups have in common and what needs are exclusive to one or other of them? How does, or should, your organisation market its products to both groups?*

7.2   *Think of a product or service you buy for which your organisation is one of the relatively small number of large customers. How does, or should, the manufacturer attempt to maintain and increase the volume of your purchases?*

7.3   *Have you been a member of a DMU at home, at work, or elsewhere? How did the various members influence the purchase decision? Suppose your organisation is thinking about buying micro-computers for the first time for a number of its offices, or is planning some other capital investment. Who would you expect to be in the DMU? How could a salesman know the right people to talk to?*

7.4   *Identify an item where you recently switched brands. Why did you do this, and how might the manufacturer of the original brand regain your custom?*

8   Are all our customers the same?

Overview

Recognising that customers differ from each other in terms of who they are and why they buy provides opportunities for market segmentation. Segmentation, it is suggested, can provide the key to profitable marketing in competitive markets. The means whereby groups of customers are distinguished from each other is clearly important and attention has to be paid to the choice of criteria for segmentation. Customers can be categorised on many dimensions, but only those criteria which relate in some way to purchasing behaviour and which lend themselves to marketing action are of any use to the marketing strategist.

Market segmentation

Once an organisation's customers, actual and potential, have been identified, the question arises of whether the organisation can satisfy their wants. The problem would be easily solved if all customers presented the same requirements or, put another way, if their wants could be satisfied by the same product sold in the same way. However, as we saw in the previous chapter, there are differences in demographic characteristics between customers and closer examination reveals that other, more subtle, differences exist as well; these include taste, life style, and so on. These differences amongst customers mean that an undifferentiated campaign to a mass market will seldom meet with widespread success. On the other hand, few organisations are in a position to be able to cater for highly specific individual requirements within the market place.

Fortunately, it is often found that, when a market is subjected to scrutiny, the members of that market fall into natural groups or segments within which customers exhibit the same broad characteristics. These segments form separate markets in themselves and can often be seen to be large enough to warrant a separate marketing strategy. Looking at markets in this way is termed *market segmentation*.

A segmented approach to marketing can bring many advantages to an organisation. In the first place, many companies have found that if they can identify a viable sub-market they can cater exclusively for the needs of that segment and gain a degree of dominance that would probably not be possible within the total market. One German firm in the specialist instrument field took this view and discovered that it was more profitable to have a 50% share of a DMk50 million market than to have a 5% share of a DMk250 million market. They realised, as many other organisations in all fields of enterprise have recognised, that market segmentation strategies can be the key to profitability in competitive markets.

Recognising that customers are different can enable the marketer to achieve a closer matching of customer needs with the firm's product or service offering. Thus, the matching process that is at the heart of marketing is in fact facilitated by adopting a segmentation approach. Segmentation strategies have an additional value in that they allow the company to relate its strengths and weaknesses to its marketing approach by ensuring a concentration of resources in those areas where the company has the greatest advantage.

Identifying customer groupings

Two approaches to segmentation suggest themselves:

– market segmentation through an analysis of the characteristics of the customer;
– market segmentation through an analysis of the responses of the customer.

Segmentation by customer characteristics poses the initial question, 'Who are our customers?' We saw in Chapter 7 that demographic features can be a useful way of describing customer differences and can, indeed, be used as the basis for a segmentation strategy. For example, a French commercial bank might decide to develop particular services that are angled at the young and newly married in the joint annual income bracket of Fr40,000–Fr60,000.

But demographic characteristics are not the sole criteron whereby we can characterise markets. In consumer markets, for example, it might be appropriate to use personality factors or 'life style' types as the basis for segmentation.

The food market, for instance, can be divided into a 'conservative' segment, such as those who eat steak and chips and drink tea, even when they are on holiday in Spain, and an 'adventurous' segment that relishes new and exotic tastes.

There are also those who like to spend a lot of time cooking and are potential customers for a great range of spices, sauces and so forth, to say nothing of kitchen utensils and cookery books. People in a hurry, on the other hand, are more likely to buy something in a plastic bag that only needs a ten-minute boil up. The 'convenience' customer and the 'connoisseur' may even be one and the same person with different needs on different occasions, since even the most enthusiastic home chefs may sometimes be pushed for time.

Similarly, industrial markets can be segmented by descriptive characteristics. A UK manufacturer of marine engines might set up approaches to the sale of marine systems to the warship market which contrast with those employed towards the container ship market.

Segmentation on the basis of responses asks the question, 'Why do they buy?' This approach can involve an examination of shopping patterns to determine how many customers shop at the retail outlet closest to their home or how sensitive customers are to price changes. An approach which is becoming increasingly popular is to examine the attributes that the customer is seeking from a product or service. This is called 'benefit segmentation' and is based on the notion that the reason a customer purchases a specific product is to acquire the 'bundle of benefits' that he or she perceives it to contain.

Different patterns of benefits sought can give rise to a basis for segmentation. Sometimes, as in the case of personal banking, the customers' needs develop and change on a 'life cycle' basis. Young people leaving school and earning their first wages are likely to need a current account, cheque card and credit card, with the benefit that they have somewhere safe and yet accessible to put their money, and can to some extent 'take the waiting out of wanting'. They are also likely to wish to make use of some form of savings arrangement. If they later marry, they will often have recourse to borrowing facilities as they establish a home and family.

These two approaches to segmentation, by customer characteristics and by customer responses, are by no means mutually exclusive. On the contrary, many organisations combine both approaches to provide a richer and fuller description of their market segments.

The UK toilet soap market, for example, can be looked at in a number of ways. It can be analysed in terms of the age and the life styles of consumers. These descriptive criteria may form useful bases for segmentation. Benefit segmentation, on the other hand, provides additional dimensions to the segments. Because individuals will have different requirements when it comes to benefits, we can see that the rationale for segmentation under this scheme is the grouping of customers on the basis of the similarity of their perception of the benefits that a particular product contains.

In the case of toilet soap, for example, market research might reveal that there is a segment that seeks mainly hygiene-related benefits, such as cleanliness, deodorant properties, freshness, etc. Another segment might be largely concerned with the cosmetic properties of the soap, such as skin care and scent. Still another segment might be seeking 'value for money' as the main benefit and therefore would be guided more by the unit price of the soap. The identification of these different benefit segments would then enable the design of marketing strategies aimed specifically at them.

Criteria for segmentation

Whatever the means whereby we distinguish between our customers, the criteria that we use for categorisation must be appropriate to the specific product/market situation. In other words, why segment a market on the basis of age of customer (in the case of consumer and service markets) or on the basis of plant throughput (in the case of an industrial market) if those characteristics fail to distinguish between different kinds of potential purchasing behaviour? Clearly, the characteristics must be related to behaviour. When segmentation is based on the benefits that the customer is seeking to acquire from a product, the criteria must be limited to those benefits actually related to purchase. Once we know the nature of those benefits and the particular combinations that the market seeks, then we are better poised to promote our product offering to those customers who are most likely to be attracted to it.

For a strategy of market segmentation to be successful, there are a number of requirements that must be met (see Figure 10):

– First, for a segment to be viable it is necessary that it can be distinguished from other segments. At the same time, the customers within each segment must have a high degree of similarity on the criteria adopted for segmentation. In other words, customers must be different on some dimensions, thus allowing segments to be isolated within the overall market, but customers within each segment must be similar on certain specific dimensions.

– Second, the criteria used to differentiate between customer groupings – market segments – must be relevant to the purchase situation. These criteria should be related to differences in market demand.

– Third, the segment should be of a sufficient potential size to ensure that any marketing investment made within it will result in an adequate return.

– Fourth, an identified market segment can only be exploited if it can be reached. It must be possible to direct a separate marketing strategy to each segment. This means that the customers in each segment could have different television viewing or reading habits, different retail shopping patterns, different responses to prices or different expectations as to the benefits to be derived from the product.

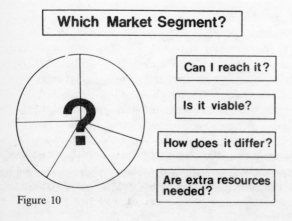

Figure 10

As has already been indicated, the realisation that customers are different has led to many successful marketing innovations by a wide variety of companies. Building societies, for example, offer different rates of interest for customers with short- and long-term financial needs. Educational institutions segment their markets successfully by using criteria of educational qualifications and career aspirations. Manufacturers of components for computers divide their market and vary their terms of sale according to the requirements and circumstances of different customer organisations. These and other examples provide a testimony to the value of market segmentation.

Segmentation in action

A Danish brewer of lager developed a new approach to its product strategy after a fresh look at its markets as a result of a segmentation analysis. The company knew that national differences existed in terms of preferences for beer and lager and it had some idea of what the criteria for preference were. Scandinavians liked a light, dry drink; the Germans and Dutch preferred a fuller, sweeter beer. Such knowledge was useful but it did not provide great insight into why some beers did better than others in some markets. The company knew also that the majority of beer was consumed by a minority of drinkers.

Evaluating its existing knowledge, the company believed that there could well be 'gaps' in the European market where minority needs, which were not being currently met, could be filled by a product aimed just at them. The questions were: who were these people and what attributes should the product possess to ensure an appeal amongst these potential consumers?

It was decided that a multi-country study should be conducted in Denmark, Sweden, Holland and Germany to ascertain the nature of current preferences and to relate them to identifiable market segments. This was done through an attitude survey which questioned existing drinkers on their preferences for beer and lager along a number of dimensions such as strength, brightness, dryness, and so on. At the same time, the survey accumulated data relating to demographic characteristics such as age, income, occupation, etc. Information was also collected which was designed to give an indication of the life styles that these drinkers associated with the consumers of various existing brands of beer and lager.

The research established that people have 'images' of the type of person who drinks particular drinks. Thus, one drink might be seen as being 'masculine', another as 'friendly', another as 'sophisticated', and so on. The segmentation study revealed that amongst occasional drinkers there was a need, particularly displayed by younger respondents, for a 'potent but convivial' drink at a price that was not excessive but high enough to give a connotation of quality.

The outcome of this research was the successful development and launch of a 'German-type' beer with special packaging in the form of a foil top and a label that was closer in its format to a bottle of Chateau wine. The promotion appeal was very much oriented towards the status aspirations of the younger, sophisticated end of the market and the price was about 25% higher than the regular beers in the market. This is just one example of the profitable exploitation of a market segment, based on a careful analysis of market characteristics and the opportunities within that market.

Application questions

8.1 *Think of a consumer product which you buy regularly. Do you, and all other buyers of the product, buy it for the same reasons? Can the manufacturer usefully classify his customers, or consumers, into different groups for marketing purposes? On what basis would he do this? How could the manufacturer appeal to each of the groups which you have identified?*

8.2 *How many different discrete types of customers buy your organisation's products or services? How are these groups differentiated? Have some greater potential than others? If so, is this balance reflected in the marketing of the organisation? If you were responsible for marketing policy, would you employ a segmentation approach? Outline your approach and explain the rationale underlying it.*

8.3 *Apply a 'benefit' segmentation to your organisation's market. How do you/could you communicate with each segment which you have identified? How do the major points being conveyed to each segment differ? Are there ways in which your organisation could make more direct use of benefit segmentation?*

9   Why do customers behave the way they do?

Overview

Marketing success depends on understanding, and being able to explain, the way in which customers behave in terms of purchase decisions. If we can understand how and why our customers buy, we are in a better position to combine in the most appropriate way the different elements of the marketing mix.

There is now a considerable body of knowledge available covering the mechanisms of customer choice in consumer, service and industrial markets. This knowledge can be summarised and distilled in the form of 'models' and theories of behaviour which can afford an effective basis for marketing action.

Why do people choose?

In a classic product test, two well-established brands of margarine were tested against each other in 400 French households. One was the brand leader and the other was a much smaller brand in terms of market share. Half the sample were given the two brands in plain foil wrappers simply marked 'X' and 'Y'. The other half received the two brands in their usual, familiar wrappers. All 400 housewives were asked to state which brand they preferred overall. In those households where the brands were given in the anonymous wrappers, there was approximately a 50/50 split in choice. Neither brand emerged as the clear leader. However, amongst those households where the brands' true identity was revealed, the preference was 65/35 in favour of the brand leader. *Why?*

A manufacturer of British defence equipment selling to the Middle East has found that price is of minor importance; that quality is taken for granted; that performance is assumed to be as specified; but that the critical determinant of the purchase order is the ability to establish a personal rapport with the buyer. On occasion, orders have gone to the most expensive tenderer where the performance levels have been lower, rather than to a cheaper competitor's bid. *Why?*

These examples are not quoted because they necessarily demonstrate anything odd or out-of-the-ordinary on the part of the particular customers cited. Rather, they demonstrate the complexity of the mechanics of customer behaviour.

How do people choose?

The study of customer behaviour in marketing is essentially the study of how people choose. What are the influences that affect choices and how do they differ from person to person or from product to product? These are questions that the marketer must answer if he is to build an effective marketing strategy; for it is indisputably true that if we know more about how a customer chooses, then we are in a much better position to present products or services that will lead to his or her choice being our offering.

This approach contrasts with the stimulus-response point of view, whereby the consumer is viewed simply as a 'black box'. Exponents of this view maintain that as long as one knows that for a given stimulus there is the likelihood of a certain response, then what goes on in between does not matter.

Such a view is too crude and limited for the development of creative marketing strategies. It postulates the customer reacting rather like one of Pavlov's dogs. If we expose him or her to a sales visit, for example, an order does or does not result. Now, in reality, we know that sales visits by themselves rarely generate orders because there are so many other elements at work as well. If there is a connection between sales visits and orders placed, it will probably not be a direct one. It is more likely that a visit might influence the customer's attitude towards the product or service and that influence, along with many other factors, might then affect choice behaviour in the way we wish.

Accordingly, it is often the case that today's marketing practitioner is looking for models of customer behaviour which attempt to describe and explain the influences of several and hopefully all marketing actions upon choice. These models need not necessarily be very elaborate or complex but they do need to be grounded upon a secure theoretical foundation. This need for theory should not dismay the practical marketer; it has often been observed that there is nothing so practical as good theory.

The requirement for a deeper understanding of choice mechanisms applies equally to industrial and service markets as it does to consumer markets. There is often a feeling that industrial buyer behaviour is somehow more rational or straightforward than the behaviour involved in the purchase of consumer goods. This has repeatedly been demonstrated not to be the case. The marketer encounters the same patterns of interplay of behavioural factors in the marketing of machine tools or printing inks as he does in marketing toothpaste, canal narrowboat holidays or education.

Models of buyer behaviour

Over the years, a considerable body of theory and knowledge has developed about customer behaviour. If the theories are taken to offer a complete picture of how the customer's mind works, it will soon become clear that they stand in opposition to each other. In other words, if the psychoanalytic explanation is believed to offer a complete explanation of behaviour, then the economic view which stresses the importance of 'utility' in purchasing behaviour cannot also be correct. However, the prudent marketer will not seek a global explanation of why customers behave in the way they do; rather, he will be content to derive insights and knowledge from the different models which have been built up. In doing this, he will usually be able to find a way of understanding more clearly the motivations operating in his own particular market, whether it be in the industrial, consumer or service sector. He can then proceed to build on this understanding to develop a marketing approach which will meet his customers' specific requirements.

The models described below summarise some of the main theories which have been used to explain customer behaviour. They may be employed or rejected as the individual marketer sees fit; it should be noted, however, that they have all provided insights which have proved invaluable in different marketing situations.

The rational, economic model The idea of the rational customer is based largely on the writings of theorists in economics. In their attempt to understand how a customer allocates his resources of disposable income, they propose a model whereby the customer seeks to maximise his satisfaction or 'utility' as return for payment.

This approach to customer behaviour suggests that choice behaviour is determined by the utility derived from a purchase compared with the financial outlay necessary to acquire the item. The model ignores all the many non-price factors that marketing practitioners know to exist in given situations. One example of this is the economists' concept of the demand curve, which postulates that, in most situations, as the price of a product goes up, the demand for it will fall. This does indeed happen in many cases but there are many exceptions to this trend (see Chapter 18 for some examples and discussion of this).

The Pavlovian learning model   According to this model of behaviour, learning is largely an associative process and most behaviour is conditioned by reward and punishment.

The modern versions of the Pavlovian model offer a number of insights useful to marketers. The model suggests, for example, that repetition and reinforcement are desirable attributes in advertising. In addition, it implies that in order to achieve its objectives, an advertisement must arouse strong drives in the customer, whether these are hunger, thirst, cold, pain or sex.

The Freudian psychoanalytic model   This model is well known in at least some of its aspects and is widely used by advertisers. Its basic thesis is that the individual human being is a divided kingdom, where behaviour rarely allows of a simple explanation. The individual maintains a precarious balance between emotion and rationality, between instinctive drives and socially acceptable behaviour.

Using this model, the marketer can construct his message so that it appeals to the parts of the psyche which are not accessible to the consciousness but which are still likely to determine behaviour. One disadvantage of this model, of course, is that it is difficult to make generalisations about any particular market segment. However, very effective advertising campaigns have been devised which appeal to the customer's private world of hopes, fears and dreams.

The social-psychological model   In this model, man is seen as primarily a social animal, open to influence from the broad culture in which he lives and from the sub-cultures with which he has chosen to identify.

In using this model, the marketer would draw on the importance to the individual's attitudes and behaviour of culture, sub-cultures, reference groups (that is, social groups to which the individual relates in his or her behaviour) and face-to-face groups.

The organisational buyer model The previous models concentrate on the drives, forces and influences which mould the individual customer. However, the organisational buyer (such as the purchasing agent) can be seen to respond to a rather different set of circumstances. These customers are buying not on their own behalf but on behalf of an organisation; their motivation, therefore, may be regarded as particularly complex.

This model suggests that organisational buyers are not impervious to personal appeals of the kind outlined earlier. However, they are also concerned to meet the needs of the organisation as satisfactorily as they can. They are, therefore, open to a dual approach by the marketer – a subject to be explored in more detail in the next chapter.

Behaviour in action

Whatever insights into customer behaviour are accepted as being useful for the individual marketer, it is a good starting point to regard such behaviour as comprising two related processes: perception and decision making.

Perception

All buying decisions are based on the perception and interpretation of information. However, perception is not a straightforward process: selection and distortion of information invariably occur when a customer perceives information.

Two main phenomena affect perception and should be thoroughly understood by the marketer. These are selectivity and subjectivity. *Selective perception* is a psychologist's term which means simply that people do not pay attention to all the information available in any communication. They pay attention only to those things which are important to them, be it price, styling or masculinity.

Subjective perception means that no two people will interpret the same communication in the same way. This phenomenon is the main reason why eye witnesses are frequently so unreliable. In the area of customer behaviour, customers are inclined to read into an advertisement what they normally expect from that source. If the customer has had a bad experience with a pre-prepared and packaged meal, all commercials for such products are likely to be viewed with suspicion. Customers selectively distort information in a manner which is consistent with previous attitudes.

Decision making

The decision-making process comprises two basic elements: beliefs and choice criteria.

All customers hold *beliefs* about the presence or absence of certain benefits among the brands available in a particular product class. It is known that customers do not notice all brands available in a given class of product. For example, if one were expected to decide rationally which deodorant to use, information on thirty or forty available brands would have to be processed. We know, however, that this never happens. Instead, what seems to take place is a phenomenon described as 'bounded rationality'. This is a short listing of acceptable brands. Out of the total set of deodorants, a customer in fact will make a purchase decision based on a group, or sub-set, of five or six brands which might possibly meet his or her needs. He or she has relatively little information about the other brands in the product class. The customer uses his beliefs about some of the benefits located in the smaller group to make a purchase decision.

A second factor influencing the purchase decision is the customer's *criteria for choice*. Potency, conviviality, high quality, for example, are all potential choice criteria for one class of product. Choice criteria are simply those attributes of a product that the customer defines as important and desirable. These attributes must also allow distinctions to be made. That is, a shopper must be able to compare an attribute, such as freshness, in one brand to the freshness of another brand. Customers may find safety in a car an important criterion; but, if they are unable to discern a difference in the levels of safety between motor cars, safety cannot be numbered among their choice criteria.

Choice criteria are derived from the multitude of experiences a customer is able to relate to the product. There are also certain outside variables such as social class, ethnic origin and religious persuasion, which can help determine and mould choice criteria. This concept is probably the single most important aspect of buying behaviour. If a marketer understands his prospective customer's choice criteria, he can then set about the business of designing products consistent with them.

Many marketers have found that the division of choice criteria into 'functional' and 'non-functional' categories is a useful basis for marketing action. Functional criteria relate to the physical properties of a product – the durability of a tyre tread, for example. Non-functional criteria relate to the non-physical properties associated with the product – the connotations which are evoked for the customer. Style, image and tone are often very important to the customer; they should be of equal concern to the marketer.

Having chosen the sub-set of products, and appropriate choice criteria, the customer is now in a position to make his decision. By comparing the products in his sub-set with the choice criteria, the consumer can arrange the various brands in an order of preference.

Customer behaviour: a review

The points made about customer behaviour can be summarised as follows:

– The first element in the buying process is the nature of the beliefs which the customer holds about the presence or absence of certain benefits among the brands available in a particular product class.
– For any particular type of product, the customer has various choice criteria. Choice criteria are simply those attributes of a product that the customer feels are important and desirable.
– These choice criteria are then used to select five or six most suitable brands from the entire product class. This smaller group of products, or sub-set, limits the purchase possibilities.
– Depending on how each of these brands in the sub-set meet the choice criteria, they can then be arranged in order of preference. Once this process is complete, the customer is in a position to make his purchase decision.

However, all these steps involve information, and information involves perception. Consequently, perception is an integral part of customer behaviour. There are two basic phenomena affecting perception:

– Selective perception refers to the fact that people tend to notice only those things which are important to them. The choice criteria are the important attributes and customers pay attention only to information about important attributes.

– Subjective perception, on the other hand, refers to the fact that different people are apt to interpret the same situation differently, depending on their fundamental attitudes.

And that, in outline form, is the way buyers behave. While the description is in no way foolproof, it does help a marketer to develop products and strategies that are consistent with customer-buying patterns.

Application questions

9.1   *What is your organisation selling, both in the 'functional' and 'non-functional' sense? What is the customer buying? How can these answers be brought closer together?*

9.2   *What criteria does the potential customer use to decide whether or not he is in the market for your type of product or service? How does he decide between alternatives once he is committed to a purchase? Why is your own market offering chosen? What could you do to increase the likelihood of purchase of your market offering?*

9.3   *What is the model of buyer behaviour operating in your market? Who needs information and at what stage of the buying process is different information needed? Is there any way in which your organisation could improve its communications with potential customers?*

9.4   *How does your organisation encourage existing purchasers to purchase its products or services on future occasions? Is your organisation providing the right information in the right form to the right people?*

10 How do organisations buy from us?

Overview

The most readily apparent distinction between organisational and consumer buying is that organisations often treat the buying process as a specialist task, to be performed by professional 'buyers'. This does not mean that the buyers' purchasing behaviour is always highly sophisticated, nor does it absolve the marketer from the necessity to consider other actual or potential members of the Decision-Making Unit (DMU). The DMU itself may be highly complex and include members who do not even belong to the customer organisation.

Organisational buying is characteristically more formalised than consumer purchasing and decision making takes longer. Distinct 'buy phases' and 'buy classes' can be identified, with implications for marketing strategy.

Some DMU members may prove invaluable 'product champions'. The personalities of individual DMU members often play a significant part in determining the nature and outcome of the decision-making process. The traditions of the buying organisation also have a strong influence. Both these factors should be recognised by sales staff. It should be remembered, though, that organisations buy as a result of an overall marketing contribution across all four 'P's, and not because of salesmanship alone.

The professional buyer

Attention was focused in the last chapter on why it is that customers as individuals behave as they do. We now turn to the buying behaviour of organisations and to the special complexities that are involved in marketing to them.

One very clear and salient distinction to be made between individuals and organisations as buyers is that the latter organise their buying as a specialist task, to be performed by one or more specialist 'buyers'. In some organisations, a whole department may be given over to buying. Specialist buyers spend their entire working week immersed in industrial buying activities, and so one might expect their professional purchase behaviour to be highly sophisticated – more so, perhaps, than when those same buyers put on a consumer hat and drive to the hypermarket for the weekend shopping, or ponder whether mowing the lawn really is more bother than a hover.

In practice, however much salesmen may doubt the fact at times, professional buyers do remain human when they are at work, and their knowledge of the products that are purchased may not always be particularly awesome or infallible. This applies especially if the buyer is responsible for buying a great many different types of product, or if an item is not of high cost in relation to others.

A buyer for a menswear manufacturer, for instance, may well purchase plastic buttons for suits and jackets without subjecting their price to careful scrutiny. This is because the cost is fairly trivial compared to that of the cloth, which it is also his job to buy, and to which he must give his greatest attention. It may accordingly be possible to achieve a very high profit margin on the buttons. A low cost item may become important to a buyer when it has to be bought in large quantities, however, and in general terms buyers tend to concentrate on areas where the overall cost impact is greatest.

Beyond the buyer

We have already seen, in Chapter 7, that customers are not always individuals acting alone, and that Decision-Making Units (DMUs) involving a range of people other than a designated 'buyer' are a common feature of organisational buying. Even in the case of apparently straightforward products such as nuts and bolts (part of the range of items known collectively as 'industrial fasteners'), it may well be that our fastener has a new design feature that could interest the customer's design engineers and the production manager, assuming that use of the new fastener could bring about production line savings. In these circumstances, it is plainly in the interests of the selling company to do all that it can to influence directly these members of the DMU, rather than have the issue decided by a perhaps indifferent buyer.

The same applies when selling a service, such as banking facilities. The usual tendency here is to perceive the company's financial director, or the corporate treasurer, as the focus for buying. But it may also make sense in such a case to go beyond 'the buyer'. If, for instance, the proposed service relates to overseas trade, it will be helpful to impress the benefits of the offering upon the export manager, as performance in his own area of responsibility could be directly enhanced by the scheme.

Organisations such as High Street multiple retailers tend to buy their stocks in consumer goods in a fairly predictable, mechanical way through the designated buyers. Initially, though, new products must surmount the hurdle of being 'listed'. That is to say, someone, perhaps called the 'merchandise manager' or 'brand manager', with a strategic responsibility for deciding the type of goods and particular items that his firm's shops should be selling, must be persuaded that the new product in question is 'right'.

Thus, a microelectronics company, say, that wishes to sell a new personal computer through Curry's or Dixon's or W. H. Smith, must first convince a strategically orientated element within the DMU that the product makes a sensible addition to the range of computers they already offer, or perhaps a suitable substitute for one that is becoming obsolete. Thereafter, the seller's attention must turn to the professional buyer element of the DMU.

Each of these examples, from the industrial, service and consumer fields, points to the necessity for marketing messages to reach customers beyond the professional buyer. The great complexity of some DMUs makes this a challenging task. A British manufacturer of 'curtain walling' (pre-fabricated wall sections hung like curtains from a girder framework) knew that the key member of the DMU for this product usually did not even belong to the contracting firms that installed it. Generally speaking, the *architect* was in effect the principal buyer, since his design specified the type of shell the building was to have. Sometimes the *client* who would ultimately occupy the building would also separately need to be convinced that the proposed building material was adequate. In one instance, the firm found that the *site owner's* influence was all important. The curtain walling was used in this case for buildings on an industrial estate owned by a pension fund, and the individual most responsible for buying the product was the fund's own *building specialist*.

The pension fund's detailed interest in a particular type of wall material may seem improbable, and would certainly have been hard to predict. The reason, however, was simple enough, and related to a product benefit that the curtain walling had been designed to provide: flexibility in use. The industrial estate was something of a speculative development. No one knew which incoming firms would prosper. Some would want to expand within a year or two; others would cease trading and give up their tenancy. It was therefore important to be able to modify any single building easily, so that one year there might be double doors at either end of the building so that lorries could drive straight through, while the following year the doorways could be walled over and windows placed all down the side for the better daylight working required by another firm.

Even in less complicated circumstances, the salesman on the ground may find it difficult to penetrate to the heart of the DMU. One study has shown that nearly 80% of board members who are important in purchasing do not see salesmen. The 'tradesman's entrance' to organisations often leads the salesman inescapably to the professional buyer's office, and it is he who can make or break efforts to go any further.

Diplomacy has a part to play in resolving the issue. It plainly makes little sense to give a buyer the impression of wanting to go over his head to someone in higher authority. On the other hand, it may be possible to convince him tactfully that a particular expert within the firm would really like to hear what the new product has to offer. The buyer might be persuaded, for instance, that a senior chemist in R & D might want to discuss a claim that a new paint had outstanding colour retention properties in extreme sunlight.

The salesman's point of view, however, is only one consideration. The answer to the question, 'How do organisations buy from us?' should not be sought solely in terms of how to sell to them, but how to conduct an integrated marketing operation. The work of a sales representative could easily come to nought as a result of insufficient prior advertising, or because the product itself had not been designed with an eye to providing distinct benefits that could be expected to appeal to particular DMU members.

Buy phases

The salesman may also fail because he is put in front of the customer at the wrong stage, after vital decisions have been taken or, almost as bad, when the buying organisation's thinking is becoming 'hardened up' in favour of a competitor's product offering. This point illustrates the fact that not all selling is about 'seller push', especially in industrial markets. Often it is a case of 'buyer pull' – an organisation realises that it has a need, perhaps for a new plant or equipment, and begins to look around for suitable suppliers. Good marketing demands that the needs of potential customer organisations are studied, with a view to anticipating fresh needs, and thereby enabling the marketer to 'get in at the ground floor'.

Studies have shown that there are distinct stages in the purchasing process that marketers should know about. These are generally known as *buy phases* and have been identified as follows:

1 A problem (or need) is anticipated or recognised and a general solution worked out. For example, designers working on plans for a new plant or machine may decide that a new system is required.

2 The broad financial dimensions of the change will be recognised, perhaps including the necessity to buy financial services as well as the plant or machinery in question.

3 The requirement is drawn up and quantified. Plant engineers, designers, architects and finance managers specify exactly what they think may be required. The process is usually formalised, documented and time consuming, as compared with the characteristically informal nature of most consumer purchases.

4 A search will be made for the required services. Various alternatives may be considered. Trade directories may be scoured to find appropriate market offerings. Visits may be made to a trade exhibition, or sales literature kept on file may be consulted. Meetings will be held at which the past experience DMU members have had with particular contending firms will be mulled over. Different types of product need will be debated in some detail. For a firm buying printing machinery, the choice at this stage might be between 4-colour and 6-colour, and whether or not ultraviolet (uv) finishing or a varnishing facility will be required.

5 The various options will be discussed with manufacturers, banks (for leasing agreements), and so on.

6 Proposals will be evaluated.
7 A decision will be taken.

Different people and different numbers of people are involved in each buy phase, and it plainly makes sense to distinguish, so far as possible, appropriate marketing messages to direct towards each of them at the appropriate time. Generally speaking, the sooner the messages begin to percolate into buyer thinking the better. The machinery moving and installation company encountered in Chapter 6 provides a good example of this. It will be recalled that this firm read about proposed new plant construction in the specialist building press, thus enabling them to anticipate in good time the prospective customer organisation's need to have machinery moved into the new plant, and to contact them accordingly.

Buy classes

One important determining factor of how many people are involved in the buying process – and how senior they are – is the degree of 'newness' of the decision to use the type of products (including services) being considered. All this means is that if the organisation has never before used such products on a similar scale, then it will be particularly anxious to have senior management deal directly with the matter. Similarly, if there is a high degree of commercial uncertainty associated with the use of the product, then once again senior management in the organisation will be careful to go into the various issues involved in considerable detail. When commercial risk is low, or the buying situation is routine, fewer people, with less status, will be involved in the buy phases.

A growing commitment operates throughout the decision-making process. Thus, as time goes on, decisions become increasingly concrete and difficult to change. Another feature of the process is that when 'newness' is high, the individuals involved in the decision tend to react to the uncertainty by using criteria that are familiar to them in other contexts. The company representative, therefore, should have a clear idea of the degree of 'newness' of the decision to buy so that he can direct appropriate efforts to the appropriate people. Just as the duration of the decision-making process can be divided into buy phases, so the decision to take up a product can be split into *buy classes*, depending on the degree of 'newness' involved.

1 *New buy, or new deal or service taken up*   Here the marketer will be approaching a company with a product completely new to it – perhaps a recent technological innovation, such as word processors. All the buy phases in such a case are likely to be followed in full. The DMU will tend to be extremely wide, involving both a range of executives and senior secretaries. The decision-making process is likely to be lengthy, and may extend until after 'test pilot' secretaries have evaluated the machine during a training programme.

2 *Straight re-buy*   Here the buying company will be familiar with the product in question. Since the need for the product will be following previously established patterns, only a limited number of people may be involved in the decision-making process. The owner of a sawmill, for instance, scarcely needs to be persuaded that he should be buying timber. The norm in these cases is for 'source loyalty' to be at its greatest. That is, existing suppliers are difficult for competitors to challenge and re-buying may be almost an automatic procedure. A potential supplier can only hope to overcome buyer loyalty if he is able and prepared to mount an impressive offering in performance terms. This may mean offering equipment on a trial basis. Or, in terms of non-technical performance, it may mean giving definitely superior terms of delivery, say, or service.

3 *Modified re-buy*   Here the customer may be so satisfied with the previous product that he wishes to extend its scope. Instead of simply buying another photocopying machine, for instance, the customer will buy one from the same supplier with a collating facility that the first did not have. Competitors may be able to break down source loyalty towards the original supplier if they are the first to introduce an appropriate scheme for 'trading up' to a more sophisticated product.

Product champions

A further finding concerning new buyers can also be put to good marketing use, namely the fact that people, including DMU members and potential members, have a wide range of attitudes to innovation. There are those who are almost immovably sceptical regarding the benefits of new product developments, and are the very last to adopt them. Others are more open-minded, but like to see a product being successfully used by others before trying it themselves. Finally, there are those (most helpful to the marketer) who are venturesome and eager to try out new ideas. When the enthusiasm of such people is tapped in order to gain wider acceptance for a product, they become *product champions*.

An international company with a strong innovative record in chemical products launched a revolutionary new form of wound dressing into a UK hospital market. A highly successful part of the marketing operation involved identifying and contacting particular surgeons within the National Health Service who were known to have been among the first in the field to adopt other medical products. Among them were surgeons who quickly appreciated the benefits of the new wound dressing. As well as being prepared to use the product in their own work, they were often keen to mention it favourably to colleagues and to write articles for the medical press describing their own successful use of the dressing.

Why do they buy?

So far in this chapter, attention has been focused on the identity of the buyer, buy phases and buy classes. Knowledge of the complex mechanics of organisational buying has an important bearing, as we have seen, on how the selling organisation goes about getting its message across.

The chapter would not be complete, however, without returning to the most obvious and vital issue – *why do they buy?* In particular, it should be remembered that the decision-forming factors for each member of the DMU are likely to be different. The production manager may be concerned with the quality of output, the works manager with the physical dimensions of the equipment, and so on. Thus, separate messages need to be addressed to each DMU member, in so far as distinctly different interests can be identified.

The fact that people may be either enthusiasts for innovation or fight shy of it, also gives some indication that, even within organisational buying, individual personalities are important. Within the same hospital, for example, one surgeon may be a product champion and another far more sceptical.

Nor are individuals necessarily immune to marketing messages, if such they can be called, which have nothing whatever to do with the product in question, but which instead make a blatant appeal to the self-interest of the buyer personally. Perks, or 'dealer loaders', such as a free cigarette lighter for store managers who take a larger than usual order for baked beans, breakfast cereals or whatever, are not uncommon. Having said that, it is by no means certain that such factors have a more than marginal influence. They may, indeed, sometimes be positively counterproductive, since there are many people who do not much care for the idea of being 'bought'.

Personality, and office politics, can also influence the size of the DMU; even corporate 'personality' has a part to play in so far as that term can be used to capture the special traditions and idiosyncrasies that influence each particular organisation's own 'way of doing things'. A dominant DMU member, with confidence in his own judgement, may view 'committee' decisions with scorn, and may be in a position to bypass other members. If a purchase is exceptionally large and risky, on the other hand, even this type of character may deem it prudent not to stand alone. The corporate tradition is frequently even more decisive than either the personalities of individuals or the type of buy class in determining the size of the DMU.

These factors must all be weighed up as matters of 'feel' and experience by representatives faced with particular organisations and DMU members. But it should also continuously be borne in mind that this exercise is a marketing effort, not purely a sales one. Organisations buy from us as a result of such factors as careful market research and product development, or the advantageous siting of a depot, just as much as from selling. Successful marketing to organisations depends on generating and communicating appropriate messages at the appropriate time to DMU members, based on planning that involves all four 'P's.

Application questions

10.1 *In relation to which types of buying would you expect the professional buyer's influence to be most dominant? Is it necessarily a good idea to seek out other DMU members in these cases? Can you think of a case where sales would be unlikely to be made unless other members of the DMU were contacted?*

10.2 *Think of a product that your own organisation markets to industrial customers. Are distinct benefits of the product communi-*

cated separately to different DMU members? To what extent does this happen? How are the messages delivered? Is there any reasonable limit to the benefit segmentation of such messages?

10.3   What examples can you think of where 'buyer pull' is more important than 'seller push'? How could marketers in these cases maximise their chance of getting in at the ground floor?

10.4   How is the buying function organised in your own organisation? Consider one product that might be bought in each of the three buy classes and how the DMU would be constituted in each case.

11   What does society expect in marketing's relations with customers?

Overview

Customers' complaints express dissatisfaction with the way in which organisations match their resources with customer needs. As such, they constitute a criticism of marketing practice. Accordingly, organised customer protest (known as consumerism) must act as a spur to redoubled marketing effort, as encouragement to the organisation to devote even more care and attention to understanding what consumers need. This involves increased attention to segmentation of markets and the development of more suitable products or services for the different segments.

It is equally important that marketing should take care to present the true economic facts about products or services offered. The avoidance of exaggerated claims and a clearer indication of what can reasonably be expected in return for a certain price are important steps in the right direction.

As society comes to expect greater 'social responsibility' from business, companies are becoming increasingly inclined to take more into account than profits alone when judging the level of their own success.

Caveat emptor

In a perfectly competitive market place, all the products or services offered by an organisation would meet the needs of its customers and consumers at the requisite level of profits. As the situation is at present, however, consumers complain with an increasingly strident voice about the way businesses operate. What conclusions are to be drawn from this? Are the major companies not based soundly on a marketing philosophy? Or are the strident voices not representative of the wishes of the vast majority of customers?

Consumerism, the name given to a wide spread of activities in the past dozen or so years, focuses our attention on the problem.

Traditionally, it has been argued that a bad product will sell only once. Its customers will reject it after unsatisfactory performance, and any organisation which persists in offering such products or services cannot long survive. Consumerists increasingly argue that a passive approach of this kind amounts to shutting the stable door after the horse has bolted. They usually want to see it made illegal for such products or services to be offered on the market in the first place. Most countries have passed a significant amount of legislation in support of this position. Up to the end of the nineteenth century, the doctrine of *caveat emptor* or 'purchaser beware' was widely accepted, although customers and consumers had always enjoyed a certain amount of protection as a result of regulations imposed on traders. However, since the end of the nineteenth century, the responsibility for the quality of the product or service sold has fallen more and more on the shoulders of the vendor.

Caveat vendor

In most countries within the EEC today, customer groups have succeeded in obtaining massive legislative support. Sweden is perhaps the most extreme example, with its Consumer Ombudsman and Market Court. However, the UK has its own Director of Fair Trading and an impressive array of legislation, including the Competition Act which became law in April 1980 and gives the Director of Fair Trading increased powers of intervention. As an illustration of legislation which supports customers' rights, we can perhaps take the concept of 'implied terms of sale'. In 1973, a statutory responsibility was laid upon a supplier of goods in the UK to ensure that any goods were indeed good for the purpose for which they were promoted and sold. This reversed the dictum, *caveat emptor*, to *caveat vendor*, or 'seller beware'.

Although many businessmen resisted this trend, it is difficult to see why they should feel that a change of this kind damaged their interests. No marketer, surely, would doubt that trust was an important element in his relationship with his customer. That customer groups, or politicians, had to lobby and get laws passed to secure this sort of relationship with suppliers is an indictment of marketing activities throughout Europe and beyond.

The marketing of children's toys provides an example of how customers, consumers and company objectives can all be satisfied by careful business practice. The successful toy companies of today are those which inform parents that their products are not potentially dangerous, not coated with lead paint, and not destroyed the hour after they are first pressed into active service.

Consumerism's way to better marketing

Consumerism is pro-marketing; it wants the marketing approach to business implemented in a sincere rather than cynical spirit. The cynical implementation, which consumerists claim has been all too widely practised, is no better than high-pressure salesmanship or misleading puffery. The sincere implementation of the marketing approach entails respect for each individual customer served. Indeed, the consumerist argues eloquently that the sort of relationship found between a manufacturer and a customer in, say, a capital goods market should be created in consumer markets. And, in so far as that is both economically feasible and what the consumer really wants, marketers must surely want it also.

Broadly, consumerists argue that recognition of the following consumer rights would ensure that a more satisfactory relationship would be built up between organisation and customer (see Figure 11).

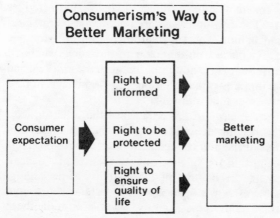

Figure 11

The right to be informed of the true facts involved in any buyer-seller relationship. Some of the key aspects, which have already been subject to legislation or regulation in Europe, include:

– the full cost of credit/loans taken up, often known as 'truth-in-lending';
– the true cost of an item, under the slogan 'unit pricing';
– the basic constituent elements of products, known as 'ingredient informative labelling';
– the freshness of foods, discussed generally as 'open-dating';
– 'truth-in-advertising'.

The case against producers is that they either mislead through exaggerated claims or fail to tell the whole truth about their products or services. Consumerists believe that the individual has the right to know these truths. Again, who can doubt that this demand, if sincerely felt, should be met? Who would be unwilling to tell an industrial purchaser the answer to basic questions about any merchandise offered for sale? What other information would our customers like? Can we not track it down before they clamour?

The right to be protected is also a major plank in the consumerist platform. All too often at present, consumerists argue, consumers' trust in organisations is abused. Safety standards (which are monitored by Government agencies) and the quality of medicines (which are subject to statutory controls) are exceptions which all businesses could learn from. It is certainly the case that the trend within the EEC is for many more product fields to be affected by legislative controls. The consumerists' argument that manufacturers should assume liability for any malfunctioning of products offered in the market place would appear to have overwhelmed the opposition. In most cases, however, good marketing will go well beyond the minimum standards required – and will not be slow to tell the customer that it does so.

The right to ensure quality of life is perhaps the most difficult demand for the marketing activity to satisfy. Nonetheless, if a meaningful segment of the market needs to perceive the products it purchases as furthering the quality of life, then that is a need that should be respected. The non-biodegradability of packaging, for example, has been shown on occasion to offend substantial numbers of customers. If a sufficiently large group of these customers is prepared to meet an organisation's research and development costs, along with the costs involved in changing to a preferred alternative, then good marketing should lead the organisation to work with these customers towards a change in its methods of packaging.

It should be emphasised that none of these rights is unfamiliar to the marketer of industrial or consumer products. He has been accustomed to responding to similar demands. What is different today is that the process of marketing is no longer done on the initiative of the marketer in a framework of *caveat emptor*. The framework is no longer *laissez-faire*. Today, the customer works through representative institutions, even unions – and the cry is *caveat vendor*.

Consumerism will affect marketing by bringing into being a more informative approach to all forms of marketing communication. It must, and will, give rise to a greater integrity in the advertising and promotional puffery of our profession without, one hopes, making life too dull, too much like a company share issue prospectus. It will give rise to a greater concern amongst all levels of business management with the long-term social implications of the materialistic bias of our society.

Consumerism as an opportunity

The social emphasis of consumerism, particularly its demands for an enhanced quality of life, is no threat to profitable enterprise. In considering this point, organisations might find it helpful to draw an analogy with changing attitudes to social factors at work. From the mid-nineteenth century, manufacturers were compelled by law to ensure that unsafe machinery was fenced in; considerable cost was, of course, incurred in carrying this out. Within the office, modern times have seen a concern to obtain office furniture and equipment designed to promote comfort at work; again, the introduction of such equipment has been an expensive business. It may well be that, in the long term, fewer accidents and a happier workforce will help improve an organisation's overall profitability. Even if this does not happen, however, the organisation should bear in mind that society expects the cost of safety at work to be included in the price of a product or service. Consumerism, like safety at work, presents an opportunity for the organisation to adjust its approach in accordance with changing social standards. As an articulate expression of customer needs, consumerism demands a marketing response.

One of Britain's most successful consumer movements is the Campaign for Real Ale (CAMRA). Britain has always been a beer-drinking nation; traditional beer, however, was fragile, difficult to transport, store and serve. The breweries' response was to introduce conditioned beers that were chilled, pasteurised and filtered for fermentation; they were then transported around the country in kegs or large tankers. The phasing out of real ales aroused a strong protest amongst certain sections of the community and eventually led to the founding of CAMRA, a lobby with a powerful voice.

Although CAMRA's attacks on lager have not stopped this segment of the market from growing, CAMRA has been successful in preventing the big brewers from phasing out real ales and cask conditioned beer. CAMRA's good beer guide which directs thousands of beer drinkers to pubs serving real ale has also revived interest in small traditional brewers. As a result of CAMRA's activities, the brewing industry has had to respond to the tastes of a small (only 14% of sales) but vocal part of the beer-drinking segment. The case of CAMRA illustrates well how the voice of dissatisfied customers can present a marketing opportunity rather than a problem.

Consumerism calls out for the reformulation and development of products and services to meet the requirements both of short-term satisfaction and longer-term benefits. A closer look must be taken at the system of marketing values which asserts that immediate consumer satisfaction and longer term consumer welfare may be opposing goals for an organisation's marketing activity. It is now necessary – and good marketing practice – to promote products which provide consumers with both short- and long-term satisfaction.

In consumer goods markets, for example, marketing specialists have devoted most of their efforts to promoting desirable and pleasing products. They have tended to ignore the long-term disadvantages to society which often accompany such products. Consumerism has reminded us vociferously of these disadvantages and, in a very real sense, has given us the opportunity to be better citizens. It is possible now to design and sell a motor car that is considerably safer than its equivalent in 1960. At that time, attempts to sell safety were conspicuously unsuccessful even though car makers emphasised safety factors in their promotional literature. It is possible now to design and sell an effective flameproof fabric for children's wear because an awareness of the need for it has been created.

Consumerism, in other words, opens up market opportunities which the astute marketing-based organisation will wish to take up. Other examples which can be cited are phosphate-free detergents, reduced lead content petrol, degradable plastic containers for a host of products, synthetic tobaccos, new nutrient based breakfast cereals and low polluting manufacturing systems.

In precisely the same way, retailing organisations have made great use of the popularisation of 'unit pricing' to help them build their business. Use of this system involves informing customers of the price charged per standard unit, whether this is 100 grams or one ounce. A major supermarket chain introduced unit pricing as a key service to its customers, inviting them to exercise their own judgements about relative prices compared with relative quality. New trade was developed and existing customers affirmed that they found the service of considerable value. It was, they reported, something they frequently tried to do themselves, but found too difficult on the basis of a fresh exercise for each shopping trip.

Marketing and society

Consumerism, as we have seen, represents not a threat to profitable enterprise but an opportunity. It helps to define and clarify customers' changing expectations, and so aids the marketer in his task of relating his company's resources to the needs of his customers.

Pursuit of the profit motive alone, however, may not be sufficient to satisfy society's rising expectations concerning the social responsibility of business. Although there is a wide range of opinion about the meaning of 'social responsibility', the implication is always that the organisation must look beyond the profit motive. Recent studies have shown that the vast majority of company executives acknowledge the interests of employees and consumers as well as the interests of shareholders. Executives are now being asked to acknowledge the interests of a 'fourth estate': that is, society.

Although unlikely to abandon the profit motive as the primary focus of their attention, company executives are now increasingly exploring ways of conducting business where 'social responsibility' is a salient criterion of success. The positive acknowledgement of the social dimension of corporate activity is likely to result in the deliberate use of marketing and marketing technology as an agent of social change. Already we have seen the adoption of a marketing approach by government agencies in attempts to gain participation in local planning decisions, to care for the countryside, to discourage the smoking of cigarettes, and so on.

When we talk about marketing, we are referring to more than just a set of techniques and procedures. We are alluding to an organised behavioural system which is constantly changing as it adapts to the evolving requirements of society.

Application questions
11.1   *When were you last disappointed in a purchase you made? Should you have been 'protected' by official regulations, or did you deserve your disappointment? What sort of protection would have been reasonable? How would it have affected the marketer?*

11.2   *In what ways does your organisation respond to consumer reactions? Is there adequate guidance for how such reactions should be taken into account? In what ways could your organisation's procedures be improved?*

11.3   *How can your organisation use consumerism as a form of free marketing research? What new business opportunities does consumerism offer your organisation?*

11.4   *Does your organisation consider consumerism as something which increases manufacturing costs or as something which leads to increased long-term profitability? Suggest some reasons for this attitude. Identify ways in which your organisation could make consumerism work for it rather than against it. What changes would the organisation have to make in order to gain from consumerism? How could these changes be brought about?*

11.5   *Think of a form of packaging or other marketing activity adopted by your organisation which could be considered socially harmful. What would it cost to eliminate the damage and would your organisation, or society at large, be willing to pay the cost? What prevents these changes being made?*

11.6   *Does your organisation acknowledge interests beyond those of its shareholders? If you feel that there is some concern for 'social responsibility', how might this be better expressed? What part might marketing have to play in this?*

12 What products should we market?

Overview

An organisation must know its market and know its customers. From there, it must proceed to a systematic yet dynamic approach to product development.

Customers are not attracted to products, but to the benefits which the product can bring. The organisation must, therefore, adopt a market-orientated approach to product development, rather than a product-orientated approach. At all times, the emphasis must be on what the customer wants and needs. This is especially important during times of technological and sociological change, when market demand will change accordingly. Developing and maintaining product-market strategies should become a major part of any successful organisation's activities.

Give benefits not products

Successful marketers try to remain open and flexible, yet there is one unchanging maxim which they share: *customers don't buy products; they seek to acquire benefits.* Those few words hold the secret of many an innovative organisation's success. It is a principle which can be applied to almost any product/market decision.

The principle itself is almost deceptively simple, which is why some marketers pass it by. The successful marketing organisation will pay more than lip service to its meaning, because it represents the most basic yet most important principle of marketing. Customers do not buy a product for the product itself. Customers buy clean floors, not floor polish. They buy security, not insurance policies; high performance engines (or status), not Ferraris; better lubrication, not industrial cutting oil.

You, the reader, bought this book not because it was a certain number of pages bound together in a card folder, but because it contained a promise to give you certain insights into marketing.

You bought the insights, not the book. The benefits which a book can bring have little to do with the product itself. The product, after all, is only printed paper. Many people produce books, and if someone produces a better book on marketing which can give better insights into the business, then this book will immediately lose its value. Books in their own right are already losing value in some areas where the customer finds he or she can gain the benefit – say, knowledge – in an easier form, such as microfilm. If the book represented the benefit of entertainment to the customer of the nineteenth century, the same customer today may find television or cinema a better provider of the same benefit. A forward-looking book publisher of the early twentieth century would have done well to buy into film rather than try to retain what was soon to be lost ground.

Another example can be taken from the banking industry. A bank's customers don't buy long-term loans, they buy the benefit of flexibility which comes through better cash flow and financial security. A different bank customer will buy the benefit of owning a house, not a mortgage. Both customers look to the bank for satisfying a want and for providing a benefit. The product itself is only the means to that end.

An innovative tool manufacturer realised, through the course of its relationship with its customers, that a major problem on the production floor was the time lost in changing abrasive discs. The company invested a great deal of time and money in seeking a solution, and invented a highly specialised system of binding grit to disc. The result was a new disc which had a much longer life and could be removed and replaced much faster than the old type. This gave the organisation's customers the benefit of more efficient production time and better value for money.

The benefit in the last example served a dual purpose; it gave the customer the advantage of time-saving and cost-effectiveness, and at the same time solved a traditional problem of changing discs. The 'problem' in this case was a customer need which had to be satisfied.

The concept of customer benefits shows the importance of an organisation being orientated towards the customer, or market, rather than the product. The organisation cannot afford to adopt a narrow view of its role by concentrating only on the product. An organisation, for example, manufacturing adding machines in a marketing environment which is moving towards calculators will soon find itself and its product obsolete. It must consider what the benefits of its product are – in this case computing sums accurately and quickly – and make sure that it is providing that benefit better than any other organisation. If a better or more cost-effective method of computing comes along, the customer will naturally be attracted to that product which incorporates those developments and can therefore provide increased benefits.

Marketers must be on guard against what one marketing specialist has termed 'marketing myopia'. Theodore Levitt described this condition as the result of confusing products with markets. He pointed out that people bought ¼″ drills to make ¼″ holes. The fact that a certain drill makes a hole that size is largely irrelevant to the customer. The mechanical drill as we know it may someday be replaced by a product developed through another technology. When that day comes, no customer will be interested in an out-dated product.

The organisation can avoid myopia of this kind by maintaining a dynamic and regular check on its product range. It must constantly assess its product by asking: 'Does the product provide the relevant and desired benefits to meet our customers' needs today?' The question will only be properly answered if the organisation conducts benefit-needs research. This will include the benefit segmentation analysis discussed in Chapter 8.

An organisation will find that it is easier to gain information on what benefits customers believe products actually bring rather than on what benefits customers would like but which are not currently provided. The amount of effort required to survey customers is, however, well worth it for the constructive input received. A French floor polish manufacturer discovered this when housewives were interviewed about the products they used. They were asked to list the benefits of the product which they now received, and the benefits which were most preferred. Benefits included:

– 'stands up to damp mopping';
– 'provides a lasting shine';
– 'no streaks';
– 'non-slip';

and so on.

A further sample was questioned on existing products and how well they provided the benefits sought. The result of this study was a detailed basis for the development of a new product and the design of a new approach to marketing it.

Matching products and markets

Marketing has been defined as the process of matching an organisation's resources with customer needs. The result of this process is a product. The need, therefore, for the organisation to remain dynamic is obvious because the product is the only key to the organisation's solvency and profitability. No matter how else the organisation runs itself cost-effectively and sensibly, if the product is not selling well then the money simply will not be coming in. Company and consumer are interdependent. The product will provide the means whereby *organisational* objectives can be met only if it simultaneously provides the means whereby *consumer* needs are met. Figure 12 illustrates this idea.

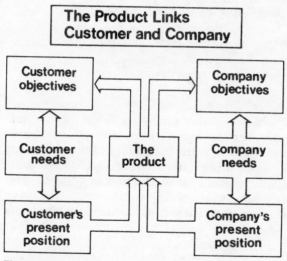

Figure 12

Successful product management depends on the organisation knowing how and if the current product range meets consumer and organisational objectives. One way of doing this, as previously described, is to conduct detailed benefit analysis segmentation. The most important attitude towards product management is to view the product as only one part of the marketing mix which also includes price, place and promotion. In this way, the product is viewed as a variable which can be adapted or even changed radically to meet a changing market. How it can be changed will depend on several factors within and outside the organisation, including the organisation's resources, market conditions and opportunities and competitive threats. Later on in the text we shall examine in more detail one of the most common techniques for doing this – the SWOT analysis for Strengths, Weaknesses, Opportunities and Threats. We consider here the most pertinent questions which can help to establish whether an organisation's current product-market strategy is appropriate.

– What benefits do customers seek in this type of product? Does our product provide these better than the product offered by our competitors?
– Does each of our products still give customers the best value for money?
– Does our product range as a whole still provide the best value for money?
– Does each product in our range still meet the corporate objectives set for it?

Product-market strategy

'Product-market strategy' is the term used to describe all the decisions which the organisation makes about its target markets and the products it offers to those markets. The use of the word 'strategy' is important, for it implies a chosen route to a defined goal and suggests long-term planning. This is quite different from 'tactical' activities which are used to achieve short-term objectives by gaining immediate results. Product-market strategy represents a decision about the current and future direction of the organisation. It is the step between the market segmentation issues discussed earlier in the text and the selection of new products to be described in Chapter 14.

As has been emphasised throughout the text, the key to success in any organisation comes with planning.

To plan for growth, an organisation implements a product-market strategy. This accounts for the two main directions of commercial growth: product development and market development. Table 1 illustrates the concepts.

MARKET	PRODUCT				
	Present	*Product Modification* - *quality* - *style* - *performance*	*Product Range* - *extension* - *size variation* - *variety variation*	*New products in related technology*	*New products in unrelated technologies*
Present	Market Penetration strategies	Product Reformulation strategies	Product Range Extension strategies	Product Development strategies	Lateral Diversification strategies
New	Market Development strategies	Market Extension strategies	Market Segmentation - product differentiation strategies	Product Diversification strategies	Longitudinal Diversification strategies
Resources and/or distribution markets	Forward or Backward Integration strategies				

Table 1 Product-market strategies

Product-market strategy must be developed in the most cost-effective manner, paying attention to cash flow and profitability requirements. To minimise costs at the outset, a sound marketing approach will usually attempt to increase profits and cash flow from existing markets. The following examples can help illustrate the total strategy at work.

Market penetration Heinz revamped its marketing strategy to increase consumption of its tinned soups. This product was traditionally a winter purchase, but Heinz successfully promoted the idea of celery soup, drunk hot or cold, as a suitable summer purchase. The product attributes of celery were linked with concepts of slimming and refreshment on summer days.

Market development   A British hotel chain opened up a new market by offering 'Leisure Learning' weekends in its hotels.

Market segmentation   A British bank promoted the idea of foreign exposure management for its international customers, thus opening up a new market segment among large corporations.

Product reformulation   Manufacturers in the US car industry responded to the market demands for increased fuel efficiency by bringing out models to compete with Japanese imports.

Product range extension   A European breakfast cereal manufacturer brought out a new 'variety' pack to appeal to young children who liked the freedom of choosing a new cereal each morning.

Product development   Manufacturers of digital watches soon combined the watch function with an alarm component. This not only attracted customers who liked the novelty of the idea, but seriously threatened the traditional watch market.

Lateral diversification   A successful French company in the materials handling market acquired a small warehouse design consultancy which allowed the organisation to offer a complete design/construction package to its customers.

Longitudinal diversification   An Irish television rental company successfully launched an office equipment leasing company. Previously, office equipment had always been purchased. Leasing became an attractive alternative, profitable for both the organisation and the customer.

Forward integration   A British wallpaper manufacturing company found that market share, profit and cash flow were all much improved by owning its own retail outlets.

Backward integration   A US fast-food restaurant chain found that buying back many of its franchise units improved service to customers and ensured that the organisation's image was preserved.

Application questions
12.1   *Identify the benefits you bought when you made your most recent purchase for your home. Did the marketer help you see the benefits arising from ownership of his product or service, or did you have to imagine them for yourself? Was there any additional information which you wished that the manufacturer had provided? Had he provided any information which you felt to be inappropriate or misleading?*

12.2 *What benefits do your organisation's products or services provide? How will people acquire those benefits ten years from now? Will your organisation still be in a position to provide the benefits?*

12.3 *How could your organisation improve its position in the market?*

(a) *By moving back in the material supply chain?*
(b) *By moving forward closer to the consumer?*
(c) *By repackaging existing products?*
(d) *By introducing new products to existing markets?*
(e) *By introducing existing products to new markets?*

At both a formal and informal level, how does your organisation identify, monitor and evaluate the possibilities? Identify ways in which you feel the relevant procedures could be changed or improved.

Action points
● *Remember* that a customer buys benefits, not products.
● *Make* a dynamic and regular check of your product range, to ensure that products continue to satisfy customers' needs.
● *Be prepared* to modify a product to meet a changing market.
● *Plan* for growth by implementing an appropriate product-market strategy.
● *Take into account* that a good marketing approach attempts to increase profits and cash flow from existing markets.

13   How do products make profits?

Overview

Products become a source of profit for an organisation when they provide customers with benefits in a cost-effective way. Products move through various stages in their development: a process known as the Product Life Cycle. Understanding this process can be useful for the marketer who combines this understanding with a thorough knowledge of the individual market. The product can be understood in terms of its growth, maturity or decline. Appropriate marketing strategies can then be developed.

Product-market strategy should be decided upon in the context of a product range portfolio, containing a good balance of growth products, mature products and declining products. Such a portfolio can give an organisation a sound base from which to plan.

The product life cycle

Integral to any organisation's successful development is the success of its products. In this sense, success is determined by the profitability of its products, a factor dependent upon customer appeal and cost-efficiency. It is first necessary to understand how products generate profits, and how their ability to do so can be best understood.

Product life cycle theory

The concept of the product life cycle has been widely employed by marketers during recent years. Although it is a hypothesis with weaknesses as well as strengths, it still forms one of the best foundations available for understanding product evolution. In essence, the concept suggests that a product, service or industry moves through identifiable stages and exhibits a sales pattern as illustrated by the 'S' curve in Figure 13.

The first stage is the *introduction* of the product into the market place. Growth is initially slow as customers must be persuaded to buy the product. The first few customers are known as 'innovators'. This period is marked by low profitability, when the organisation is faced with the costs of product development and introduction, coupled with low sales.

If the product is successful, then the next stage marks its *growth*. The graph here shows a dramatic increase in sales as the product quickly achieves popularity and rapid purchases ensue. The customers who rush to buy the product are termed 'early adopters'. The industry growth is also marked here, as competitors often imitate the product and join the promotional fever, thus helping boost total sales.

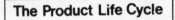

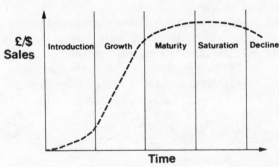

Figure 13

After the new buying spree settles down, the product enters its period of *maturity*. Few new purchases can be expected here, with the impact on the market lessening and the product being purchased by loyal customers.

The curve then levels off to the point of *saturation*, when the market has been almost completely exhausted. Sales expansion can only be expected here if the organisation modifies its marketing mix.

After this period of saturation, the product moves into a state of decline. The product is replaced in the market by a new generation of product resulting from the organisation's or its competitors' innovations.

Using the concept

The concept of the product life cycle has many good uses for the marketer and the organisation. It does, however, have its limitations; and these should be pointed out before the theory is embraced wholeheartedly. First of all, it presumes a cycle and a pattern which cannot, in actual practice, be totally relied upon. It would be a mistake for the marketer to assume that the product life cycle, or indeed the life cycle of an industry, will always follow the well-defined stages outlined above. For example, a product may be launched on the market and achieve instant, almost unprecedented success. The recent innovation of a new cheese in Britain, Lymeswold, illustrates this case. The producers promoted the product so well, and it took off so quickly, that initial supplies were exhausted. Similarly, a product may be launched and may never get beyond the introductory stage because it is unacceptable, poorly presented or untimely.

The product life cycle as described will vary from industry to industry, with some products by their very nature quickly reaching, or even by-passing, the various stages. Examples of this are the motorcycle and bicycle businesses which, after a definite period of decline, experienced a massive return to popularity. Examples such as these show that external influences will affect product life cycle and cannot always be accounted for by the organisation. The 'craze' for fitness which began sweeping North America in the 1970s spread to Europe in the 1980s and has influenced the buying patterns of many consumers. New market segments for sportswear and equipment have opened up, and products such as weights and track suits have suddenly become popular amongst young women.

Another point which must be made is that the life cycle does not constitute an inevitable progression; it *can* be manipulated. As has been mentioned, the stage of decline can be altered if the organisation redeploys the marketing mix in a more effective way. The case of Turtle Wax in the United States is a good example of using the marketing mix to influence product life cycle.

When the product was initially launched, its price was low in comparison to other brands. Instead of making the product more attractive, this low price caused consumers to view Turtle Wax as an inferior product. When the manufacturer increased the price, the product suddenly took on a greater value for the consumer and sales soared.

Similarly, the marketer can look at the other elements of the marketing mix for modification. Perhaps the product would sell better if it was made more available (place) or was presented in a different light (promotion).

With all these qualifications understood, the marketer can still make effective use of the product life cycle concept. Errors and confusion can be minimised by careful analysis of the particular product, the current market, the nature of the industry and competition within it. Having done that, the marketer can use the concept as a guide, rather than a rule.

Correct use of the cycle can be promoted by distinguishing between the life cycle of the product *class* (e.g., reprographic equipment) and the product *form* (e.g., photocopying) and the specific *brand* (e.g., Xerox). Each of these factors generally follows a different pattern in terms of life cycle. The life of the product class will usually be longer than that of the form or brand. The form generally follows a pattern most resembling that in Figure 13. The brand tends to be more influenced by changing competitive strategies and therefore exhibits a less stable pattern. By distinguishing these stages, the marketer can see that a certain brand movement may have no relationship to the market trends.

While the concept of the product life cycle cannot be used as a hard and fast rule, it can be a useful tool for management. The concept at least gives an organisation an idea of one likely turn of events which will probably occur. This then allows management to take a corrective course of action. Figure 14 shows how one manufacturer was able to affect the life cycle of a type of automobile lubricant. When the organisation saw the product in its growth stage, it actively worked to prevent the usual pattern of decline and saturation by introducing product innovation and increasing the range of product.

Keeping the product in perspective is also helped by understanding the life cycle. If an organisation works on the basis of typical product life cycle, it can avoid the mistake of haphazardly juggling the marketing mix when sales decline. It is sometimes tempting to vary the other variables, such as price, as soon as sales decline. By considering at what stage in its cycle the product

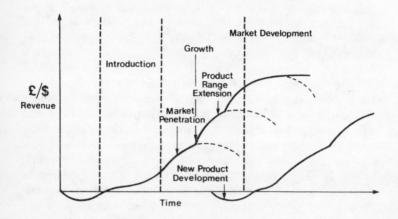

Product Market Strategies and Product Life Cycle

Figure 14

may be, the organisation can consider if modifications to the product itself are necessary. Has it passed its growth stage? Is its initial slow growth inevitable? Perhaps the product has indeed reached its natural conclusion and should be allowed to die rather than have money wasted on redevelopment. Such moneys may be better used to create a new product which better meets customer demand.

As we have noted earlier, marketing is simply the process of matching an organisation's resources with customers' needs. A product is the result of this resource management, and the organisation must always be sure that it is indeed meeting the customers' needs. The decline stage in its cycle may be the result of changing customer needs.

The product portfolio

Several techniques have been developed to help organisations analyse the effectiveness of their various businesses. This is usually done by viewing products as a group, taking into consideration those at different stages of growth, maturity and decline. The group which is analysed in this fashion is known as the 'product range portfolio'. The balance of that portfolio will reveal an organisation's current stage of profitability and allow it to create sound strategic plans.

A product range portfolio is in many respects similar to an investor's portfolio of stocks and shares. The investor may want a portfolio with a good mix to provide a balance between yield or income and capital growth. Or he may choose to create a portfolio based on risk, with some shares bearing a high risk of capital loss offset against their potential for high earnings.

In a similar way, the organisation may choose to assemble or maintain a portfolio to meet its long-term strategy. Objectives may include growth, in which case investment will be carefully monitored, or cash flow, in which case initial high sales will be wanted, or risk. The organisation can examine the product's life cycle and the life cycle of the industry to see how components of the portfolio are growing, maturing or declining. In doing so, the organisation can manage the whole portfolio in terms of strategy. This can only be done through a systematic process of monitoring and analysis. Most organisations today use the following method of doing this.

The Boston Matrix

One technique commonly adopted for product portfolio review has been termed the 'Boston Matrix', after its initiators, the Boston Consulting Group. Also known as the growth/share matrix, the technique offers a simple yet effective way for organisations to assess their portfolio.

The basis of the matrix is that different types of products will generate different levels of cash flow for the organisation. This goes beyond the initial assumptions about products in terms of sales achieved and profitability, because profitability is not always a good indicator of portfolio performance. Profitability is a factor affected by other influences, such as changes in the non-liquid assets of an organisation. Cash flow, however, is a key factor associated with the organisation's ability to develop its portfolio management. The Boston Consulting Group went on to develop a way of showing how different businesses generate different levels of cash flow and should, therefore, be managed differently.

According to the Boston Matrix, products can be classified according to their positions on two dimensions:

– relative market share;
– market growth rate.

Market share indicates how well the product can generate cash, and is measured against competitors. It therefore shows how dominant the product is in the market place. Market growth will show the cash requirements of the product. Figure 15 illustrates the concept.

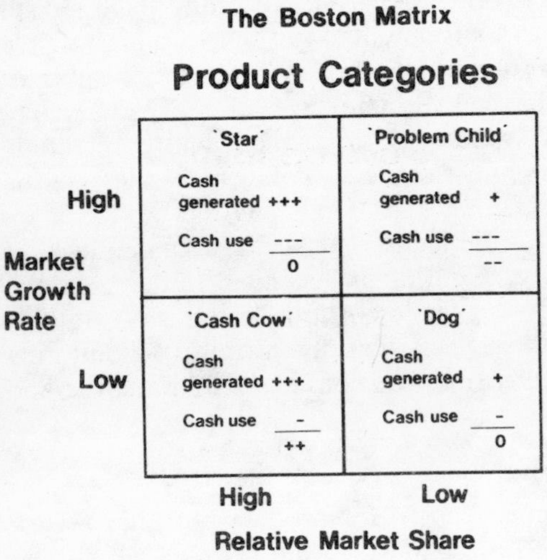

The Boston Matrix

Product Categories

	High Relative Market Share	Low Relative Market Share
High Market Growth Rate	`Star` Cash generated +++ Cash use --- 0	`Problem Child` Cash generated + Cash use --- --
Low	`Cash Cow` Cash generated +++ Cash use - ++	`Dog` Cash generated + Cash use - 0

High   Low

Relative Market Share

Figure 15

Each quadrant contains a description of the product provided by a descriptive label.

Problem child   This is a product, either newly launched or in a period of difficulty, requiring a great amount of financing and representing a drain on the cash flow within the organisation.

The star   This product will have a relatively high share in high-growth markets and is still growing. This means that it is still needing significant cash input, but its own cash generation has brought it almost into cash balance.

The cash cow   This is a product, yesterday's 'star', which has a high relative share in low-growth markets. This means it can help develop other products by producing a healthy cash flow.

The dog   As the name implies, this product has a low relative share in low-growth markets and will be a drain on the organisation's cash. Because its decline is likely, it is a product ripe for divestment.

A proper balance in the portfolio will mean that the products will be more or less self-sufficient in cash terms. The ideal product development sequence is shown in Figure 16, with products moving through the matrix in a controlled fashion. The cash flow within the organisation would ideally centre in the Cash Cow quadrant, with funds being channelled to the Star and Problem Child. Dogs would be divested before they drain too much off the organisation.

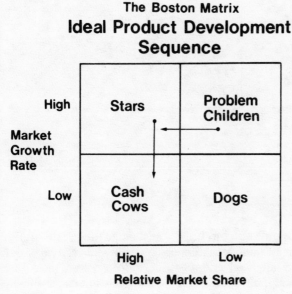

The Boston Matrix
Ideal Product Development Sequence

Figure 16

The matrix can be used to help the organisation forecast its portfolio. Figure 17 shows how a manufacturer of office equipment identified the current position of its product range and has predicted the range for five years hence. The area of each circle is proportional to the product's contribution to the organisation's sales volume.

The definition of high relative market share is taken as a ratio of 1 and above relative to the nearest competitor. The cut-off point for high versus low market growth must be defined according to the specific circumstances prevailing in the markets in which this organisation operates. In this case, the organisation has taken a figure of 10%. Using the Boston Matrix allowed the company to form a policy for new product development and decide how to manage existing products.

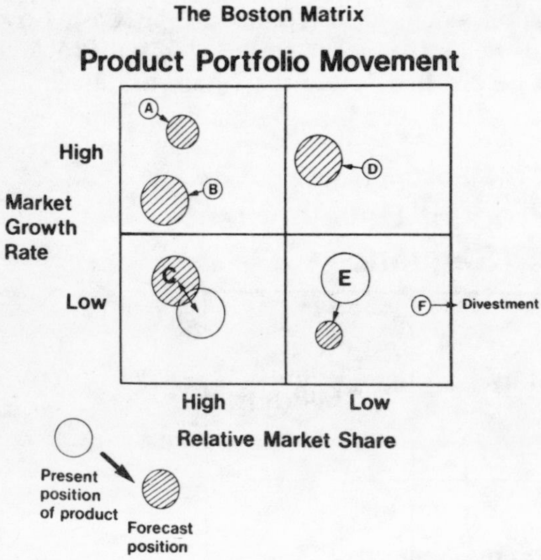

The Boston Matrix

Product Portfolio Movement

Figure 17

To use the Boston Matrix to its best advantage the organisation must ensure that the market is understood and the relationships between markets are well grasped. The industry, too, must be appropriate in that its structure would make relative market share a fair determinant of a product's success. The best use of the matrix would be in helping develop a corporate plan when the implications of different product-market strategies must be clearly understood, and potential weaknesses of existing strategies must be identified.

Planning for profits
Ideally, a product portfolio should contain the following:

– a substantial number of new products to provide major future profits;

– a sufficient number of mature products to finance the growth products;

– planned divestment of products which no longer generate enough profit to pay their way, and are unlikely so to do.

Such a balance in a product portfolio will benefit the organisation by providing a sound basis on which to plan for future development.

Application questions

Note The word 'product' is used in these application questions to include services. All the questions are as relevant to the marketing of services as they are to the marketing of products.

13.1 *Briefly analyse and define your organisation's product portfolio in terms of the Boston Group's categories. Is the portfolio evenly balanced? How could it be improved: by elimination, by addition or by attempts to change the positions of existing products?*

13.2 *How would you define your organisation's products in terms of the stages outlined by the product life cycle concept? How much of your organisation's profitability is coming from products or additions to the product range being developed to replace yesterday's 'breadwinners'?*

13.3 *Where do you see your organisation being in five years' time? Which products will have been phased out or re-launched in a modified form? What new products or product extensions will have been added to the range?*

13.4 *Who is responsible for the balance of the product portfolio in your organisation? Is there adequate provision for 'managing' new product developments and product re-launches? How could product management in your organisation be improved?*

Action points

● *Remember* that a product may have a life cycle, starting with low profitability, reaching maturity and saturation, and then declining.

● *Take into account* that a product life cycle can be manipulated.

● *Analyse* your group of products to find which stages of growth, maturity and decline each is in.

● *Analyse* how different products generate different levels of cash flow.

● *Devise* a product portfolio in which products at different stages of their life cycles can together produce sufficient profits to ensure sound future planning.

14   How can we manage
our new product development?

Overview

An organisation which does not wish to remain stagnant will be concerned with the selection and development of new products. To do this effectively, it will have to take a general view and a specific view of product market development – a dual process involving a macro and a micro approach. The former requires the organisation to identify gaps between its current performance and its objectives; the latter assesses the product's position within the organisation's portfolio and its contribution to the organisation's objectives.

New product ideas come from customers, scientists, competitors, salesmen and top management. A number of techniques can be used to generate and develop new ideas. These must then be critically evaluated and screened.

Testing new products is another process consisting of several stages. Each stage helps the organisation look at the product in different lights, including its impact on the organisation, the potential customers and the market place.

Product-market development: the macro view

In thinking about new product development, it is important to make the distinction between those products which are new to the organisation and those which are new to the market. Many organisations will be involved heavily in Research and Development and will find that this preoccupation suits the objective of being first on the market with new products. Other organisations will favour another approach more firmly based on adapting existing products or improving on competitors' products.

Whatever direction the organisation pursues, it must have a product development programme which is coherent, well thought-out and based on the corporate plan. It can ensure that this happens by taking what is known as the 'macro view' of product-market development. We have discussed before the importance of setting objectives before market development or product development strategies can be created. The usual way of doing this is to conduct a *marketing audit* of the organisation. This means that the organisation's external and internal operating environments are evaluated through use of the SWOT analysis mentioned earlier in the text.

The SWOT analysis basically consists of analysing the organisation's Strengths and Weaknesses as they relate to Opportunities and Threats. Strengths and weaknesses are counted as internal factors; opportunities and threats as external factors over which the organisation has no direct control. The Boston Matrix can be used to establish some of the strengths and weaknesses within an organisation. A product which enjoys a high market share and generates good profits is obviously a strength; one which is in a poor market position and drains cash from the organisation is a weakness.

Opportunities and threats are often less obvious, as they require serious evaluation of existing and potential factors. An example may be opportunities overseas; is the organisation pursuing the advantages of a licensing agreement, and would such a move be in its best interests?

Those in the banking industry will understand the complexity of such an analysis because they are faced every day with the problem of weighing opportunities against threats. The political, economic and cultural factors operating in different countries must all be taken into consideration when large amounts of money are involved. Another example of an external factor over which many have no control is the oil business; the massive increases in the cost of crude during the 1970s seriously affected manufacturing organisations all over the world.

Earlier in the text an outline was given of the marketing planning process. The marketing audit comprises the first three steps of this process:

– relevant information about the external environment and the organisation's internal resources is gathered;
– the organisation's internal strengths and weaknesses are identified, especially in relation to the external market opportunities and the competitive threats;

– assumptions about the future are formed.

The audit can then be used as a basis from which to go forward. It will show an organisation where it stands; objectives will state where the organisation intends to go. Naturally, there will be a gap between the two. In order to bridge that gap, the organisation can use a technique known as 'gap analysis'. This helps the organisation find the direction in which it should move towards its objectives. It assesses which of the organisation's products are meeting which customer needs, and how unsatisfied requirements can be met. Figure 18 illustrates the procedure.

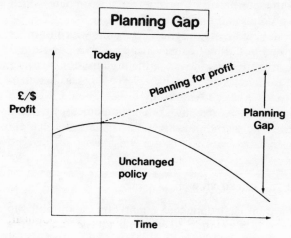

Figure 18

There are three major product development strategies which the organisation is likely to consider. The first can be a Research and Development (R&D) route which will mean heavy investments in research, experimentation and development. Rewards can be slow at first, with the organisation always running the risk of being copied by competitors who have not spent the time or money on development. Another route will be development-intensive but without the total dedication to R&D which the first option demands. The organisation in this case will take previously developed research and use it to create products which suit the organisation's particular objectives. The third route is one of pure application where the organisation takes products which have already been developed and adapts them slightly to a particular market. This approach is heavily market-orientated and entails no research or development costs.

An example of how the approaches work in the market place can be taken from the computer industry. Here, only a few organisations were involved in massive R&D, with other organisations taking the basic product and developing software to match. Yet other organisations took both hardware and software and, simply through packaging and marketing, opened up new markets.

Beyond development strategies lies another method of filling the gap between the organisation's current position and its desired position. This is the alternative of buying another company which already has the product and market in place.

Gap analysis can help an organisation determine which of these approaches it would best adopt to meet its objectives. The question will revolve around how innovative the organisation wants to be: does it want to invest heavily in R&D? Would it do better to be development rather than research intensive? Should it take a market-intensive approach or/and buy other companies which have already achieved some of the objectives the organisation has set for itself?

New products: the micro view

Once the organisation has conducted a marketing audit and gap analysis, it will be in a position to go from the general to the specific. 'Micro' considerations of new product development include those factors which must be taken into account to assess the product's position in the product portfolio and its contribution towards the organisation's objectives.

New product development can consist of six steps:

Exploration   A search for product ideas to meet the organisation's objectives.

Screening   Analysis of those ideas to determine their relevancy.

Business analysis   Examination of the idea to determine its commercial appropriateness in the business.

Development   Putting the idea into practice (making the product).

Testing   Verifying initial business assessments through market tests.

Commercialisation   Full-scale product launch, committing the organisation's reputation and resources.

Product conception and exploration

The major sources of new product ideas are customers, scientists, competitors, salesmen and management. The organisation can tap into and encourage these sources through a number of methods:

– sponsoring market tests to gauge consumer demand;
– funding research in universities;
– analysing competitors' products and directions;
– providing clear channels for salesman to feed back information from the market place to management;
– encouraging management to brainstorm (see below).

A number of techniques have been developed to stimulate and develop new product ideas.

Attribute listing means that the attributes of an object (e.g., a hand food-mixer) are listed and then individual attributes are modified in search of a better total product (e.g., interchangeable beaters).

Forced relationships means that product ideas are first listed and then considered in relation to each other. An insurance company, for example, listed household effects insurance and personal effects insurance. By combining the two it arrived at a lower per unit cost for each insurance policy issued but a higher value per policy sold.

Brainstorming simply describes a process of intentionally generating ideas in a 'free-for-all' environment. Ideas are not criticised or evaluated, but offered spontaneously by members of the group.

One criticism of brainstorming is that ideas are accepted too quickly without enough consideration of different perspectives. A method of overcoming this problem is 'synectics'. This means that the brief is defined very broadly so that participants do not know the precise nature of the problem. When the initial perspectives are exhausted, the co-ordinator can introduce a few more facts which further refine the problem.

Screening

New product ideas must be screened to determine their suitability for the market and the organisation. One consideration should be whether the new product *complements the existing range*. This can be important for several reasons. Complementary products can boost total sales of other products because they focus customer attention on the organisation. Too much diversification can confuse the products in the customer's mind and, if they offer no great improvements, they may appear simply as gimmicks and so erode the organisation's reputation. Complementary products can take advantage of existing customer relationships, salesmen, trade and retail outlets and distribution channels.

Products which produce an uneven level of demand should be avoided unless the manufacturer has products which have complementary patterns of seasonality. An *even level of demand* for the product is usually preferable.

Products should also ideally offer some *protection from imitation*. This can be attained through patents and through innovation. If the product itself is an imitation, then the organisation should ensure that the product has been carefully assessed for strengths and weaknesses.

Service requirements must be considered to ensure that the new product can be serviced adequately and immediately. Nothing destroys an organisation's credibility more than to launch an exciting new product which has no back-up. Smoothing out the wrinkles should be the organisation's problem before the product is launched, not the customer's problem afterwards.

Financial considerations will include the product's ability to repay initial investment in terms of payback, average return, net present value or internal rate of return.

Manpower requirements will cover problems of industrial relations when new technology is introduced, and also the use of existing technical and expert personnel.

Procurement factors are important. This requires consideration of material supply, agents and vendors, and supplier concentration. In all these cases, known qualities are preferable to unknown. The organisation must be careful to guard against erratic lead times in supply and delivery, and the effect of inflation on pricing.

Once the product ideas have been generated and deemed to be appropriate, they must be tested before a full-scale launch is planned. New product development involves a significant investment of the organisation's financial, physical and human resources. There is no guarantee that such investment will provide an acceptable return, but the organisation can work to attain the best odds.

Research into the success of new product development is not encouraging. Some 80% of all new product launches fail in that they do not meet marketing targets and are soon withdrawn. Reasons for failure can vary, with some industries such as grocery or cosmetics being more prone to failure than others. An example can be taken from a major food manufacturer which launched a new dessert after careful market testing. Retailers were unwilling to carry the product since its packaging posed problems in stacking on the shelves. This existing distribution channel was, therefore, blocked and the organisation was forced to withdraw the product.

New product testing

An organisation can avoid some of the major pitfalls of new product development by adopting a systematic approach to product testing. This can follow clearly defined stages as described below.

Concept testing The product idea can be tested on groups representative of the target market. The test can cover many features of the product, including technical specifications, colour, flavour, size, packaging, and so on. While positive reaction at this stage does not necessarily mean the product will be a total success, it can at least eliminate the non-starters.

The qualitative screen This is the process mentioned earlier when management must again review the product's suitability in terms of the organisation's objectives and resources. It must also extend the economic analysis discussed earlier and embark on a more detailed examination of investment appraisal.

If the tests thus far have proved positive, then the organisation can enter into a *product test* which involves considerable expense as quantities of the product must actually be manufactured. The test will sample a portion of the target market and gain the reactions of prospective customers and users. Aspects of the product to be tested would include its physical characteristics, the range available, suggested usage, price and image.

If a select group of people, including distributors and technicians, approve the product at this stage, the organisation may decide to *launch the product on a small scale*. This often involves selecting a town or other market segment to observe the progress of the product. This stage is still experimental; accordingly the segment chosen should relate as closely as possible to the actual market. All effort expended, in promotion and packaging for example, should be proportional to that expected on the grand scale.

The sequence of tests described here can vary, according to the organisation's needs, or can occur simultaneously. The time, however, must come when management will take a decision on whether the product is indeed viable. A careful balance is created between the natural reticence of investing too much of the organisation's resources into a product and the need to actually go ahead if tests prove positive. Delays can be costly, both through profits lost and through additional development expenses. If the organisation follows a systematic and thorough testing procedure, then it will reach a stage where it has the best idea possible of the product's eventual success. That is then the time to launch the product.

No product will ever be a 'sure thing' until it has been tried and proven in the market place. The organisation can do no more than conscientiously develop and test a product which it believes will meet customers' needs and wants. It must make every effort to 'get the bugs out'. From that point onwards, it will have to go ahead with the product and let the market place be the final judge.

Application questions

14.1   *What was the most recent new product introduced by your organisation? How do you explain its success or failure?*

14.2   *What procedures were used to generate and develop the idea of your newest product? With the benefit of hindsight, how would you have changed these procedures?*

14.3   *In what respects is your newest product compatible with the rest of your product range? Are there other new products which would complement the range?*

14.4   *What was the most recent new product purchased by you which was subsequently withdrawn from the market? How do you explain its failure? Could research have indicated that the product would fail? If you had been the brand manager responsible for the product, what research programme would you have recommended?*

14.5   *Consider the most recent new product launched by your organisation. Were all aspects of the product thoroughly researched? What research was done? What were the advantages and disadvantages of the research methods chosen? Would you have reduced the risk of the launch by undertaking any other research?*

14.6   *Who has responsibility within your organisation for the research and other decisions associated with a new product launch? Are any changes needed to make the new product launch less of a risk?*

Action points

- *Plan* a product development programme based on the corporate plan.
- *Know* how to conduct a marketing audit.
- *Know* how to make a gap analysis.
- *Remember* the steps and methods necessary for new product development.
- *Remember* the stages in systematic product testing.

15 What routes could lead to our customers?

Overview

Distribution is an integral part of marketing and involves much more than physical distribution alone. It has the potential to negate or reinforce other aspects of the marketing effort; distribution policy can also stimulate demand.

The channel of distribution is the route taken by a product in reaching its end users. The channel involves both trading and physical aspects, each of which should be subjected to careful scrutiny by the marketer. Planned decisions should be made concerning choice of channel and use of intermediaries.

Channel structures are complex, usually affording the producing organisation a considerable degree of choice and flexibility. Management must develop a distribution channel policy which ensures that channels match customers' requirements and the firm's capabilities in the most cost-effective way.

The importance of place

Our previous discussions of the marketing mix emphasised the need to understand the impact of the mix elements on an organisation's marketing effectiveness. However, it is often the case that organisations concentrate on three elements – product, price and promotion – and leave the fourth element, *place*, almost to look after itself. In the quartet of the 'P's, place is the shorthand description for the means by which the matching process between the needs of the market and the offering of the firm is finally achieved by getting the product to the right place at the right time.

The questions addressed by marketing under the heading of place are wide-ranging. They include decisions as to the type of routes that are to be used (e.g., should we go via wholesalers and retailers, or by direct mail?), questions related to physically moving the goods to the right place (via lorries, warehouses and so on), and policy regarding the level of service to be offered to the customer, in terms of such factors as the quantity and reliability of deliveries.

Thus, from a marketing standpoint, the word 'distribution' refers to much more than physical distribution alone, and represents a major strategic area of marketing. Indeed, in recent years, which have seen a slowing down in the growth of many markets, and shrinking margins, it has become a focus of ever greater attention.

There are signs that, in some markets, distribution is being asked to provide the key to long-term survival. The chairman of Monsanto's European operations states, for example: 'We in Monsanto increasingly regard distribution as having the same significance and making the same contribution to our success as skilful advertising, aggressive selling, efficient manufacturing and innovative research and development.'

Distrubution is an integral part of marketing. Its impact can negate or reinforce other aspects of the marketing effort; even more significantly, distribution policy has the potential to stimulate demand.

Much promotional effort might be spent, for example, on giving a perfume an expensive, exclusive image. But unless an appropriate distribution policy is chosen, this effort could be wasted. The brand image of the perfume would be strengthened by its appearance in up-market stores, such as the UK's Harrods, Selfridges or Rackhams. But if the perfume were at the same time distributed through down-market stores, its image might well be severely damaged, leading to loss of sales.

Consider too the grounds on which an industrial customer might buy steel forgings for the valves that his company has just started to make. There may be little to choose between competing suppliers in terms of price or product quality. In these circumstances, the customer may well choose a particular supplier because he knows that the firm is strong on delivery reliability.

The channel of distribution

The channel of distribution is the route that a product takes (remembering that the word 'product' in our usage includes services) in reaching its end users. Outlets must be created which enable the product and the customer to be physically brought together, and which enable the customer to buy.

Television advertising for a light travelling iron succeeded in interesting one would-be customer, known to the authors, who went along to Currys, Dixons, Dickens and Jones and other likely shops on the assumption that the iron would be in stock. It was not. The shops chosen had other travelling irons, but not the brand that had been advertised. Was the customer going to the wrong shops? Or had the producer advertised before sorting out physical supply to retailers? Or had the producer failed to 'sell' the product to the retailers? Whatever the reason, the lack of availability of the product in the right place at the right time meant that a sale was lost; in the end, the consumer settled for a competitor's brand.

Marketers who wish to avoid such miscalculations need to take into strategic account two main aspects of the channel of distribution.

– The trading route, through which the product is made available for *purchase*. This concerns the sequence of negotiation, buying and selling that goes on. Goods nowadays are sometimes bought and sold by intermediaries who never actually see or handle the merchandise; their task is to ensure that the product finds buyers, and then to effect sales.
– The route through which the product is physically moved from factory gate to end-user, by pallet-load and forklift, by crane and container lorry. This is the concern of physical distribution management as well as of marketing management: an interesting interface to which we shall return. The function of this aspect of the channel is to make the product available for *use*. Services, such as banking facilities, are not moved by the same means, but they nonetheless do need to be made available in a physical sense. Banks need to have branches, 24-hour cash tills and so on, that are convenient for customers to use, and these are channel considerations.

A fundamental issue regarding channels of distribution, whether on the trading or the physical side, is whether the producer should take the product direct to the end-user himself, or whether intermediaries should be used. For a variety of reasons that we shall soon come to, intermediaries are in fact used more often than not, and channels of distribution often amount to chains of such intermediaries.

Trading intermediaries include middlemen who are merchants in the full sense – those who buy and sell merchandise on their own account – and various kinds of agents and brokers who do not take title themselves but who are nonetheless instrumental in bringing about the change of ownership from producer to consumer. In addition to trading intermediaries, non-trading inter-mediaries, such as distribution companies like Cory and SPD, may be used. These intermediaries are not involved in the buying and selling but offer specialist services; distribution companies, for example, offer services like bulk-breaking, storage and transport-ation. Whereas intermediaries who buy and sell can expect to receive a proportion of the profit on the product (i.e., their margin), non-trading intermediaries tend to receive a straight payment for services rendered.

Frequently the distribution channel will have taken its present form as a result of unplanned and haphazard development, reflecting the fact that channel choice has in the past tended to be overlooked as a variable in the marketing mix. Such disregard for this vital area of marketing decision making means that many opportunities for the profitable development of market potential are passed over. For example, one international chemical company selling to Europe through its own sales office direct to customers found that the use of a chemical merchant or middleman would reduce selling costs and allow the company to take advantage of a ready-made sales organisation.

Another company, a British shoe manufacturer producing better-quality shoes, found that it could open up a new and profit-able market segment by including its products in the catalogue of a national mail-order firm. Soon, the manufacturer was selling the same shoes, at the same prices, to two, largely distinct, markets: to the up-market speciality shoe shop and to the wider down-market audience reached through the mail-order catalogue.

Here, then, are two examples of the benefits of taking a fresh look at channels of distribution. Both involved a reappraisal of the route by which the customer acquired the product and a comparison of the costs and benefits of using alternative routes.

Many companies use multiple channels of distribution to get their products to the market place. These companies may, for example, sell to different markets by means of different outlets or they may approach the same market through a dual distribution channel, with some products taking one route and others taking another.

For example, L'Oreal markets its branded items such as Elseve shampoo, Recital colourants, Elnette lacquer and Ambre Solaire suntan products through chemists, chain stores and supermarkets. However, only in the hairdressing salon will most customers come into contact with L'Oreal products such as Coloral colourant, Influence waving lotion or Kerastase conditioning. Of this dual approach, the distribution through hairdressing salons reaches markets for sophisticated prestige higher-priced items, distributed through exclusive outlets where customers expect a certain amount of personal service. On the other hand, the customer who buys products for use at home is offered the type of point-of-sale service common to mass distribution outlets.

Alternatively, a company may habitually use one particular channel of distribution but may wish to consider the possibility of using a different one. Whatever the situation, it is a necessary and valuable exercise to look at the costs and benefits accruing through the use of any particular channel of distribution. The alternatives depicted in Figure 19, for example, have quite distinctly different costs and revenue profiles.

The cost/benefit appraisal must be undertaken in the widest possible context. It needs to consider, for example, questions of market strategy and the appropriateness of the channel for the

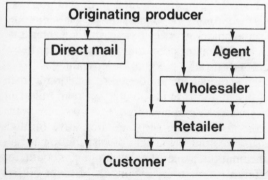

Figure 19

product and customer requirements, as well as the level of comparative costs of selling and distribution.

Channel structure

What are the variables of structure?

Channel structures differ in terms of:

– the number of 'levels' of intermediaries; i.e., how many firms handle the product, either in a trading or physical sense, on its way from the producer to the end-user?
– the types of intermediaries that are used, whether wholesalers, retailers, agents or others;
– the intensity of distribution at each 'level'; for example, is every available outlet to be used (i.e., saturation coverage), or is distribution to be on a selective or exclusive basis?

Most producers of consumer goods do not sell direct to the end user. There is normally at least one level of intermediary, frequently a retailer. It is in industrial markets, especially capital goods markets, that direct sales tend to predominate.

The strategy for choosing any particular pattern of channel structure will be examined later in the chapter. At this point, it should simply be noted that the three variables cited above give a high level of choice, at least in theory. For instance, in a situation with three available levels, three possible degrees of intensity and five established types of intermediary, there would be $3 \times 3 \times 5 = 45$ possible channel structures. In practice, the number of feasible alternatives is often limited, but there may still be half a dozen or more that warrant serious consideration.

Why use intermediaries?

The use of any intermediaries at all is bound to result in some degree of loss of direct contact with the market place and loss of control over key areas such as customer service policy. So why, in fact, are intermediaries used?

One reason for their use is that intermediaries specialise in particular activities. Hence, economies of specialisation are achieved and the channel as a whole benefits from division of labour. The intermediary may also achieve economies of scale through high volume at high throughput levels that are normally unavailable to a single firm doing the same tasks on its own account.

The use of intermediaries also reduces 'contactual costs'. These are the costs of the contacts that need to be made between buyers and sellers to distribute a product. Simple channel geometry illustrates the way in which these costs can be reduced by using intermediaries.

Figure 20 illustrates two distribution structures. Channel structure (a) is one of four manufacturers each distributing their products direct to retailers. 16 contacts are required in this case. Structure (b) also comprises four manufacturers distributing their products to four retailers, but this time using a wholesaler. In this case the number of contacts needed is eight, half the number in (a). Assuming that the costs attached to these contacts are similar, then considerable savings are associated with this reduction in the number of contacts.

Bulk-breaking and sorting are specialised activities that intermediaries are especially well-placed to undertake. Typically, the producer supplies a narrow range of products in bulk quantities. At the final point of sale, a wide assortment in small sizes is generally required. These differing requirements are reconciled by breaking bulk and assembling assortments of products, to varying degrees, along the channel of distribution. This enables each successive stage to purchase suitable arrays of products in appropriate quantities.

Some channel characteristics and developments

Channel structures are not static or universal; they can and do change over time and vary from market to market. Distribution channels servicing rural markets, for example, tend to have more intermediaries than channels serving urban markets. This is because in densely populated urban areas sales volumes are often sufficiently large to warrant direct distribution to retailers, whereas the lower volume demand of retailers in rural areas makes distribution far less attractive. Other rules of thumb for channel structure are that the lower the gross margin of the product and the higher the frequency with which it is purchased by consumers, the longer the distribution channel (i.e., the more levels of intermediaries) and, conversely, the longer the time an end-user is willing to spend looking for the product and the lower the frequency with which it is purchased, the shorter the distribution channel.

An important example of a change in channel structure over time is provided by the UK grocery trade. In the 1950s, the

Channel Geometry

Four manufacturers contact
four retailers **directly**

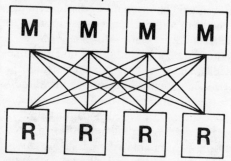

Number of contacts needed for all
manufacturers to contact all
retailers = (number of
manufacturers) x (number of
retailers) = (4) x (4) = 16 contacts

Four manufacturers contact
four retailers **indirectly**
through a wholesale intermediary

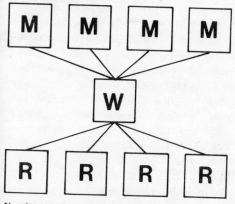

Number of contacts needed for all
manufacturers to contact all
retailers = (number of
manufacturers) + (number of
retailers) = (4) + (4) = 8 contacts

Figure 20

majority of groceries were sold to consumers by independent retailers. These retailers were typically supplied by wholesalers, the wholesalers buying the products from manufacturers. Today, more than 60% of groceries are bought by consumers from supermarket chains that obtain their merchandise from the manufacturers. This has brought about drastic changes in food wholesaling, such as the emergence of the cash and carry, an innovation soon imitated in non-food markets.

There are many different routes which may be taken to the final customer, some of which have already been illustrated in Figure 19. Some of those producers who choose not to use intermediaries at all both sell and deliver direct to end users; others sell direct but use third parties to aid in the physical distribution of their products. For example, an English manufacturer of fitted bedroom and kitchen furniture uses a mail order catalogue to sell its products, but uses a combination of hired vehicles, common carriers and the postal services to deliver its products.

Recently, there has been a growth of yet another approach to distribution. With this approach, intermediaries are used to reach the market and sell the product to end users, but these intermediaries do not handle the product itself. The delivery of an order to a final customer is undertaken by the original supplier, using either his own or third-party facilities, especially when the order is large. Despite this development, however, if trading intermediaries are used, in most channels they are also involved in the physical distribution process.

It should be remembered that producers often use more than one channel, and that the channels of distribution can be very much more complex than those illustrated in Figure 20, especially where there is a separation of the trading channel and the channel of physical distribution.

Criteria for the selection of channels

The ultimate purpose of the distribution channel is to reach the customer in a way appropriate to his or her requirements and to the firm's capabilities. The channel, in other words, finally brings together these requirements and capabilities, and the best choice of channel is the one that does the job effectively at the least possible cost.

Six broad categories of variables which influence the decision to choose a particular channel may be identified. These relate to the nature of the market, the product, the company, the middlemen, the environment and, finally, to the ways in which channel members relate towards each other.

Market variables In general terms, the main factors to be considered are the size of the market, the extent of its geographical dispersion and the buying behaviour of the customers. Who does the buying? When? Where? And how? If buying is highly seasonal, for example, intermediaries may usefully be employed to perform storage functions, so that production can go on steadily, instead of being affected by the peaks and troughs of short-term patterns. Sometimes the firm's market segmentation policy will necessitate the use of particular channels of distribution. If a company is marketing an insurance counselling service in Germany to individuals in the higher tax brackets, then it would probably not be appropriate to set up a network of door-to-door salesmen. The company may well prefer to use an indirect channel of distribution which might rely upon intermediaries such as bank managers and accountants.

Associated with the question of segmentation is that of coverage or penetration. In other words, how far do we wish to gain distribution penetration in our target segments? To gain maximum coverage may well require the involvement of an intermediary. A specialist book publisher, for example, was having only limited success in developing sales through mail order. Eventually he identified three major booksellers who had long-established positions as suppliers of libraries, overseas customers and others. The booksellers agreed to add the publisher's books to their list and actively to promote them to their customers. The publisher had to offer the usual trade discount but in return he had available a distribution network of a size and effectiveness that were beyond his own limited resources.

Product variables Perishable products, such as fresh fish or vegetables, require as short a channel as possible to ensure swift handling. Confectionery, by contrast, is typically marketed through longer channels. The priority here is to distribute intensively to all available outlets; to reach them all at low cost may require several intermediaries.

Company variables Large firms tend to have a stronger power base in terms of their expertise and their ability to reward or coerce other channel members; as such, they have greater flexibility with regard to channel choices. A particular firm's objectives, however, may work in the direction of limiting this choice. A short channel is indicated, for instance, if tight control over an aggressive promotional policy is required.

Middlemen variables   Middlemen vary according to both their cost and the extent of the services they provide; clearly, a trade-off between these two variables is needed. Sometimes it may be necessary for a company to set up its own intermediary chain where none presently exists.

Environmental variables   The legal environment, for example, has an impact on channel choice. In some countries it is virtually impossible to distribute to intermediaries on a selective or exclusive basis. The adoption of vending machines for the sale of confectionery, snacks, drinks and so on, illustrates the role of both the technological and the socio-cultural environments. In affluent societies, with convenience-orientated cultures, consumers are willing to pay the extra cost of buying from vending machines. The advent of electronic data-processing systems has also enabled manufacturers and middlemen accurately to assess their distribution costs and redesign their respective channels.

Channel relations variables   The relative power of channel members, with the implications this has for channel membership and control, is enormously important and is considered below.

Reappraising channels

Given these considerations, and assuming that we are in a position to choose rather than be chosen, what are the circumstances that might prompt a reappraisal of an organisation's existing channel strategy?

Reconsideration of channel policy is all too often a matter that is forced upon companies by changing circumstances, rather than the result of positive planning. Typically, new thinking tends to come about only when the producer is faced with inroads made by competitors, the appearance of major new products, increasing costs or shifts in the pattern of demand.

However, channel design should be considered under a great many other circumstances too, such as when an existing product is aimed at a new market, or when a major change is made in some other component of the marketing mix. The introduction of a new product, or even a merger with another company, should similarly involve a careful analysis of the costs and benefits of utilising present channels compared with possible alternatives.

Likewise, a change in marketing strategy might involve similar consideration. For example, an Italian manufacturer of specialist outdoor and climbing gear decided that the need for greater promotional and service support at the dealer level required a move from intensive to selective distribution. Or again, the identification of new potential market segments might require a channel reappraisal. The market, too, can change, necessitating a reaction by the distributing firm.

One firm that was adversely affected by too rigid a policy towards channels was an old established Belgian company in household products such as polishes and scourers. The company had traditionally sold its products through hardware wholesalers who distributed the products to hardware shops. When approached by a leading supermarket chain to produce 'own label' brands for them, the company refused on the grounds that such a move might not be well received by their existing outlets – the hardware shops. The problem was that hardware shops were a declining feature of the Belgian retailing scene and much of the business that had formerly gone to these stores had been captured by the supermarkets. Thus, the company was locked into a channel of distribution that was accounting for an ever-falling share of the market.

Channel leadership and control

In most channels one member will emerge as the leader, determining the policy of other members of the channel and even sometimes extending its control over them. *Vertical integration* is a common phenomenon in marketing channels. This process could involve a company in absorbing those firms who are its sources of supply (that is, backwards integration) or in extending its control towards its markets (that is, forwards integration). Such a movement backwards or forwards need not always require ownership of the firms involved. Marks and Spencers, for example, is a retail operation in the UK which, through its massive buying power, exerts an almost total control over many of its suppliers. When you sell 100 per cent of your output to one customer you are to all intents and purposes 'owned' by them. The motor car industry has a very similar relationship with its component suppliers.

Traditionally, it was assumed that the manufacturer was always the channel leader, but in an age of large retailers this is no longer the case. This is not to say that manufacturers no longer have channel leadership powers; it merely means that they do not have a monopoly of them.

There are four bases for channel leadership:

1 *Brand ownership* The owner of a brand establishes the quality specifications for manufacture of the physical good and the service standards that surround them. There are three types of branding, each with different implications for channel leadership:

– Unbranded or commodity products. When a producer sells these he gives up a large measure of his leadership authority because the unbranded product can be sold however the new owner chooses. The outlet, the price and the promotion are all up to him.
– Branded products. Manufacturers give up title ownership but not brand ownership. The distributors' own customer loyalty may outweigh brand loyalty, in which case the distributor rather than the manufacturer has a dominant position.
– Own label products. Here the manufacturer becomes a production agent whilst the distributor becomes the channel leader. The manufacturer, however, may be able to compete with his branded product.

2 *Economic power* Coercion or persuasion? Both are forms of motivation and effective leadership uses both. Economic power has diverse forms such as: massive purchasing power, patents, financial strength, technology and market dominance.

3 *Positional authority* Position in the channel can give advantages which result in an ability to dictate channel policies. For example: very strong brand loyalties, raw material monopolies, low operational costs, large market shares.

4 *Technical skill* Any competence sufficiently exclusive to a channel member can be the basis for channel leadership. For example: R & D, managerial expertise, ability to generate demand, physical distribution capacity.

One of the most important, yet difficult, functions of the channel leader is to manage the conflict that exists between members of all channels. There are several reasons for this conflict, including channel members having different ideas about what the channel should be doing, what the channel is doing and what rewards each should receive from the channel. This conflict tends to focus on issues such as: Who should hold inventory? How should the available margin be split? Can intermediaries lower down the channel be relied on to follow through desired marketing strategy and promotional plans? The likelihood of conflict is enhanced if each level of channel attempts to maximise its own return. In situations such as this, the return enjoyed overall in the channel may be reduced.

Managing the distribution channel is clearly a task of some strategic importance. Decisions taken about the nature and type of channel to use in the distribution of a particular product will considerably affect its profitability. For this reason alone, therefore, part of the distribution management function must be to review constantly the effectiveness of current channels of distribution and to recognise that they need not be fixed for all time but that they can, and should where necessary, be altered.

Application questions

15.1   *How do your organisation's products and services reach your customers? What do you see as the advantages and disadvantages of these channels?*

15.2   *Who is responsible for deciding the channels of distribution to be used for your products and services? How are the requirements of customers reflected in these decisions? Are there any cases where the channels used may not be the most appropriate? How could a situation of this kind be rectified? Is there any case to be made for marketing personnel being more closely involved in these decisions?*

15.3   *Is there any opportunity for your organisation to integrate its channels of distribution? What integration would you recommend? What advantages would result?*

15.4   *If your organisation were new to the market, what channels of distribution would you establish? How would your recommendations differ from the existing channels? What prevents your organisation from making these changes?*

Action points
- *Consider* the importance of differing distribution channels.
- *Appraise* the costs and benefits associated with each particular distribution channel.
- *Know* the variables of distribution channel structure.
- *Know* how to select the most appropriate channel.
- *Keep in mind* the bases for channel leadership.

**What levels of service
do our customers want?**

Overview

*Customer service needs to be defined more widely than has tradi-
tionally been the case, so as to take greater account of the factors
that customers themselves consider to be important. Instead of
assumptions as to what these factors may be, there needs to be
research into the overall service package that customers really
require.*

*Such investigation is a marketing function, as are the strategic
decisions involved in the control of the customer service offering.
Properly defined and measured, customer service can be a valuable
marketing tool. The level of service to be provided depends on
achieving a satisfactory cost-benefit balance. In judging where the
balance lies, objectives must be set and information gathered.*

What is customer service?

Customer service is measured by the brewers of Oranjeboom beer
in Holland in terms of how frequently their sales outlets are out
of stock. The National Westminster Bank in the UK considers
their customer service offering in terms of the location of their
banks, the availability of cash dispensers, the provision of budget
accounts, and so on. Monsanto Chemicals European Division,
based in Brussels, defines customer service in terms of the
percentage of orders that they are able to fulfil within a specified
period of time.

All these measures express a concern with the *availability* of
the product to the customer, and reflect the traditional definition
of customer service as the service provided to the customer from
the time an order is placed until the product is delivered.

Availability is indeed a key variable in customer service. If the
company's product is not available at the time the customer needs
it, and in the location he or she specifies, then the probability of

making a sale is much reduced. In product/market areas where competing products are only weakly differentiated (as in the case of, say, sugar or butter) availability will be the largest single determinant of sales. Research has shown that in many product fields availability considerations will overcome brand loyalty. For example, if a particular brand is out-of-stock, many consumers will abandon their search for the brand and switch to the next most preferred brand. For an industrial company selling sockets, holding stock of unusual sizes enabled them to charge high prices for immediate delivery. This policy helped establish the company's reputation for immediate delivery and encouraged engineers to contact them whenever their normal suppliers were unable to give prompt service.

Important as availability is, however, it does not comprise the whole of customer service. Research has shown that customers often regard other factors as significant aspects of service – and so too should astute marketers.

Companies engaged in valve and pump manufacture, for instance, were asked to rank in order of importance the elements of customer service provided by the firms that supplied them with steel castings and forgings. While all of them ranked delivery reliability as a major concern, many other factors, such as technical advice offered by the supplier, test facilities and replacement guarantees, were mentioned significantly often as important factors, as shown in Table 2.

Table 2

Service factor	Importance scale (proportion ranking in top 5)
Delivery reliability	100%
Technical advice	60%
Test facilities	60%
Replacement guarantee	60%
Willingness to manufacture a wide range	50%
Ease of contact	50%
Prompt quotation	50%
Sales representation	25%
After-sales service	25%
Credit	10%
Pattern design	10%
Machining facilities	4%
Discounts	0%

In a different environment, that of the retail store, another study discovered that the customers' image of a store's service offering is affected by a number of factors. Particularly important were customers' evaluation of the staff, the amount of queueing involved, the stocking policy in terms of the range of items carried, and the layout of the store as it facilitated the location of goods for self-selection. Interestingly, the study suggested that customers of the retail store would be grouped in three ways according to their service needs. One group reacts mainly to the quality of the staff, whilst the service requirements of the second group are met in an impersonal environment which encourages speed, efficiency and minimum risk in purchasing. The third, much smaller, group seeks service enabling them to delegate parts of the purchasing process to the store.

These examples point us towards a broader definition of customer service which encompasses every aspect of the relationship between a supplier and his customers. Under this definition, sales representation, after-sales service, product range offering, product availability, and so on, are all dimensions of customer service. Customer service can then be seen as the total activity of serving one's customer.

It is also clear that it often pays to *investigate* what the customer wants in terms of customer service in any particular case. The customer service package should comprise what customers actually want, not merely what marketers assume they should want.

Improved standards need not be costly. Analyses based solely upon product availability have tended to emphasise that the cost of improving this factor beyond a certain level is often prohibitive. But adjustments to other aspects of the service mix may cost comparatively little. Instead of a very high level of stock availability and fast delivery, for instance, a customer, particularly an organisational buyer, may be just as happy to have *consistency* or *reliability* of delivery. If he can predict accurately *when* the product will be available, perhaps regularly at the beginning of each month, he will be able to plan his own operations more satisfactorily.

Finally, there is often confusion as to where the responsibility for customer service should lie. Improved customer service can provide a competitive cutting edge in the market place. It is thus quite clearly a marketing concern, and indeed constitutes the reason that distribution itself can be described as a marketing variable.

Yet customer service is commonly looked upon as the outcome of physical distribution activity, and the task of managers whose primary concern is the efficient running of transport, warehouses, invoicing and the like. To a great extent this is true. Physical distribution plays an enormously important role in customer service, and if the management task in the physical distribution area is viewed as one of moving products efficiently, i.e., to acceptable levels of service at the lowest possible cost, it might at first sight be wondered why marketing should be involved at all.

Table 3

Factors influencing industrial purchase decisions (400 EEC purchasing agents)		Factors influencing export sales	
Factor	Rank order	Factor	% respondents
Product quality	1	Delivery	16.3
Distribution service	2	Supplier prices	13.8
Price	3	Supplier's support	9.1
Efficiency of supplier	4	Demand	9.1
Distance to supplier	5		
Order size constraints	6		

But marketing has to be involved for two reasons. Firstly, as we have seen, customer service covers a wide range of factors, all of which – both those inside and those outside the scope of physical distribution – need to fall within the strategic area of marketing. Secondly, decisions as to what constitutes an acceptable level of service are precisely what marketing, with its customer-orientated approach, is all about. It is in order to define appropriate levels of customer service that marketing needs to involve itself in the physical distribution process.

Customer service as a marketing tool

Many companies have no customer service objectives or strategies and the poor level of service often provided is a reflection of this. But customer service is an important factor to customers, as indicated in the results, summarised in Table 3, of research surveys. Customer service might indeed provide the way in which a company can really distinguish itself from its competitors if, say, the other aspects of its product are very similar.

In Scandinavia a study found that poor distribution service to grocery supermarkets invited 'retaliation' by the retailer. This took the form of reduced shelf space allocation, the de-listing of the product, or a refusal to accept or list new products.

One means by which the concept of customer service can be used as a marketing tool is to regard it as a focus for segmentation. As we saw from the example of the retail store, some people like fast, anonymous service; others are more interested in the quality of the staff, perhaps preferring to be given a certain amount of time-consuming personal attention. Astute organisations have the opportunity to capitalise on such differences of taste, by recognising and catering for them separately.

An extremely low-cost example of service segmentation is provided by supermarket checkouts at which those customers buying a large number of items pay at different tills to those buying only a few. This system very sensibly recognises that the one or two item customer may well resent being kept waiting behind trolleys loaded up to the gunwales. Paradoxically, this is a case in which it makes sense to give a *higher* level of service (i.e., speedier) to customers buying *fewer* products. Usually, the reverse of this will be the best policy. Some grocery stores, for example, give free deliveries to the homes of customers – providing that they have a large, regular order. Service segmentation of this kind is also very common in sales to other channel members.

The customer service package

Experience in the market place suggests that, from the customer's point of view, customer service is a subjective phenomenon that comprises a host of tangible and intangible features. The customer's perception of service is formed by all the points of contact that the customer has with the company in his or her search for solutions to buying problems. Customer service can in fact be seen as a *package* in the sense that, whilst diverse, the constituent parts all have an effect on the customer's perception of physical distribution performance.

Considering service offering as a package has a number of advantages, chief of which is that it forces us to take a global view of the customer's service requirements and thus encourages us to develop cohesive and integrated service policies. Inherent in this approach is the idea that the service package can vary from customer to customer, from market to market or from area to area. Thus, some of our customers may warrant special delivery service, or greater technical back-up or more formalised procedures through which they can provide feedback on their specific requirements. The service package can be designed with any of these requirements in mind and need not be the same for all customers or all segments of the market.

It is not easy to assess how the market will respond to a proposed customer service package. The concept of marketing experimentation is well established in other areas of the business. We are used to thinking of test markets for new product launches, advertising testing, and so on. The development of similar experiments to identify cost-effective service policies is more unusual. However, a number of companies have conducted experiments of this type and found the results to be extremely valuable.

One company manufacturing a wide range of grocery products in the UK had developed good cost data which enabled it to estimate accurately what the cost implications of different levels of stock-level service would be. What they could not predict, however, was the likely effect of those various service levels on sales revenue. They tackled the problem by identifying two areas of the UK, each served from a different depot and nearly identical to each other in terms of sales, retail structure and demography. In one of these areas they deliberately reduced the level of service in terms of safety stock maintained at the depot; in the other area no change was made from the existing level. The outcome of this experiment was that there was no significant difference in sales between the two areas. But there was, of course, a major reduction in the stock investment of the test region. The experiment indicated, therefore, that a lower level of service was considerably more cost effective.

How can we measure customer service?

Before any decision can be made as to the appropriate level of customer service to be offered, there has to be some way of measuring such levels. We encountered some possible measures in the opening remarks of this chapter, and it should now be added that the best measure of customer service is one which reflects both the importance of the product to the customer and the importance of the customer to the company.

Let us take the case of product availability – bearing in mind, however, that this is only one factor and that other items in the customer service package can be measured too. A manufacturer of farm implements, say, has received an emergency order from a farmer whose combine broke down just before harvest. If 20 items were ordered and 19 were shipped, customer service could be recorded as 95%. Similarly, if the total value of the order was £100 and the value of the item out of stock was £1, customer service could be recorded as an impressive 99%. However, if all 20 parts were needed in order to repair the combine, from the farmer's viewpoint the manufacturer has achieved a zero service level.

Customer perceptions are also a vital consideration when contemplating a *change* in the service package. Again taking product availability as an example, there is considerable evidence to suggest that even the professional buyer cannot always distinguish between, say, a 97% level of service and a 95% level of service. The difference would be that for 100 orders for a particular item it would not be available on average on five of those occasions rather than three. If the customer only orders that particular item once a week, for example, then we are saying that over a period of two years he would only experience two more stock-outs on that item than was previously the case. It is perhaps not surprising, therefore, that such small service changes might pass unnoticed.

What is the right level of customer service?

The simple answer to the question of what level of customer service is to be provided is that a balance must be found between the benefits, in terms of marketing advantage, of a particular level of customer service and the cost of providing it. Usually, that balance will be at the point where the additional revenue returns for each increment of service are equal to the extra cost of providing that increment. The principle then is simple enough; but actually finding this point of balance is a difficult task.

So far in this chapter, we have been concerned almost exclusively with one side of this equation, that of the marketing benefits of good customer service. The cost aspect is just as fundamental. It must be recognised, for instance, that by offering to deliver goods, costs are borne that would otherwise have fallen on the customer. If, for example, Nestle deliver orders to Albert Hijn, the Dutch supermarket chain, twice a week instead of once a week, they are relieving them of a necessity for holding stock. Similarly, if the manager of an Albert Hijn store knows that when he places an order with Nestle they will rarely be out of stock on that item, then again his stock holding can be lower. The cost of holding stock can be as much as 25% of its value a year for the retailer. By their service offering Nestle are absorbing some of this customer cost.

It is also essential to realise that once the level of product availability is stepped up beyond the 70–80% mark, the associated costs tend to increase far more than proportionately. Offering a 97% level of service instead of a 95% level may have no discernible effect on customer perceptions, as we saw earlier. But although the effect of this change on demand is negligible, the impact on physical distribution costs will be huge. For normally distributed demand, this 2% increase in the level of service would lead to a 14% increase in safety stock requirement alone, as is illustrated in Figure 21.

As has already been pointed out, the cost-benefit equation is simple enough in principle. In practice, there are considerable practical difficulties. On the one hand, there are the problems of generating accurate cost data relating to service policies; on the other hand, there are problems in determining the response of the market place to service offerings – that is, in assessing the benefits.

What therefore tends to happen is that most companies attempt to find a *satisfactory* balance of costs and benefits that meets a number of declared objectives rather than trying to devise *optimal* policies. Adopting the former approach leads necessarily to a choice between two options. Either management can go for a *cost-minimisation* approach or a *service-maximisation* approach. How do these approaches differ?

The cost-minimisation approach requires management to lay down specific objectives for customer service and then to ask the question: how might those objectives be met at minimum cost? The alternative approach, that of service-maximisation, is based upon the notion of a fixed distribution budget with the consequent

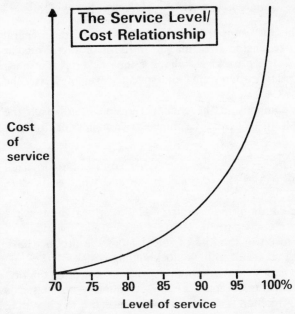

Figure 21

budget constraint. It is not possible to lay down hard and fast
rules as to which of these two approaches is preferable. In those
market situations where customer service is very competitive, then
the cost-minimisation approach may well be the only viable
strategy. Alternatively, given a situation of limited corporate
resources, the firm may well have to work within the constraints
of a tightly controlled distribution budget, thus necessitating a
service-maximisation approach.

A further complication in the question of how much should be
spent on customer service is that the development of any customer
service strategy within a company must take place in the total
context of the business. It will be self-defeating to attempt to
implement a customer service strategy that is not integrated with
the other areas of the business. Marketing, financial, production
and purchasing considerations will impinge most heavily upon the
development of a cohesive service strategy.

Some key questions when setting service levels

Given that the distribution manager can identify the general requirements of a customer or market in terms of any particular element of the service package, what are the questions that must be asked in order to determine the specific level of service he should offer?

One Dutch company in the chemical business asks itself the following questions to help determine service policy for products and markets:

1 *How profitable is the product?*   What contribution to fixed costs and profits does this product make and what is its sales turnover?

2 *What is the nature of the product?*   Is it a 'critical' item as far as the customer is concerned, where stock-outs at the point of supply would result in the loss of sales? Does the product have characteristics that result in high stockholding costs?

3 *What is the nature of the market?*   Does the company operate in a sellers' or a buyers' market? How frequently purchased is the product? Are there substitutes? What are the stockholding practices of the purchasers? Which markets and customers are growing and which are declining?

4 *What is the nature of the competition?*   How many companies are providing an alternative source of supply to our customers? What sort of service levels do they offer?

5 *What is the nature of the channel of distribution through which the company sells?*   Does the company sell direct to the end customer, or through intermediaries? To what extent does the company control the channel and the activities of its members, such as stock levels and order policies?

The answers to these questions provide the basic information upon which the service level decision is made. To take an example, a product with a low level of profitability will not justify a massive investment in customer service.

One UK food manufacturer carried a low-price, low-margin product line only because it was believed to complement the whole range of his products and because it would typically be sold along with high-margin products. A distribution cost analysis revealed that many delivery locations were unprofitable because they bought only the low-margin items. The food processor also discovered that in some cases his standard of service was too high. As a result he discontinued the delivery of 'balance' consignments of goods not available when the first delivery against their order was made: customers were asked to include these items on their next order. Furthermore, the frequency with which orders were delivered was reduced, particularly when the delivery location was relatively distant from the depot. (It had also been found that no delivery locations situated more than 55 miles from the depot were profitable). This action led to encouraging small and other unprofitable accounts to use wholesalers.

Application questions

16.1 *What is your organisation's policy on customer service levels? How does the service level compare with that offered by your competitors? What is the rationale underlying this policy?*

16.2 *Do you* know *what your customers mean by customer service? How does this match with the customer service your organisation currently provides? What changes should be made?*

16.3 *Can groups of your organisation's customers be identified with similar service requirements? Can the service offering be differentiated? Do all your customers require the same level of service?*

16.4 *With the benefit of hindsight, what would you consider a satisfactory service level for each of the markets you supply? How could any changes identified be achieved? What implications would these changes have for customer service policy?*

Action points
- *Take account* of *all* the factors involved in customer service.
- *Know* how to measure the different levels of service available.
- *Know* how to choose the most appropriate level of service to offer.
- *Aim* to achieve a satisfactory cost-benefit balance.

17 How can we get our products to the customers?

Overview

Getting the product to the customers cannot be viewed by marketing management as the concern of others, since physical distribution can have a major impact on marketing performance. Seen in this light, the means by which the product reaches the customer assumes a vital importance in marketing strategy.

It is also suggested that the key to the successful development of the firm's physical distribution effort is the adoption of a total systems approach, whereby an integrative view is taken of the various activities involved.

The importance of physical distribution

The process of physically distributing products has been given a number of different names. Physical Distribution Management (PDM), Marketing Logistics and Materials Management are some of the descriptions that have been used in discussions of this neglected area of management. There has been a tendency in many organisations to treat physical distribution as something of a necessary but mechanical activity that incurs costs and is something to do with transport. Too few companies have seen their distribution effort as potentially contributing in a vital and positive way to company profitability through its capacity for generating revenue via its impact on customer service.

Let us see how one British company in the food business released the profit potential that was latent in its physical distribution system. With a sales turnover of £100m a year from four major lines, the manufacturer was using a combination of 15 public warehouses and company-owned facilities to distribute 100,000 tons of goods each year. The company had separate order processing organisations for each line, with a total annual warehousing and transport bill of over £3m. In recent years this figure had been growing alarmingly and yet turnover in real terms was static. A review by a team of consultants resulted in a complete reappraisal of the way the company distributed its products. A consolidation of deliveries reduced transport costs by 20%.

In addition, the number of warehouses was cut to seven, a move which both reduced the total inventory holding in the system and cut storage and handling costs by 40%. The end result was a vast improvement in delivery performance and, hence, sales effectiveness, plus overall reduction of one-third in total distribution costs.

Similar examples can be cited from markets as diverse as fuel pumps and baby foods. As more and more companies take a fresh look at the role of distribution in their marketing effort, they are coming to the conclusion that there is considerable scope for profit enhancement through improvements in distribution. When it is considered that studies have estimated that the average European manufacturing company spends 21% of its sales revenue on distribution-related activities, it is not difficult to imagine the benefits of such a reappraisal.

These benefits need not always come from cost savings in distribution. Frequently, profitability can be improved by spending more rather than less on some aspects of the total corporate distribution activity. International Computers, for example, have found that it pays to ship their computers from the UK to continental European customers by air freight rather than by surface transport. Although the cost of transport is clearly higher, savings are made on packaging and port charges.

Furthermore, faster deliveries mean lower inventory carrying costs for goods in transit as well as improved cash flow as a result of a reduction in the time before customers can be invoiced.

The logistics concept

The emphasis behind the logistics concept is on systems. It suggests that the 'movement' activity in a company is so widespread and pervasive that it needs to be considered as a single system. Figure 22 highlights the spread of these activities within a firm.

The logistics concept rejects the traditional situation where marketing, production, distribution, purchasing, and so on, attempt to optimise their own particular set of logistics activities, quite oblivious to the others' involvement in the flow of materials.

Instead, the concept suggests that it may be necessary for some, or all, of these to operate sub-optimally in order that the whole system may be more effective. For example, the marketing manager must, if necessary, be prepared to accept a lower level of service than he would like; the production manager must be prepared to schedule shorter runs with more changeovers; or the transport manager must be prepared to make more frequent deliveries, if it benefits the overall effectiveness of the logistics system.

One of the major problems of conventional approaches to physical distribution is that responsibility for the task remains spread over the many discrete functional areas. Accepting the integrative systems-based approach which characterises the logistics concept implies a recognition that an inter-relationship exists

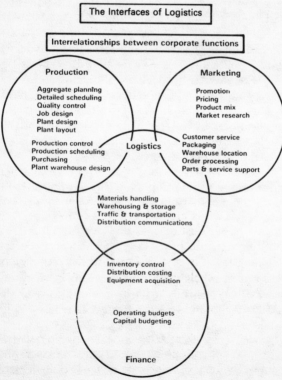

Figure 22

between the parts of the whole such that action affecting one part may well affect all the others. Any action, therefore, must be considered in the light of its effect on all parts of the business and on the overriding objectives of the company. Thus, the company can be viewed as a number of interlinked sub-systems which must somehow be united if overall effectiveness is to be maximised. Those who accept this approach must be concerned with the flow of materials through the whole business process, from raw materials through to the finished goods arriving at the customer's premises.

The logistics mix

Customers not only want products physically available; they also want them in the right unit sizes, in good condition and at the appropriate time. To meet these requirements, five key decision areas, which together constitute the *logistics mix*, have to be co-ordinated. These five elements are facilities, inventory, communications, unitisation and transport.

Facility decisions These decisions are concerned with the problem of how many warehouses and plants the organisation should have and where they should be located. Obviously, in the short term, most organisations must take the location of existing plants and warehouses as given; but the question assumes importance in the longer term and when new plants or warehouses are being considered.

Inventory Stock holding is central to physical distribution. How much inventory should be held, where the inventory should be held, in what quantities and with what frequency inventory should be replenished – these are just some of the decisions that have to be made. Stock levels are of particular concern as they have a direct bearing on the customer service that can be offered and, at the same time, are the prime determinants of inventory holding costs. Holding stock is costly; it ties up working capital and can perish or become obsolete if sales are not made according to plan. The management task is, therefore, to determine a level of stock at which its associated costs are balanced by the benefits for customer service.

Communications decisions It must always be remembered that logistics is not only about the flows of materials through the distribution channel. The flow of information is just as important to an efficient logistics system. Here we are talking about the order processing system, the invoicing system, the demand forecasting system, and so on. Without effective communications support, the logistics system will never be capable of providing satisfactory customer service at acceptable costs.

Unitisation decisions   The way in which goods are packaged and then subsequently accumulated into larger unit sizes (such as a case load) can have a major bearing upon logistics economics. For example, the ability to stack goods on a pallet which then becomes the unit load for movement and storage can lead to considerable cost savings in terms of handling and warehousing. Similarly, the use of containers as the basic unit of movement has revolutionised international transport and, to a certain extent, domestic transport as well.

Transport decisions   Last, but seldom least, are those decisions surrounding the transport function of the firm. The transport decision involves such issues as what mode of transport we should use: should we transport by road with our own vehicles or should we lease them? Should we ship overseas by air freight or by container ship? The organisation of delivery constitutes another major issue: how should we schedule our deliveries? How often should we deliver? Perhaps because it constitutes one of the more obvious facets of the distribution task, transport has received rather more attention within the firm than have the other four decision areas of the logistics mix.

Together, these five areas constitute the total costs of physical distribution within a company. It is frequently the case, however, that a decision taken in one area will have an effect on the other four areas. Thus, a decision to close a depot, a facility decision, will affect the transport costs, the inventory allocation and, perhaps, data processing costs. Managing the logistics function involves a continual search for such situations, the intention being to secure a reduction in total costs by changing the cost structure in one or more areas. This is the principle of a *cost trade-off* amongst the elements of the logistics mix.

One important feature of this logistics mix concept is that transport is seen as being just one element amongst five. Conventionally, in many companies transport *is* distribution; yet viewed in this total sense, it may account for only a small proportion of the total logistics costs.

The logistics system

Figure 23 brings together those aspects of a company's operation that are the core concern of an integrated approach to logistics management.

The diagram also shows the relationship between physical distribution and logistics. Whilst physical distribution management is concerned only with those flows from the end of the production line to the customer, the integrated approach of logistics encompasses the total flow of materials and related information into, through and out of the corporate system.

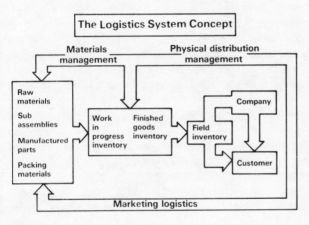

Figure 23

Application questions

17.1   *How is the logistics system managed within your organisation? In what ways could the integration of the logistics system be improved? What would be the consequence of such improvements?*

17.2   *Is logistics management adequately represented at board or senior management level in your organisation? How could representation be improved? Where you can identify changes, how could they be achieved?*

17.3   *What co-ordination takes place between the logistics and manufacturing functions within your organisation? What problems arise because the co-ordination is inadequate? How can problems encountered be minimised?*

Action points
- *Remember* that there is an inter-relationship between all parts of the organisation, such that any action can affect other parts of the business.
- *Know* the elements of the logistics mix.
- *Keep in mind* that physical distribution management covers a product's flow only from production line to customer.
- *Remember* that marketing logistics encompasses the *total* movement of materials and information through the corporate system.

18

What price should we charge our customers?

Overview

Pricing decisions are of paramount importance in marketing strategy. Like the other elements in the firm's marketing mix, the price of the product should be related to the achievement of marketing and corporate goals. Thus, the role of price must be established in relation to such factors as the product life cycle, the requirements of the total product portfolio and sales and market share objectives.

The procedures and methods adopted to meet these goals are as dependent on the market and competitive circumstances as they are on costs. Indeed, the market-orientated approach to pricing, described in this chapter, sees costs as a constraint which may determine a lower limit to the firm's pricing discretion rather than as a basis on which price is determined.

Pricing should be planned across the whole product line, rather than for single products separately. Finally, a step-by-step approach to arriving at an exact price can eliminate the potential confusion of trying to ponder too many variables simultaneously.

The price decision

In the economists' view of the world, price is regarded as the chief determinant of the level of sales of a product. Price is central to many of their models and the mechanism whereby prices are set has become a major field of study. At the governmental level too, the price of goods and services is subjected to great scrutiny, in this case because of the implications of inflation and general social welfare.

In the light of this external interest in prices, it is perhaps all the more surprising that many organisations adopt relatively unsophisticated approaches to the determination of price. Surveys in several countries have shown that the price decision in the firm often tends to be automatic, to be based upon some rudimentary formula or rule of thumb. Only infrequently, it would appear, do pricing decisions form part of an overall integrated marketing strategy where price is related in some specific way to the achievement of defined objectives.

The pricing decision is important in a number of ways but, clearly, its main importance lies in its direct and indirect effects on profits. It directly affects profits by determining the revenue that can be obtained. Its indirect effects lie in the way in which it influences demand, thus affecting the quantity sold, and the way in which it interacts with the other elements of the marketing mix. We can see from this latter consideration the importance of ensuring that the price set is appropriate to the company's marketing programme.

The way in which price can interact with other elements of the marketing mix, notably place, and to some extent promotion, can be seen in a ticket-selling scheme used by London's West End theatres. From mid-afternoon, theatre-goers can obtain half price tickets (if the seats are not already all reserved) from a single kiosk situated in the centre of the city. When the scheme started there were fears that the already existing market for theatre tickets would be undermined, but these anxieties were soon recognised to be unfounded.

Many customers were happy to pay the full price for theatre seats in order to eliminate the uncertainty and inconvenience of having to queue for tickets on the day of performance. The scheme by which reduced tickets are sold appeals successfully to a market not already reached.

Relating pricing objectives to marketing strategy

If an integrated marketing strategy is to be achieved, the pricing decision must be taken in the light of the objectives underlying that strategy. This implies, first and foremost, that the price of the product must fit the *market position* planned for that product. 'Market position' in this context means the place that the product occupies, in comparison with its competitors, in the eyes of the organisation's customers or potential customers.

Sometimes this position will be determined mainly by the perceived physical attributes of the product; for example, a grade of industrial steel may occupy a particular market position by virtue of its product characteristics. On other occasions, the market position of a product may be considerably affected by perceptions of less tangible attributes; for example, a toilet soap may have connotations of gracious living associated with it. Because price is one of the marketing mix elements that will contribute to a product's market position, it is necessary that price should be consonant with that position. In the above situation, for instance, it would hardly be appropriate to set a rock-bottom price on the toilet soap.

The price of the product must also relate to its *life cycle* and to the organisation's strategic views on that cycle. Let us take the example of video recorders. The first producers in the field were faced with a decision as to pricing policy. They could go for an initial high price or *skimming policy* or for a lower price aimed at gaining maximum *market penetration*.

A skimming policy, as the name suggests, is based on entering the market at a high price and then later, if necessary, lowering the price to gain acceptance in other price segments. It is a strategy appropriate to several circumstances; for example, if the company feels that it has a sufficient lead over its competitors in the introduction of the product and can take advantage of this lead to achieve an accelerated rate of recovery on its investment. It is important in a situation of this kind for the innovating firm to be aware that a skimming policy can provide encouragement for other manufacturers to enter the market. The key to success in these situations is to plan for a steady reduction in price once an initial market penetration has been established and cost recovery is under way. Such price reduction will normally be made easier by the unit cost reductions that should occur once cumulative output starts to grow; this is known as the experience effect. This effect was classically reflected in the falling price of video machines some time after their appearance on the market.

On the other hand, a chemical company introducing a new type of plastic film might take the opposite route by going for a penetration pricing policy. Here, the price is deliberately set low with a number of objectives in mind. An initial low price makes it very difficult for would-be competitors to imitate innovations, particularly in technological product areas. A penetration policy also ensures maximum adoption of the product in its early life, thus leading to a more rapid experience effect. The problem associated with such a policy is chiefly the 'opportunity cost' of possible additional revenue foregone.

The appropriateness of either of these policies will be determined to a large extent by the elasticity of demand in the market place; that is, the responsiveness of demand to relative price levels. In some markets demand does not seem to be affected by price – up to a point at least. In such circumstances, we say that demand is inelastic, as it is, for example, in the market for technical journals sold mainly to libraries. On the other hand, some markets are more sensitive to price as, for example, in urban bus services. Price elasticity by itself does not explain the response of markets to price levels but it should at least be included as a criterion in the choice of pricing strategy. Whereas the earliest producers of video recorders, for instance, could count on at least a section of the potential market to pay almost any price to possess the new gadget, the chemical company could make no such calculation.

A further consideration is the nature of the competition. The market for plastic film is an established one, with a relatively large number of manufacturers supplying diverse markets around the globe. There are established price brackets for specific types of film and, within these brackets, there are a number of firms competing. Thus, the question must be asked: are we a price 'maker' or a price 'taker'? In other words, does our position in the market provide us with room to manoeuvre on price? In markets where the competitive product offerings are relatively undifferentiated, this becomes a very real consideration.

Finally, it must be recognised that pricing policies have a strategic importance in the context of sales and market share objectives and the revenue requirements of the rest of the firm's product portfolio. If, for example, the chosen marketing strategy was to establish as quickly as possible a sizeable share of the market, then sales maximisation through a penetration pricing policy would seem to be indicated. In this case, the company might even decide that the benefits of market share over-rode the need for initial profitability; that is, that market share should be bought by a deliberate pricing policy. On the other hand, in the case of an established product well into the maturity stage of its life cycle, the product might be viewed as a source of cash for financing the growth of other products. In these circumstances, the pressure would be to maintain price, and even to increase it, at the expense of sales and market share.

The firm's market profile is likely to have a great influence on pricing decisions. A British manufacturer of car radios, for example, was considering what price to set for an extension to its product range. The firm had considerable accumulated production expertise. It also had an outstanding distribution network; this was particularly important in its market since retailers may have considerable influence on their customers' choices. In addition, the company had built up a reasonably high reputation for its radios. In order to avoid damaging its reputation, the company was obliged to offer a price towards the upper range which would imply high quality. It was felt that a reduced price would not necessarily lead to an increase in the volume of sales. On the contrary, there was considerable evidence to suggest that price is seen by many consumers as an indicator of the product's quality.

In this latter context, we are seeing price in its true strategic role (see Figure 24), as a variable that enables the achievement of corporate marketing objectives across the complete product portfolio. The pricing decision on a specific product should be viewed in relation to the strategic requirements of the company's global market strategy as well as in terms of the product's own needs.

Influences on Pricing Policy

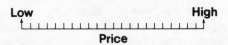

Low   High

Price

What are our competitor's prices?

Where is the product in its life cycle?

What is our market positioning policy?

Is the market developing, saturated or declining?

Figure 24

Pricing procedures and methods

Cost-orientated procedures

Given that pricing objectives have been established, how might the decision on a specific price be taken? The conventional profit-maximising model of the economist tells us that price should be set where marginal cost equals marginal revenue – in other words, where the additional cost of producing and marketing an additional unit is equivalent to the additional revenue that its sale would generate.

In its theoretical form, the logic is indisputable; as a practical pricing tool, however, its use is somewhat limited. Why is this? It is because the economist's model requires a knowledge of the demand curve facing the product in the market place; it is based on a notion of cost behaviour strictly limited to the short-run; it does not take cognisance of any strategic objectives of the firm save profits; nor does it recognise that long-run goals can, and frequently will, be met by sacrificing short-run goals.

In practice, we more often encounter pricing procedures which are based on simple, although often equally unsatisfactory, precepts. Many of these procedures are what might best be termed 'cost-orientated'. One frequently encountered approach, based on costs, is the *target return on costs* method; this is commonly known as the 'cost plus' method of setting prices. Using this approach, the company would set itself a target level of profits to be achieved at a given level of sales, such that an adequate return on costs would be obtained. A specialist book publisher in France uses this method, for example, when it makes a decision to produce 1,000 copies of a book at a total production and marketing budget of Fr30,000. The firm requires a 20% return on this investment – that is, Fr6,000. Thus, the required level of total revenue must be Fr36,000, which, on a sale of 1,000, implies a price of Fr36.0. This method is based in effect on a breakeven analysis of the form illustrated in Figure 25.

The problem with this approach is that it assumes that if 1,000 copies of the book are produced, they can then be sold at the given price; whereas in fact the price itself is likely to have some effect on sales. Another problem occurs in some cases in the determination of total costs. This is particularly true in multi-product companies where many costs are common between products. The allocation of overheads between products can be difficult

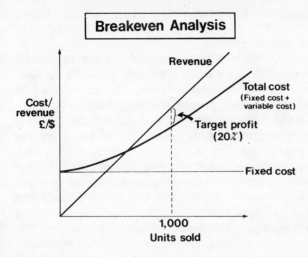

Figure 25

to determine; the allocation chosen is frequently arbitrary for the individual product. There is also the danger that the method might lead us to seek a return on 'sunk' costs; that is, those fixed costs which represent outlays made in the past and which should have no bearing on the price.

The market-orientated approach

The *market-orientated approach* to pricing stands in contrast to those methods which are based mainly on costs. In this approach, costs are viewed solely as a constraint on the lower limit of pricing discretion. The emphasis here is placed on such notions as what the market will bear, competitive activity and price/quality perceptions, as well as the overall strategic marketing goals of the sort outlined earlier.

The idea that a product should be priced according to market considerations rather than cost considerations is not new; it is surprising, however, to find that many companies enter a pricing decision by first talking about costs. In a sense, this is understandab'e: costs are tangible inputs to any decision process and appear to be easily quantifiable. Market factors are usually harder to pin down. Getting a feel for what the market will bear can really only come through experience in a product field. Few companies know enough about their markets to enable them to construct demand curves. It is more likely that the organisation will be able to identify broad bands within which the price will be acceptable to the majority of the chosen market.

Some researchers have developed operational methods for determining what these price bands might be. They simply ask a representative sample of the target segment whether they would buy the product at a certain price and, if they answer 'no', they are questioned with a view to finding out whether the refusal is due to the price being too high or too low (in the sense that the quality of the product might be in doubt). These researchers have reported that the consumer intent on a purchase enters the market not with a set of demand schedules in mind, but simply with two price limits. He has a lower limit below which he would distrust the quality of the product or service and an upper limit beyond which he would judge the article unduly expensive.

This later point emphasises that the concept of price has a qualitative dimension. In other words, in many markets price is used by the customer as an indicator of quality. For example, Stella Artois is a Belgian beer marketed under licence in Britain. A major promotional campaign was based, amongst other things, on the premium price of the product. The advertisements suggested that this was a high-quality product and they deliberately emphasised the fact that the price exceeded that of competitive products. Other manufacturers too have found that raising the price can have a beneficial effect on sales if the market cannot accept that a relatively low-priced product can in fact meet the claims that are made about it. Thus, the traditional view of price and demand being inversely related need not always hold good in a particular section of the market.

The market-orientated view of pricing attempts to relate the price of the product to the value that the customers believe they will derive from its purchase. This concept is discussed more fully in relation to conditions of strong price competition (Chapter 20), when it is especially important to exert an influence on the customer's perception of the value he derives.

The principle of relating price to perceived value also holds good in industrial markets. For example, the Glacier Metal Company in Britain uses a method of pricing, known as *product analysis pricing*, which is based on the concept that the price the buyer pays for a product must be directly related to the various utilities (such as reliability in use, or good after-sales service) that the user is seeking from the product. Here cost is seen solely as a lower limit beyond which the long-term price should not fall.

In almost all markets, the competitive structure of the market influences the price decision. Often, pricing discretion is limited by the fact that a going rate exists within a market and, unless the organisation occupies a dominant position in that market as a price-leader, this single fact will of necessity determine the price at which the company must operate.

Product line pricing

One vital area of pricing policy not so far touched upon is that of pricing not just one product, but an entire product line. A fundamental determinant of the strategy involved relates to two possible ways in which the sales levels of individual products in the line are very often inter-dependent. Specifically, they may be *competitive* with each other, or *complementary*.

Competitive items are close substitutes for each other, such as butter and margarine. Usually, a customer who buys more of one will buy less of the other.

Complementary items are those whose sales boost, or are boosted by, another product. An increase in camera sales, for instance, can be expected to increase the sale of photographic film.

Complementary and competing products are found not only in trade between rival companies; they also influence patterns of sales, and hence pricing policy, within a company's product line.

Competing items

Curiously, most companies are in active competition not just with other companies but with themselves as well. If a butcher runs a special promotion on beef, he may well lose sales on lamb and pork. Extra sales of a particular model of cassette player may depress the sales of others in the same range. On the other hand, by adding new items to a product line, it may be possible to increase sales across the whole line by becoming a preferred source of supply. Having a good idea of what will happen in any particular case will depend on the collection of detailed market research data on substitution effects.

One safe generalisation is that buyers of any product give consideration to buying closely related items offered by the same seller.

If they buy his line of lathes, or trousers, or typewriters, they will examine and compare several items in the line, especially those most closely related. This being so, one important price consideration is that the differential prices between items in the line should 'make sense' to the customer, i.e., they should appear reasonable and fair. Care should also be taken to make sure that there are no yawning price 'gaps' between items that a competitor might fill, and that prices are not so close to each other as to cause an irritatingly difficult choice for the customer.

An important distinction is to be made between 'end' and 'in-between' items in a product line. At the bottom end, for instance, the lowest-priced item usually affects the total sales of the whole line far more than does the price of any other product in the line. It acts as a 'traffic builder', drawing marginally interested customers to the place of purchase. It appears that the lowest price is usually the most frequently remembered and 'perceived' price, and some customers will compare it with the lowest price charged by rivals. Consequently, reductions in the price of the lowest price item tend to have a very stimulating effect on sales.

Complementary items

There are many types of complementary linkage, and they frequently give rise to opportunities in which premium prices can be obtained. There is the 'quality supplement' phenomenon, for instance. Customers who have bought an expensive piece of equipment will often be anxious to look after it, and will be prepared to pay extra for further items in the same maker's product line designed for its maintenance. For example, manufacturers offer 'special' own-brand lubricants for delicate engines, and there is evidence to suggest that other, low-priced products will be avoided.

In some cases, the purchase of one product virtually requires the customer to buy the complementary item from the same supplier, because only his supplies fit the original equipment. Duplicating machines, for example, will often take only the maker's brand of stencil. Under these circumstances, the seller can afford to offer the equipment at a low, or even subsidised, margin, while demanding a high return on the supplementary item.

The concept of treating the entire line as a unit and subsidising the sale of some items to increase the sale of others is in many cases the key to pricing complementary products.

Multi-stage pricing

For the marketing manager, these various aspects of the pricing decision can be seen as providing a framework for manoeuvre. At the same time, it can be a confusing business trying to weigh many variables against each other, and what is also needed is a systematic way of narrowing down the options. One such method is known as *multi-stage pricing*, in which the major elements in a pricing decision are handled in a logical sequence of stages. As will be seen, this method also has the advantage that it gives weight to the price implications of such intangible but vital factors as brand image. By contrast, the arithmetic of costs is seen as an important *final* consideration, but one which is far from dominating the pricing process. These are the main stages:

1 *Selecting market targets*   This first stage begins with defining the extent to which an organisation is already 'committed' in the short and medium term, in ways which have pricing implications. A company may well have built its entire trade, for example, through a particular chain of retail outlets associated with upper end prices, and there will be customers with definite views about the reliability and quality to be expected from the firm's products. Such commitments limit and define the market segments, and hence price range, at which a company should realistically be aiming.

2 *Choosing a brand image*   Once management has defined the market segments it wishes to cultivate most actively, it must select the methods to achieve its goal. In particular, the firm's selection of a brand image should be consistent with the type of customer it is trying to attract. The image selected – 'style leader', 'solid dependability', 'technical innovation' might be choices in, say, hi-fi equipment – will need to be reinforced by an appropriate price. This is because, as the Stella Artois example showed, price itself helps to create brand image.

3 *Determining pricing policy*   Armed with clear ideas as to target market position and brand image, policy questions such as, 'Should our price be around 5% above, or 2% below, the industry average?', can be approached with definite goals in mind, and the answers will be that much less arbitrary than might otherwise have been the case.

4 *Arriving at a specific price*   After all other considerations have been weighed, the price setter's choice will be a narrow one, and only at this final stage does the arithmetic of price come into play. Arithmetic, that is, to calculate, so far as possible from sales forecasts, the likely revenue to be gained from each of the remaining price possibilities. Costs of production must also be calculated, so as to address the question, 'Would this price be sufficient to cover costs and yield at least a minimum level of profit?'

Application questions

18.1   *When the most recent product or service was introduced into your organisation's range, how was the price established? In retrospect, was this decision correct? Was there any additional research which could have helped you establish the correct price?*

18.2   *Do customers' perceptions of your prices coincide with your declared pricing policy? If there is a variance, how can it be explained and rectified?*

18.3   *How do your prices compare with those of your competitors? Is this intended organisation policy? How is your pricing policy justified?*

18.4   *How should your prices be altered:*

(a) in times of inflation?
(b) as your product or service enters different phases of its life cycle?

How would you justify these recommendations? How could these changes be implemented?

18.5   *Think of the products in one of your organisation's lines. Do they include items competing with each other? Could their prices in relation to each other be improved? How? How would you price any complementary items that your organisation sells?*

18.6   *To what extent is your organisation committed to a particular price range? By what factors? At what stage should costs of production be considered when pricing? Why?*

Action points
• *Take* pricing decisions in the light of the marketing strategy objectives.
• *Remember* to price products according to market considerations rather than cost considerations.

- *Take into account* the pricing of an entire product line, rather than just one product.
- *Know* the steps in the multi-stage pricing method.

19

**What margins
should we negotiate with
our distributors?**

Overview

*The margins negotiated with intermediaries in the channel of distri-
bution should be viewed in terms of the* value-added *by them as
product or service passes along the channel. In return for the
performance of various functions necessary to the efficient comple-
tion of the exchange process, the firm is obliged to make available
some of the total channel margin available to it. The various types
of margins that are commonly encountered are trade, quantity,
promotional and cash discounts.*

*It is suggested here that the overall policy towards distributor
margins should be considered in the wider context of the need of
the firm to achieve its declared marketing goals.*

*The margins offered to distributors overseas in practice often need
to be larger, and it is sensible to operate a currency equalisation
scheme to offset problems caused by fluctuating exchange rates.*

Reward structures in the distribution channel

Chapters 15, 16 and 17 have shown the vital importance of the
choice of distribution channel to the success of the marketing
effort. The intermediaries that constitute that channel perform a
number of functions that enable the exchange transaction between
producer and consumer to be carried out. In return for the
functions that they perform on the firm's behalf, these intermediaries naturally seek a reward. Put in its simplest terms, this reward
amounts to the margin between the price of the goods at the
factory gate and the price the end-user eventually pays.

It is common to refer to this margin as the *value-added* by these
intermediate functions. In conditions of perfect *competition*, i.e.,
if the producer could freely choose from any number of intermediaries equally well able to perform the task, the reward for the

value-added would never rise above the bare minimum required
to make it worth while for the intermediary to stay in business. If
a higher reward were to be demanded, the other channel members
would simply take their trade elsewhere.

The actual situation in most markets is, however, quite different
to this. Instead of perfectly competitive market structures, one
usually encounters *vertical marketing systems*, where varying
degrees of control and integration are administered by the more
powerful members of the channel. This situation need not result
in a loss of economic strength. Indeed, it may often lead to
improvements in total channel efficiency. In the fragmented and
unintegrated market structure implied by perfect competition, the
typically small size of intermediary units will not allow for
economies of scale in purchasing, handling and distribution. A
fragmented structure can also lead to each individual unit in
the channel attempting to maximise its own reward – a tendency
which could result in a less than optimal situation in the channel
overall.

Ideally, the reward structure in the marketing channel should
involve an acceptable rate of return on investment being earned
at each level in the channel: a 'win-win' situation where all channel
members gain.

Available discount options

Most organisations have a number of devices for rewarding the
intermediaries in the channel. These will usually take the form of
a number of discounts against some nominal price list.

Before enumerating these discounts, it should be pointed out
that the issues are being examined here from the point of view of
a manufacturing company contemplating its margins to 'down-
stream' distributors. Furthermore, we have in mind a company
which, in line with the way vertically integrated marketing systems
usually operate, has a definite policy as to what the price of its
products will be to the ultimate consumer, and is able to negotiate
margins with intermediaries on the basis of such a price, (although
it should be borne in mind that retailers cannot nowadays be
compelled to sell at a manufacturer's nominated price, as was
once the case). In other words, discussion as to the share of
rewards within the channel is conducted on the basis of the difference between the factory gate price and the end-user price.

Bearing in mind, then, that the following is not the pattern for *all* companies, the most commonly encountered discounts are:

1   *Trade discount*   This is the discount against the list which the company will give to a channel intermediary in return for the service he makes available. Thus, a wholesaler might purchase goods from the manufacturer at a 20% discount, in return for which he will provide such services as bulk-breaking, storage, and retail order-filling. In turn, the wholesaler will offer a trade discount to the retailer. In some cases, the wholesaler will be bypassed and the discount normally passing to the wholesaler will either be retained by the manufacturer or passed on directly to the retailer. In some markets, such as groceries, the retailers have taken on the functions of wholesalers and demand an increased discount to reflect this fact. The precise level of the trade discount is an issue to be explored later in this chapter.

2   *Quantity discount*   A quantity discount is one which is offered in relation to the size of the order: the greater the order the greater the discount. A manufacturer offering this discount does so in order to encourage larger purchases than might otherwise be made. A discount of this kind can be to the benefit of both parties.

Let us take the example of a Dutch manufacturer of household electrical appliances who offered to wholesalers a discount of 5% on orders for Fl6,000 or more, a 7% discount on orders for Fl10,000 and a 12% discount for orders over Fl15,000. These discounts were in addition to the normal 20% trade discount. The rationale for such additional discounts on price was simple. In the first place, the competitive environment demanded that discounts over and above the normal trade discount be given on larger orders. In addition, the company believed that there were a number of economic advantages associated with a quantity discount structure.

The first of these was that they felt that the wholesaler would be encouraged to buy more and thus sell more. Secondly, by ordering in larger quantities, the wholesaler would carry a greater proportion of the total costs of holding inventory – costs that would otherwise have to be borne by the manufacturer. Thirdly, the company felt that the encouragement to purchase in larger quantities could well lead to a decline in the number of orders placed by an individual wholesaler in a given period. This would have the effect of reducing the manufacturer's costs of meeting orders.

Naturally, the wholesaler would want to be sure that the size of the discount more than compensated for his increased inventory carrying costs. A successful quantity discount scheme is a good example of a 'win-win' situation.

3 *Promotional discount* In a number of markets, other institutions join the manufacturer in promoting the sale of that manufacturer's products. Promotion might take the form of advertisements in various media informing the public that products are available at particular outlets. Alternatively, and this is frequently encountered in fast-moving consumer goods markets, the promotion may be in the form of in-store displays, 'money-off' offers, competitions, and so on. This latter form of promotional activity has come to be known as *below-the-line promotion* and in some markets is more important than the more traditional media promotion.

It might be argued that these various types of promotional activity benefit both the channel institution and the manufacturer. However, in a number of situations the channel institution requires an additional discount in order to become involved in activity of this kind. This often happens when a particular channel member holds a great deal of power. Thus, in the UK, a manufacturer of convenience food products has to offer an additional discount to the large supermarket chains in order to persuade them to participate in a promotion that he is planning.

4 *Cash discount* Organisations often attempt to encourage the prompt payment of accounts by offering a cash discount to their customers.

A typical example is a Belgian manufacturer of office equipment whose terms were 30 days credit but who offered a discount of 2½% for payment within ten days. In inflationary times, when the management of cash flow becomes as important as making a profit, the speedy payment of accounts by customers is vital to the manufacturer. With the cost of capital of 20% or more, this office equipment company, with Fr600m annual sales, was facing an average account payment period of 40 days; in other words, some accounts were always overdue. 40 days represented approximately Fr96m accounts outstanding at any one point in time (40/ 250 × 600) which represented an opportunity cost of Fr19.2m a year (96 × 20%). Clearly, the 2½% incentive to settle within ten days was having little effect. The customers were in effect using their trade credit as a source of working capital; and, even at a discount of 2½% foregone, it was cheap at the price.

The problem of the level and structure to be used in determining cash discounts is difficult to solve. There is a limit to the extent to which the firm can eat into its own margin in order to increase the discount for prompt payment. Likewise, in competitive markets, it is difficult to reduce the period of credit – or even to persuade the customer to respect the period of credit offered.

Margin management

As we have just seen, there are a number of problems surrounding the allocation of margins amongst channel intermediaries. In a dynamic distribution channel, there will be constant pressure for the improvement of margins at all levels. The ultimate effect of this is often a shortening of the channel, with the functions of some intermediaries being absorbed by others.

Because of this pressure, the question of margins must be seen at a strategic as well as a tactical level. In those markets where there is a proliferation of products (say, breakfast cereals in Europe) the problem of gaining distribution has to be solved by offering the largest part of the total margin available to the retailer. Strategic implications such as these will often determine the policy towards margins.

This whole area of *margin management*, as it is coming to be called, can be viewed as a series of trade-off decisions which determines how the total channel margin should be split. The concept of the total channel margin is simple. This is the difference, already described, between the level of price at which the organisation wishes to position its product in the ultimate market place and the cost of the product at the factory gate. Who takes what proportion of this difference is what margin management is about. The situation is illustrated in Figure 26.

It can be seen that the firm's channel requirements will only be achieved if it carries them out itself or if it goes some way towards meeting the requirements of an intermediary who can perform those functions on the firm's behalf. The objective of the firm in this respect can be expressed in terms of a willingness to trade off margin in order to achieve marketing goals.

If, as may well be the case, channel functions are performed better as a result of such a trade-off, the company's gain in terms of faster turnover may lead to greater profitability (overall rate of return on capital invested) rather than less.

Margins for distributors abroad

Distribution in overseas markets frequently presents the marketer with a margin policy dilemma. The very remoteness of the market means that it is difficult for the home company to know what is going on; frequent visits may be undertaken, but the distributors may even so be left to their own devices more than the producing company would ideally wish to see.

This factor of remoteness often leads in practice to less effort being exerted by distributors at any given percentage margin than

The Main Factors Involved in Margin Management

Firm's Marketing Goals

e.g. Sales
    Market share
    Return on investment

Firm's Channel Requirements

e.g. Distribution coverage
    Inventory holding at point of sale
    Promotional & sales support

Intermediaries' Requirements

e.g. High stockturn
    Maximum margin
    Return on investment

Figure 26

would apply to those nearer at hand. The obvious solution is to offer greater incentives by means of a more generous margin, and such a policy is in fact often adopted. The question then becomes one of whether the whole exercise is worth the candle, given the extra costs of shipping, documentation and so forth, that are involved in international marketing.

It may be. The distributor's extra efforts in return for a larger margin may pay handsome dividends, but every case is a matter for individual judgement. No fresh principle applies to this judgement that is not inherent in the comments already made on margin management.

On the other hand, the problem of which currency to price the goods in, and hence which of the parties is to bear the risk of exchange rate fluctuations, does involve a fresh issue: the end price of the product, and hence the whole marketing strategy, may be affected by the way in which this matter is resolved.

Suppose, for instance, that the Australian agent for a UK publishing company has an agreement to buy in sterling prices. He buys 1,000 books at £3 each, with a view to selling them to Australian retailers at A$10. For the sake of simplicity we will say that £1 is worth exactly A$2. Buying at sterling prices, the agent therefore parts with A$6,000 in anticipation of sales at A$10,000. Thus he makes (if he sells all the books) A$4,000 profit.

The Australian dollar now falls in value so that the rate is A$3 = £1. In order to buy the same number of £3 books as before, he now has to pay A$9,000, reducing his profit to A$1,000, unless he raises the price to his retailers.

So it is the agent, in this example, who is taking the currency risk, and not the UK publisher.

But can the publisher *afford* to let the agent take such a risk entirely on his own shoulders, bearing in mind that the only satisfactory arrangement in the long term is 'win-win', not 'win-lose'? What would be the effect on overall marketing strategy of allowing the distributor to pass on the entire effect of the devaluation to his customers? Would the books still sell at the full extra price?

A more sensible policy, which allows for a reasonable, planned margin for the distributors, and for greater control over marketing strategy, is to allow the agent compensation against currency losses, while also ensuring that he hands over windfall currency gains to the UK company. Currency equalisation enables a more controlled and equitable *de facto* margin to be established between producer and distributor in international markets.

Application questions

19.1 *What margins are expected by the intermediaries with whom your organisation has to work? Are these margins justified? Is there any way in which the margins can be reduced without undermining the efficiency of your channels of distribution?*

19.2 *Could your organisation replace its intermediaries in any way? What costs would be incurred and what benefits would be gained? Should such changes be considered seriously by your organisation?*

19.3 *Over the last ten years what trends have occurred in margins operating in your industry? Are these trends acceptable? What policy does your organisation adopt towards these trends?*

Action points

• *Know* how to use the reward structure in the marketing channel.
• *Bear in mind* the most commonly encountered discounts.
• *Consider* how the total channel margin should be split.
• *Take account* of margin policy problems in dealing with distribution abroad.

20 How can we market in the face of price competition?

Overview

Price cutting wars are destructive. Price competition can often be countered effectively by the deployment of an imaginative marketing approach, aimed at differentiating in the eyes of the customer the value of one's own product from other market offerings.

The first requirement is to know what aspects of the product customers particularly value, and then to build the marketing strategy around these perceptions. Price cutting can sometimes be used strategically to build market share, but there are many pitfalls. In some markets pricing decisions must be made without information about competitors' prices.

Is price all that matters?

'Price cutting,' it has been said, 'is a technique for slitting someone else's throat and bleeding to death yourself.' Price cutting wars erode profits right across the industry in which they are waged, and are often started by a wholly unnecessary panic reaction to price competition.

The view that a competitor's prices must always be matched in order not to lose market share is an unduly pessimistic one, based on the false assumption that the customer is only interested in price.

Even in price sensitive industrial commodity markets this is so far from being the case that price is not even the *most* important marketing variable in the eyes of customers. Surveys in the UK and elsewhere have shown that in excess of 60% of DMUs would not change their best suppliers for a drop in price of 5% plus, and for some the figure would be 10%.

Sulphuric acid, for instance, is a bulk commodity that can be described as price sensitive. The large buyer is likely to be involved in running a continuous process. The acid cannot be stored in large quantities, except at prohibitive expense, because it is corrosive, and so if the supply is interrupted for any length of time the customer has to stop production. For this reason he 'multisources' – that is, buys from several suppliers. Even so, supplies are far from guaranteed because at peak business periods they will all be stretched. So the wise customer chooses suppliers primarily for reliability, not price.

The example demonstrates an important principle: 'The cost to my customer is not necessarily the price I charge.' The customer's costs include the risk of interrupted supply, poor quality, ordering difficulties, and so forth. The buyer's decision, in other words, relates to many more factors than price alone.

It follows that knowledge of precisely which factors it is that customers regard as of greatest importance, will enable the marketer to concentrate attention on these points, and steer the buying decision away from price.

Knowing what the customer values

What the customer regards as important is sometimes far from obvious, and can only be reliably uncovered through detailed market research. Products that seem entirely identical to their producers may not rank equally in the eyes of the purchaser. For example, a same-day developing and printing service for film would have a very high value to a short-stay tourist who wished to see how successful his photography had been while he still had the chance to re-take the pictures. That same person at home would place a totally different value on such a service.

Research by a technique called 'trade-off analysis' enables studies to be made in the relationship between price and the customer's perception of value. A range of attributes that are likely to be of importance to the buyer, such as quality, service back-up and company reputation, are selected, and the respondents (actual or potential customers) are asked to consider a situation where all the factors are offered at a high level, but where the suppliers, faced with increased costs, will eliminate one factor rather than raise the price. The respondent is then invited to state which features he would prefer to be kept. Values are assigned by respondents to the price differential they would tolerate to retain the higher level of performance of each feature. In the case of reprographic equipment, for instance, a potential buyer might say: 'I absolutely must have consistency of quality of output and a fast repair service, but I could just about get by without quick delivery of consumables, such as paper. However, I would be prepared to pay an extra £150 if this service were available.'

Forearmed with information of this type, the producer of reprographic equipment who suddenly finds himself undercut on price to the extent of, say, £100 by a rival with a product offering of equal merit, need not respond in kind. He is able instead to increase the desirability of his own product, perhaps by making his own delivery of consumables more attractive than his rival's and making a sales feature of this fact, in the knowledge that the value of this service in his customer's eyes will outcompete the rival's lower price. He must of course be sure that the extra cost of providing a superior delivery service is not prohibitive. The aim must be to differentiate his own product offering in a way that is of high value to the customer but not of disproportionate cost to himself.

Differentiating the product (that is, the overall product offering, including service) is just one of the available options. Analysis of value perceptions can provide the information base for other types of differentiation too. It may be, for instance, that a product already has an attribute that the customer is discovered to value highly, but that not much has been made of this attribute in promotion. In this case, the marketing task is clear: to differentiate the value of the product from that of cheaper competitors by changing the promotional approach to emphasise the valued attribute.

Finally, market information can be used to provide a segmentation base. The product can be forcefully and successfully marketed to segments where the offering's attributes are highly valued, giving either premium price or an improved market share in that part of the market where the attributes are appreciated.

A new competitor in a heavy apparatus industry in the UK was able to expand market share against the dominant producer while commanding a premium price that started at 3% and grew to 8%. The key to this success was management's recognition that its company's products offered significantly lower fuel consumption under extended high-speed operating conditions. Traditional market segmentation was in terms of the geographical location of major users. The new company instead segmented the market across all user areas in terms of types of applications where its products would significantly lower costs of operation. It then concentrated its marketing efforts on helping users measure the difference. The dominant competitor could not match this performance without abandoning its own technical approach.

Competing on value, not price

Given that the marketer has a sound appreciation of what it is that the customer values most, what should his response to price competition be? The uses to which information regarding the customer's perception of value can be put have already been touched upon. Boiled down into a single rule of thumb they amount to this: when faced with price competition, distract attention from price. Or, to put it more positively, do everything possible to concentrate the customer's mind on the superior *value* to be derived from your own product. This is a marketing task in which the aid of each of the other three 'P's can be invoked.

Product

Price competition can be inflicted very suddenly by a rival, whereas product development is typically a longer-term business. Nevertheless, it is often the case that the product can be differentiated in value by relatively small modifications, such as added bran in breakfast cereal, providing that these differences are promoted vigorously enough. Detergents, light bulbs and personal stationery provide further examples of successful differentiation from the consumer field.

At first sight, true product differentiation would seem a hopeless task with regard to many 'standard' products, such as screws or paper clips, and in some cases this may be so. But there are often opportunities for differentiation by way of the 'product surround', such as more ready availability, delivery twice per week, or a wider assortment of pack sizes.

Guarantee policy bears looking at too. Companies should ask themselves how long their guarantees are, and why. Could they be extended in length at nil or low cost to give a marketing lead? Would a self-imposed penalty for unreliable delivery or products create a differentiation that would be meaningful to customers?

Promotion

The creation of a brand franchise is the classic promotional answer to price competition. That is to say, the use of advertising and other promotional means to convince the customer of the special value of a branded product, so that he will be prepared to pay a premium price for it.

Examples abound, but to take just one from the pharmaceuticals industry, the chemist supermarket chain, Boots, brought out their own brand of antacid in competition with the market leader, Alka Seltzer, at two-thirds of Alka Seltzer's price. On the face of it, Boots' product ought to have done well, given not only their price advantage but also Boots' strong company image in the medical field and their control of retail outlets. But Alka Seltzer did not engage in panic price cutting, nor did they change the product. Instead, an advertising campaign was undertaken, designed simply to reinforce Alka Seltzer's image as *the* drink for settling stomach upsets. It worked, and eventually Boots withdrew their brand.

Another consideration under the heading of promotion is that a firm's sales force may itself be a source of unplanned price cutting, as the method of their remuneration may encourage them to offer reduced prices even when they are not asked to do so. One way to avoid this problem is by offering bonuses to those sales staff who do *not* offer price reductions.

Companies can also pay attention to the quality of the sales force. Because there is thought to be little to say about standard products such as duplicating paper, plastic tubing or ball bearings, industry tends to use order takers rather than sellers. There may be some scope for persuasive selling, though, particularly, as we have seen, with regard to elements of the 'product surround'.

Place

Differentiation by place has in recent years assumed major proportions. That is to say, taking up new means and places of sale that are attractive to customers and have not hitherto been exploited by one's own company or competitors. One of the most celebrated successes was the adoption of vending machines in public conveniences for the sale of contraceptive sheaths, whereas previously barbers' shops had been the principal outlet, far ahead of chemists' shops.

'Racking' is another possibility. Trading sites, notably garages, previously unused for selling such products as books, or ladies' tights, now provide a market place for such items. This is thanks to enterprising companies who have offered the site owners a share in the profits of a rack filled with the item in question. The stock remains the property of the supplying company until bought by the consumer, and the rack is re-filled regularly by the supplier's representative.

Most interesting of all, from the point of view of the producer facing price competition, is the provision of ·a merchandising service at supermarkets, when these outlets have already bought the product, perhaps at head office level. The merchandiser's job is to go around the supermarkets to make sure that the goods are being properly displayed and to keep an eye on the warehouse stock needs at the store in question. To provide a merchandising service adds to costs, but it may well enable a producer to out-compete a price cutting rival whose goods fail to secure shelf-space and therefore do not sell at all.

When should price cutting be considered?

The first response to price cutting by rivals should be, as we have seen, to examine all the market variables to see how we might be able to differentiate the product in value so far as the customer is concerned.

In some circumstances this may not be possible. Petrol companies in the UK, for instance, have recently found that price is the dominant issue, in a market where brand franchise, trading stamps and free gifts used to be of greater significance.

When the competition on price is fierce and unavoidable, survival in the short term may depend upon reducing costs, by working on the manufacturing process to reduce unit cost of production, or else by cutting down on overheads. Longer-term prosperity, though, depends on the renewed deployment of creative marketing.

Sometimes price cutting can be used strategically, in order to generate market share for a product, particularly if it is thought unlikely that major competitors will be either willing or able to match the price. But there are many calculations to be made and pitfalls to be avoided.

The first requirement is to see what volume of extra sales is required in order to offset the loss in profits from a particular drop in price. Figure 27 shows how the relationship between volume and profit can vary between different products. The comparison is between a product in self-adhesive labels and a stapling machine. The self-adhesive labels, with a low profit margin, need a 25% increase in volume to offset a 5% fall in price, while the stapling machine requires only a 10% volume increase to offset the same price decline. Thus the stapling machine producer gets greater leverage from market share gains than the adhesive label producer.

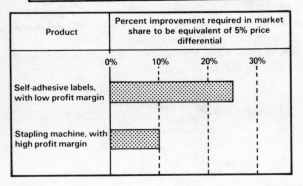

Figure 27

It should always be remembered that adding market share may cost more than it is worth, depending on where the added share is obtained. For example, after-sales support costs may be less costly, or already in place, in one part of the country, whereas achieving higher market share in another geographic area may involve higher future support costs because of the area's remoteness or the lack of an existing support network within it.

Well-planned strategic price cutting can sometimes open up a valuable market niche for a concern with a more favourable underlying cost structure than its rivals, such as discount warehouses offering a cash-and-carry service.

One famous example of price competition that was taken too far, and ended in the initiator's collapse, is that of Laker Airways. The retaliatory power of well-financed rivals, as evidenced by the major airlines' counter price-cutting against Laker, and the latter's ultimate demise, could scarcely provide a more vivid picture of the risks of fierce price competition. It should also be noted that the major airlines who were the 'winners' lost far more revenue in absolute terms than the firm that went to the wall.

An interesting comparison is provided by Pan American Airways' reaction to the advent of a Laker-style airline, 'People Express', in the US. Instead of panicking on price and jumping into a damaging price war to drive its new competitor out of business, Pan Am's public response has been much more confident. They have explained the difference, as they see it, between their own product, aimed largely at regular business travellers, and that provided by People Express, which they see as appealing typically to young, back-packing tourists on a first flight. Whereas it is important to the regular traveller to get through his flights without too much personal wear and tear, so that he requires higher standards of comfort and service, the holidaymaker in high spirits is unlikely even to notice minor discomforts, much less to worry about them. Pan American, in other words, feels secure in its own major market sector, provided that it continues to reinforce its traditional brand image of high quality.

When the competition's price is not known

Contracts offered for general tender, typically by public bodies such as local authorities, offer an example of a situation in which a company can be faced with an uncertain level of price competition. A number of construction companies will each submit a written bid to build a new sports centre, for example, or a block of flats, and, because these bids are sealed and private, no company knows what the other's price is. The system also frequently operates in relation to major engineering projects, such as land drainage schemes and the installation of North Sea oil rigs, and is also to be found in the field of maintenance contracts.

So, short of industrial espionage, or the bribery of officials, or some other leakage of information, how is a bidding company to decide what policy to adopt in the face of this unseen price competition? In the first place, the market intelligence situation is not quite as bleak as it appears, since much can be gleaned from publicly available information about contracts actually awarded by the particular local authority in question in the recent past.

Much more problematic, in practice, is the fact that bidding for contracts from public bodies usually allows all too little scope for competing on anything but price. Whereas a consumer, or a company, can freely choose to buy items other than the cheapest on the market, if they wish to obtain a quality product, public bodies are under much greater pressure to justify every penny of their expenditure, and cannot favour tenders other than the lowest without incurring either accusations of extravagance or the suspicion of corruption. It is, however, open to a bidder to propose ways corresponding to his firm's distinctive strengths in which the tender specification itself could be modified or improved, thus providing scope both for the customer to obtain better value for money, and for the company proposing the change to put its best foot forward.

Sometimes, though, the combined result of the sealed bid system and a lack of opportunity for product differentiation, is that contractors over-reach themselves in their anxiety to secure a tender. In one major local authority in recent years, as many as 40% of the contracts awarded were going uncompleted, largely due to bankruptcies. One firm's answer to this fierce price competition was to tender only the 'second time around', after the initiating firm had collapsed. At this stage, with the initial price provenly unrealistic, this firm was able to win contracts with bids an average of some 30% higher than the bid that was successful the first time. A rather ingenious special case, this, of successful differentiation by place.

Application questions

20.1   *Do you have a clear idea of what it is about your organisation's product offering that customers value most highly? Can you be reasonably sure that your judgement is correct? How?*

20.2   *Faced with a sudden challenge on price by a major competitor, could your organisation make an effective marketing response without resort to a price war? Think of particular products in your range and what opportunities there might be to differentiate their value vis-à-vis that of competitors' products.*

20.3   *How can price cutting be used strategically? Under what circumstances? Some hazards and advantages of strategic price cutting have been considered in this chapter. Does your own experience suggest any others?*

Action points
- *Remember* that price cutting wars are destructive.
- *Know* how to carry out a trade-off analysis.
- *Concentrate* the customer's mind on the superior value to be derived from your product.
- *Use* promotion rather than price cutting.
- *Take up* new means and places of sale.
- *Consider* price cutting when – in the customer's view – it can differentiate your product in value.
- *When faced* with an uncertain level of price competition, concentrate on emphasising your firm's distinctive strengths, thus offering the customer better value for money.

21

**How can we communicate
with our customers?**

Overview

*Communications between an organisation and its customers can
involve a variety of methods and approaches. They include the
direct means of communication, such as advertising and promotions, and the indirect means, such as corporate image and customer
service. The organisation must be aware of the impact created by
different deployments of the communications mix, and must work
to control the type of message being transmitted. This means
that objectives must be set which will match the aims with the
means.*

*In approaching communications, the successful marketer will keep
in mind the nature of communications, the importance of objective
setting, appropriate use of the communications mix available, the
impact of indirect communications and the value of word-of-mouth
communications.*

The nature of communications

Any organisation would like to believe that the message being
transmitted about itself or its product is the correct one: correct
for the corporate image, correct for the product image and correct
for the target market. How then can an organisation ensure that
this is so?

Communications cover a wide range of means, with the end in
sight being the correct transmission of a pre-determined message.
But it is not always possible to control that message or its delivery.
Communications involve not only direct and planned methods,
such as advertising or sales promotions, but also unplanned or
inadvertent communications. This latter sort can take the form of
publicity, either negative or positive, about a product or organisation. Clearly, unplanned and indirect communications of this
type often seem to be beyond the organisation's control; neverthe-

less, they play an important part in influencing customer perceptions.

There is a need, therefore, for the organisation to consider carefully the nature of communications and decide which forms of communication are most appropriate. The conscientious marketer will also take into account the variables which may occur through inadvertent or indirect communications, and be aware of how these are affecting the market.

An example of one approach used to transmit a particular message can be taken from the German recycling industry. A particular company decided to adopt a direct approach when trying to reach its potential customers. There were three distinct stages to its approach. First, the manufacturer identified its potential customers and designed a special event to attract them to its plant. Invitations were sent to public health and sanitation engineers, and to the heads of local government committees throughout the EEC.

Upon their arrival, they were greeted by the managing director who spent two days with them explaining the principles of recycling. He illustrated the process by showing them an installation in operation, and concluded by leading a discussion on the commercial and social advantages of recycling. The third stage involved the company's economists and technical officers in spending a full day discussing the particular nature of the problems each guest had in his own local government activity.

As a result of the two-day programme, each guest had the chance to see for himself the process at work. He had been shown the general advantages which the system could bring to his own sphere and to the wider community. Finally, the guest had received a highly personalised evaluation of his own special problems and the opportunities involved in using the system. This meant that each individual had been conducted through a direct, *person-to-person* exploration of the organisation's product and its relevance to a specific application.

Of course, not all organisations would find it possible or even productive to follow such a detailed, elaborate form of customer communication. But for this particular organisation and its customers it worked – and illustrates one method of *personal, direct* communications.

In contrast, when the British banking system launched its two major credit cards – Barclaycard and Access – a mass advertising campaign was undertaken. Few bank managers invited their customers for tea to discuss the merits and demerits of a credit card from the clearing bank compared with American Express. Instead, the national press was filled with display advertisements which were predominantly concerned with emphasising that credit cards could 'take the waiting out of wanting'. In fact, strict control of credit limits ensured that each customer could only take advantage of this claim once or twice. But the advertisements did not stress that the amount of credit offered was carefully adjusted to an individual's total financial position: this information might have deterred too many potential card holders. Instead, all holders of existing bank accounts which had been relatively trouble-free were either encouraged to take a card, or sent one automatically. This was an *impersonal* approach to communicating with one's customers.

In both examples, *point-of-sale promotional literature* was also employed. In the case of the German manufacturer of recycling equipment, guests at the conference were provided with technical documentation and costs and benefit data. The British banks ensured that the counters of their branches and the doormats of their customers were amply covered with explanatory leaflets.

The above examples deal with situations when a new product was being launched. The initial thrust was to create a high level of awareness about the product, but this is by no means the end of the story. As we shall explore further in the next chapter, awareness must lead to interest, and interest to the desire to acquire the product. Finally, the potential customer must be persuaded to buy it.

Once the customer has shown interest, as in the case of the guests who attended the German recycler's event, that interest must be capitalised upon. This means that the communication must be followed up, possibly by a different form of communication. This may involve the characteristics of the product or service in use, the nature of personal contact at point of sale, the after-sales service, and so on. All these factors will communicate with the customer. They may reinforce his judgement that he was correct in buying the product, or cause him to regret his decision and not repeat it. However the customer feels, he is likely to discuss his purchase with those around him. That message is another form of communication about the organisation and the product.

We have seen that the nature of communications means many things. It is not simply a matter of the organisation deciding on a message and launching it on to the market place. Messages will be put across in many ways, some intentionally and some inadvertently. It will be helpful first to examine how the organisation can plan its communications in the most coherent and effective manner.

Objective setting

Given that the organisation communicates with its customers in a variety of ways, how can it determine the most appropriate and effective method?

When we talk about communications in a promotional context, we can easily fall into the trap of referring to 'marketing' or 'selling' or 'advertising' in the same breath.

As we have discussed earlier in the text, marketing is the process by which an organisation seeks to match its resources with a customer's wants. In the organisation itself, the marketing process usually occurs as a distinct activity from, say, the selling function. Marketing will soften the market for the sales team by ensuring that the salesman meets those customers who want and can use the product or service.

Both marketing and selling involve different forms of communication and each will use different techniques. One of the techniques widely used by the marketing function is *advertising*.

Advertising's purpose is to improve sales potential. In this way, it takes the function of marketing into a more focused area. The organisation's resources have already been matched with the customer's needs; it is now a matter of appealing to the customer to make him or her aware of the specific product which can satisfy those needs. While the purpose of advertising is to create a positive sales environment, it is often difficult to relate advertising directly to sales results. This is because many marketing operations adopt a 'total approach' which means that the effect of any one element is difficult to assess. If a product, for example, fails to sell as had been expected, then the impulse is to change the packaging, revamp the advertising and sell it in a different manner. This means that it is impossible to say which method of communication was incorrect in the first place.

Before an organisation decides to adopt a particular method of promoting its product or service, it must consider the task in hand and set objectives for it. If it fails to do so, the risk is run that its marketing, selling and other promotional activities will be lumped into one indistinguishable mass with no coherent plan or aim.

There is no point in adopting a particular approach to communications without first ensuring that it will satisfy the objectives of the organisation. If, for example, a product's real market is those people who prefer to shop in more exclusive places, then mass-distributing the goods through low discount outlets will convey an inappropriate message about the product (a point already discussed in Chapter 15). Any target market will be reached earliest and most directly by a particular type of outlet. The organisation must set its objective – in this case, to reach an exclusive market – and then choose the best way to handle communications. Later on in the text we shall discuss objective setting in relation to measuring the effectiveness of advertising. But whatever form of communication the organisation uses to present itself, its product or its service, it should be as clear as possible about the goals which are desired. Once these objectives have been set, the organisation can move towards considering various elements of what is known as the communications mix.

The communications mix

Different products will require different orientation of communications. Industrial products, for example, are most often sold through personal selling contacts which rely heavily on the salesman's own expertise in the field and his company's ability to be innovative and competitive. Other products, such as milk, may be fairly indistinguishable in the market place, and therefore the communications effort will rely more heavily on other forms of communications, such as price, place and promotion. This situation holds good in the banking sector, where the rates and services are so similar that the organisations have to appeal almost entirely on differentiation of image: Midland, for example, is the 'listening bank'. In the consumer sector, communications can be varied more extensively, with messages about price, availability and quality all being communicated.

In the communications mix, as in the marketing mix itself, the marketer will arrange the basic elements to achieve an emphasis which will best meet the objectives of the organisation.

The major methods of communication which are widely available in Europe include the following:

National and regional newspapers These appear daily or weekly. Typically, they are confined to just one country but in recent years a number of links between the serious or quality dailies have appeared.

Trade and professional magazines These cover everything from architects' materials, computers, caravans and model railways to the accountancy and professional marketing periodicals.

National, regional and Pan-European radio and television In particular, commercial television and radio.

Exhibitions These are held either on a national, European or international basis and cover everything from dairy products to offset lithographic printing equipment and machine tools. Many are open to trade members only; others restrict the attendance of the general public to a specific time during the exhibition.

Direct mail This employs circulars or leaflets conveyed through the post or delivered door-to-door. The main advantage of direct mail as a method of communication is that it can allow the development of a personal relationship between company and customer.

Public relations This includes the dissemination of information to the press and television for possible news coverage and the general development of an organisation's image with the public. This latter activity can often constitute a major asset in marketing terms.

Back-up/point-of-sale literature This covers the supporting literature produced by organisations to supplement other communications. It includes catalogues, price lists and technical specifications, as well as special displays at the point-of-sale in consumer goods markets.

Packaging This is a particularly important influence in consumer markets. Packaging must be viewed not only in terms of how it helps to persuade customers to purchase but also in terms of the extent to which it minimises damaged goods that need to be returned or replaced. The consequences of inadequate packaging upset customers and significantly damage the effectiveness of communications.

Personal selling We have left this aspect to the last but it is by no means the least important. It is given full discussion in

Chapters 29–32. Suffice it to observe here that it embraces the activities of individuals travelling to established and potential customers; the use of telephone selling, increasingly common in consumer and fast moving industrial goods markets; and the activities of any person who sells to customers, such as the managing director of a capital goods industry, or a giant food manufacturer selling to major supermarket chains that control 10 to 20% of his total business volume.

Marketing communicates with its customers by employing some or all of these possible methods. The use of one approach on its own will seldom suffice.

A pharmaceutical manufacturer who sought to gain widespread sales for his ladies' hair colouring found that the chemist outlets into which he wished to sell his product were unwilling to respond to the blandishment of his sales ladies in a personal selling approach. The chemists required reassurance that a major advertising campaign would be launched both on television and in the fashionable women's magazines. They believed that only in this context would they be able to sell the product.

If we look closely at this example, we can see the importance of the distinction we made in Chapter 7 between customers and users or consumers. The hair colouring manufacturer had to communicate to two quite different groups – his customer and his customer's customers. The manufacturer's customers, the chemists, were not confident that point-of-sale display and elegant packaging would be adequate as a total communications effort to put the product through the channel of distribution to the women who wanted their hair coloured. Accordingly, they were unwilling to stock the product until an additional communications effort was made.

An alternative way of expending an organisation's communications budget would be by direct personal selling on a home-by-home basis. The Avon organisation has pioneered this system in Britain for a wide range of cosmetics. Their system is in fact typical of that used in industrial markets where sales or technical representatives combine their sales activities with advisory services on how best to tackle and solve problems.

The effective marketing organisation is continually experimenting with the mix of communications media it employs to find out either how to make a fixed expenditure more cost-effective or how to reduce its budget in achieving a similar level of effect. It achieves this by setting objectives, judiciously using the communications mix and monitoring the results.

Indirect communications

Organisations also communicate with their customers in a number of less obvious ways, which we can term indirect. We have already referred to the *image* which an organisation creates in the mind of potential customers prior to their receiving any new message about it. If it exists at all, that image will have been built up from a range of past experience and hearsay. It will affect not only how customers perceive any particular communications message but will also affect their behaviour or response as a result of receiving a communication. This indirect communication from the corporate image is supplemented or reinforced by the way in which any enquiry or order is handled. In technical markets, where products require installation, or in service industries, where a service relationship takes some time to settle down, the kind of service which customers receive from the employees of the organisation communicates its own definite message. Efficiency and courtesy, for example, promote a positive image of the organisation; inefficiency and rudeness work in the opposite way.

Another major means of communication is, of course, the *product or service itself*. The type of arrangements which KLM, British Airways or SAS make for their customers, both on the ground and in-flight, are vehicles for communication with the customers. Such arrangements influence customers' attitudes and perhaps their subsequent behaviour towards the particular carrier. This also holds good for the freight forwarder who uses the air cargo facilities of these organisations. If delays, damages or misdirection occur, these misfortunes communicate to him an impression of the airline which cannot fail to influence him later on.

Pricing is also an extremely meaningful communications cue to customers. In unsophisticated markets, where customers are unsure of the criteria for judgement of a product or service (say, wines, restaurants or hotel accommodation), price will frequently be used as an indication of quality. As the customer becomes more certain of himself, he begins to rely more on his own judgement and does not fear to take a more discriminating view of price. Where the price is known to other colleagues or friends, however, the fact that it has been paid can also act as a communications message about the customer.

Different levels of pricing can convey a good deal about a product. If the price is low, the product may be seen as being too cheap to be satisfactory. If the price is high, the product may be assumed to be of correspondingly high quality. Certain price levels may prompt the customer to believe that the product or service is a bargain not to be missed.

The complexity of customer reaction to price levels can be illustrated by the fortunes of Turtle Wax car polish, a product encountered earlier in the text. When it was launched in America at 59 cents, the polish was considered to be so cheap that its quality was suspect. The manufacturers increased the price to $US1.59 but made no changes in the product itself or in the channels of distribution used; the result was that the polish rapidly became the most highly priced car wax on offer, and took a major share of the market.

The point was made earlier, but can be emphasised here, that the importance of *word-of-mouth* communications should never be underestimated. Such communications can occur not only after a purchase has been made, but during the buying process. For example, in some retail outlets products which have been purchased already are left conspicuously on show with a large 'sold' label. This often prompts customers to discuss the product more specifically, sometimes with the actual purchaser. The organisation will benefit from this interchange between potential customers and satisfied customers.

Word-of-mouth communications are particularly important in industrial buying.

During such transactions, great store is put on the opinions and experiences of colleagues and peers, within the organisation and in other compatible organisations.

Summing up

In summary, the successful marketer will approach communications in a planned, systematic manner, paying attention to:

– the nature of communications;
– objective setting;
– powerful employment of the communications mix;

– indirect communications;
– word-of-mouth communications.

Application questions

21.1   *What was the last major purchase you made for your household? When you were considering alternatives, how did the product manufacturers communicate with you? Which of the communications used influenced your final choice?*

21.2   *Within your organisation, how do you communicate with your customers? Are there other ways in which you could communicate? What is the purpose of each form of communication which you presently employ? In what ways do they:*
(a) Complement each other?
(b) Act as reinforcements to each other?
(c) Fulfil a specific task which could not be undertaken by any other form of communication?

21.3   *Are your organisation's communications co-ordinated in any way? Who is responsible for the co-ordination? Do you encounter any problems when co-ordinating your organisation's communications? How can these problems be solved?*

21.4   *In what ways does your organisation communicate indirectly with your customers? Are these indirect communications compatible with your stated communications strategy? In what ways could you affect the image of your organisation presented by these indirect communications?*

Action points
● *Remember* the wide range covered by the types of messages available as communications.
● *Set* objectives *before* adopting a particular method of promotion.
● *Make* your communications mix cost-effective and be sure to monitor the results.
● *Appraise* your organisation's image by analysing its indirect communications with customers.
● *Pay attention* to word-of-mouth communications.

22

**How can we persuade
                     our customers to want our products?**

Overview

*Once an organisation has reached a target market, it must then
persuade the customers actually to acquire the product or service
on offer. The organisation must sell its product by understanding
how the customer reaches a decision to buy and the nature of
the stages involved: initial awareness, interest, attitude formation,
intention and the decision to act. These stages are often passed
through by several people forming what is known as the Decision
Making Unit (DMU). The marketer must be able to identify the
DMU in any organisation, and adjust the message accordingly.*

*Customer groups have traditionally been studied and classified
according to their socio-economic backgrounds. This method of
classification can only be used on a limited basis; more consideration should be given to the behavioural characteristics of buyers
since these determine their buying patterns.*

*Once the marketer has identified the buying process and buying
patterns of prospective customers, various forms of persuasion can
be considered. These may include short-term methods, such as sales
promotions, or long-term methods based on strategic planning.
Whatever method is used, the organisation must ensure that it meets
both long-term and short-term objectives.*

The process of persuasion

In the previous chapter we discussed how an organisation communicates with its customers about its products. In terms of persuading customers to buy products, the first stage is to *create an
awareness of the product*. This can best be done by appropriate
use of the communications mix. But awareness alone is not
enough. The customer must then be persuaded to go through to
the next stage and actually buy the goods or service.

A distinction must be made between the *needs* and *wants* of the customer. An industrial manufacturer will *need* certain components to make the factory or production line work. But the industrial salesman is all too aware that some of these components will be sold by a number of organisations. It is his organisation's goal to sell their component to the customer. The customer, therefore, must be persuaded to *want*, and therefore buy, one product in preference to all others.

In the same way, a shopper doing the weekly round of the supermarket will have certain items on the shopping list. But what makes him or her purchase a particular brand of coffee? Sometimes it is habit; sometimes it is in response to a sales promotion; and sometimes it is a matter of where the coffee is placed on the shelf.

Research into buying patterns has shown that few of these decisions are haphazard. The buying process can be analysed and conclusions drawn about buying behaviour. Before we look at these findings in detail, it is important to consider the basic elements of the customer's decision-making process.

We discussed earlier in the text the concept of the decision-making process and we saw that this process is usually founded on beliefs and choice criteria. Particular customers' approach to decision making will vary across business sectors, across industries and across organisations. An organisation trying to persuade an industrial customer to buy a large item of machinery, for example, will have to be aware of the decision-making process which exists in the customer's organisation. The salesman may actually speak only to the production manager at one stage, but this manager alone will not make the final decision.

As we have seen, a typical industrial organisation will contain within it a Decision-Making Unit (the DMU) which is likely to be composed of the production manager who is interested in the performance of the item; the finance director who is concerned about its cost-effectiveness; the operator who is concerned about ease of operation and safety; and a chief executive responsible for the overall efficiency of the plant. The DMU may be a formal body, or may be composed of a number of people who influence the decision-making process in different ways. In any case, the organisation selling its product must be aware of the different concerns which each member of the DMU holds and must tailor the message accordingly.

Using a different example, the bank manager will encounter quite a different type of DMU with a different decision-making process. He may be discussing the advantages of a business development loan with a corporate treasurer, but must realise that the corporate treasurer will be a member of a DMU which can include a senior finance director and an export manager. Again, the bank must cater to the different interests of each member of the DMU and alter the message accordingly.

Understanding, then, that the decision-making process will occur in different ways for different customers, the marketer must consider the second stage of the process of persuasion. Having achieved customer awareness of the product, the marketer must note that without a favourable attitude and intention and opportunity to purchase, awareness by itself will not bring about the desired result. Figure 28 illustrates some of the many factors involved in the decision to buy.

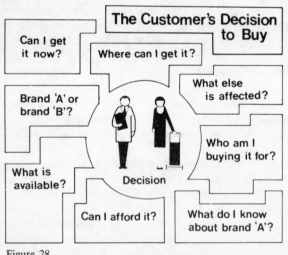

Figure 28

The example of a British brewer's misdirected advertising campaign will be remembered from Chapter 2. The brewer distributed his draught beers through a limited number of public houses. Most of these were in the South, although some were located in other areas of the country. In order to promote his product the brewer initiated a national television advertising campaign. An extremely high recall of the product and the message was achieved but, since the beer was only available in limited areas, much of this investment in awareness was wasted. Similar waste occurs in industrial markets when product advertising creates awareness but no further activity is undertaken to build upon it.

Once awareness has been created in the mind of a potential customer, *interest in learning more* about the product or service will normally follow if the product or service appears relevant to the customer's needs. Frequently, the medium used for arousing awareness will include enough further information to satisfy this interest. Technical details or demonstration of potential benefits that can accrue can be an integral part of the initial communications message. In the context of these first two steps, *attitudes* may begin to form. Potential customers may reject the service offered, not believing that a draught beer brewed in London could possibly slake the thirst of an Anglian farmer. Equally, the emergent attitude could be that an up-and-coming Anglian farmer might well want to drink what the smart young men in London drink to wash down their ploughman's lunch in Fleet Street or on the King's Road.

The significance of *understanding* how the Anglian farmer will react when he becomes aware of the draught beer will not have escaped notice. Successful persuasion requires the most careful attention to how attitudes towards particular products are formed. All the evidence available indicates that only a few generalisations can be made which cover more than a limited group of products or services. However, these generalisations tell us a great deal about how to create successful persuasive appeals. As was discussed in Chapter 9, customers' attitudes are in part dependent on their purchase or choice criteria (that is, the attributes judged most desirable and important in a product or service) and their belief about the presence or absence of those attributes in any given brand. Appropriate material, it appears, can indeed use the customer's initial interest to stimulate the formation of favourable attitudes and beliefs. Information of itself never seems to change attitudes. If an attitude is well entrenched, it will lead to a distorted perception of any information which is at variance with it, in order to make it fit. Hence, persuasive appeals must either *create fresh attitudes* or *build upon those which are already there.*

Once the relevant attitudes have been located and understood, the appeal can concentrate on offering the arguments which match the attitudes. Favourable attitudes, like unfavourable attitudes, affect the perception of information received. If the audience is well disposed, it will use the advocate's information to confirm and reinforce its own prior attitudes. It is reassuring, after all, to know that one is right – a point, incidentally, which must not be overlooked *after* the purchase when reinforcement of attitudes is vitally important.

We should perhaps pause here for a moment to reflect on the timing of these two stages, interest arousal and attitude development, as far as the potential customer is concerned. Purchasing officers in industrial companies, housewives acting on behalf of their families, service organisations acting on behalf of clients – all may be both aware and interested but in no position to act. There may be no need for the product or service at the time when interest is at its height. Evidence from this field clearly indicates that the investment made in taking customers up these early steps of the persuasion process can be all too easily dissipated. The favourable attitudes, the interest, even the awareness can decay. A good filing system or a conscientious housewife might preserve the information for a time, but persuasion processes are not static. Accordingly, a crucial part of the marketing effort to persuade is to first pinpoint those who are potentially in the market or who can be brought to the market by one's efforts. This point can be summed up in the expression *intention to buy*.

Identifying the appropriate market can be done by segmentation, which was discussed earlier in the text. The organisation must analyse which particular part of the total market will respond to marketing of the product. According to the business, segmentation can be conducted on the basis of geography, company size, nature of household, age, sex, income and so on. Baked beans can be considered as a product with mass appeal. Almost everyone has a tin of baked beans in the house at some time or another. This makes the job of marketing baked beans more difficult rather than easier. Each manufacturer of baked beans wants to achieve the highest market share, and therefore must consider in detail who the prime market is. It is not the person who 'always has a tin in the cupboard' and has an income upwards of £10,000 a year. Surplus cash flow and frequency of baked beans purchase do not correlate. This is a product with a high snack consumption, and therefore the most significant market will be the young housewife with growing children who buys baked beans at least once a week. The marketer must decide how to appeal to that person in order to increase market share. This involves a process of persuasion which must be tackled systematically. It will only be successful if the marketer understands the elements of buyer behaviour.

Buyer behaviour

Traditionally, marketers have segmented the population according to income and social status. They grouped people into 'A', 'B', 'C1', 'C2', 'D' and 'E' categories, starting with the upper middle class (e.g., professional or independently wealthy) at the top of the scale and leading down to the 'E' category of people existing at the lowest level of subsistence (e.g., old age pensioners or casual labourers). Hence, we had a 'C2' type who was someone with a certain income and a certain social class. Products were directed at each supposedly static audience.

But more extensive investigation by the Marketing Communications Research Centre (MCRC) arrived at different conclusions which have changed traditional marketing assumptions. The MCRC research was conducted on behalf of several companies who were seeking new approaches to marketing. It was realised that the traditional classifications no longer hold good. Different social classes are now achieving higher incomes than has traditionally been the case, and are therefore influencing buying patterns. For example, the type of person who traditionally had little disposable income and therefore was not ranked as a potential customer of more expensive, luxury goods has today a greater disposable income than some people further up the scale. There are skilled workers in the 'C2' categories who are now making more money than semi-professional people in the 'B' households. Class barriers are changing, and people are less restricted by the status awarded at birth.

Many organisations are now adopting a more dynamic approach to buyer behaviour based on the MCRC research. This revealed that customers can be classified according to their behavioural characteristics and responsiveness to various stimuli. Some people by nature are more responsive to sales promotions, while others exhibit stronger brand loyalty. Size of household can also play an important part, with shoppers who have pre-school children at home making less frequent trips to the shops, buying larger units of goods and responding to sales promotions only if they coincide with these infrequent outings.

What the research showed was the need for organisations to adopt a more thorough and systematic approach to marketing, based on a more detailed analysis of their customers. This means that organisations must decide how to approach their market in a more realistic manner than has been employed in the past.

Examination of buyer behaviour is not restricted to the consumer sectors. We discussed earlier in the text the models which can describe types of buyer. The industrial customer does not, as one might assume, make decisions purely on the basis of practical, rational thinking. Every customer has certain behavioural characteristics which will determine how he or she can respond to the process of persuasion, both on the wider level of marketing and the more focused area of personal selling. Selling is one part of the process of persuasion which we will examine in more detail further on in the text.

Planned persuasion

Once the marketer has become familiar with the customer's needs, wants, decision-making process and buying behaviour, the process of persuading the customer to buy the product can begin in earnest. Once again, the most important consideration should be *objective setting*. In deciding upon any approach, the marketer should consider whether it satisfies a strategic or tactical aim. An example is the use of sales promotions.

Sales promotions are a unique form of promotion in that they offer something to a defined group of customers or consumers within a specific time limit. The offer must be made over and above the normal terms of trade, with the objective being to increase sales beyond what would normally be expected. They form part of a tactical approach to marketing and can make use of the communications media or of price, product or place.

A tactical approach has its advantages and disadvantages. Used correctly, it can provide fairly immediate and often profitable results. But sales promotions used in a purely tactical way can amount to little more than a series of gimmicks lacking any coherence. The same managements who organise spasmodic sales promotions may also hold the general belief that pricing, distribution or advertising should conform to an overall marketing strategy enshrined in an annual plan. The reason for the discrepancy may be that marketing plans have always been based on a philosophy of building a long-term customer and consumer franchise, whereas the rationale of sales promotions is to help the company gain and/or retain tactical marketing initiative.

Sales promotions can be used strategically as well, with each promotion increasing the effectiveness of the next. In this way, a bond between seller and buyer can be established and tactical objectives can be linked to the broader plan. This means that all resources are better deployed and can be more effectively evaluated.

Special attention should be paid to sales promotions which involve brands. An example can be taken from the fruit squash market, which traditionally had been highly branded. In a period of fierce competition, the branded manufacturers cut their prices drastically until they were almost indistinguishable from the own-label brands. The manufacturers also ran a series of promotions, including competitions. The result was that consumers concluded that the branded squashes were no better than the own-label varieties and therefore there was no justification in paying a higher price. Eventually, this spelled the death of branded squashes. The example shows the need for organisations to consider carefully the use of tactical strategies within their overall strategies. The importance can be seen, once again, of objective setting.

Branding is an area of marketing which has been subjected in recent years to intensive research. One valuable finding can help organisations plan their promotions in the most cost-effective way. It has been shown that customers respond most strongly to what has been termed 'consumer franchise building' activities. This includes advertising and promotions which serve to build a feeling of value about the brand, its qualities and its superiority over competing brands. Types of promotion include samples, coupons, demonstrations and recipes. All are directed at the consumer and relate only to the brand. Organisations which adopt this approach have shown corresponding increases in sales and profitability.

Sales promotions are rarer within the industrial sector, as most products are sold to organisations rather than directly to the consumer or end user. But in recent years, this has been changing, with industrial manufacturers becoming less reluctant to make 'special offers'. An advertising campaign by 3M, for example, offered a £50 coupon to prospective buyers of photocopiers.

Another firm dealing in fast-moving industrial goods has developed a large range of special promotion schemes, including trade-in allowances, desk-top giveaways and custom-built guarantees.

Making featured sales promotions effective

There is widespread acknowledgement that sales promotions are often badly mismanaged. The main reason for this is that confusion about the exact nature and purpose of a sales promotion often results in expenditures not being properly recorded. Some companies regard sales promotion as part of advertising, some as part of sales force expense, others as a general marketing expense, and yet others as a manufacturing expense (as in the case of giving extra quantity for the standard price or producing special labels to announce a special offer). The loss of unit sales revenue from special price reductions is often not recorded at all.

Few companies can afford not to set objectives for sales promotions or to fail to evaluate results after the event. For example, a £1 case allowance on a product with a contribution rate of £3 per case has to increase sales by 50% just to maintain the same level of contribution. Failure to attain this, or to meet alternative objectives set for the promotion, easily results in loss of control and a consequent reduction in profits.

There are two essential steps to the more effective management of an organisation's sales promotion expenditure. First, current spending must be analysed and categorised by type of activity, such as special packaging, special point-of-sales material or loss of revenue through price reductions. Next, within a total strategy for sales promotions, objectives for each promotion must be clearly stated, such as trial, repeat purchase, distribution, display, a shift in buying peaks or combating competition in a specified manner.

Thereafter, the following procedure must always be followed:

- select the appropriate technique;
- pre-test the ideas;
- mount the promotion;
- evaluate its impact in depth.

A leading manufacturer of self-assembly kitchens embarked on a heavy programme of sales promotion after a dramatic reduction in consumer demand. While the firm managed to maintain turnover, the managers involved were worried that their sales promotional activities had been carried out in such a haphazard and piecemeal fashion that they were unable to evaluate the cost-effectiveness of what they had done. They were also very concerned about the effect of the promotion on the company image and on their long-term franchise with consumers.

Accordingly, they made a concentrated study of this area of expenditure which had come to represent over half their total communications budget. Next time round, they had clear objectives, a clear promotional plan fully integrated into their marketing plans and an established on-going means of assessment. The company took their competitors by surprise and made substantial gains in market share. In one promotion alone, they hired an entire hall in an international exhibition centre. They converted it into a giant showroom with 40 kitchen displays and a 250 seat theatre. For an expenditure of £90,000, the company presented a new range to over 2,500 customers, obtained 900 display orders against a target of 750, and sold to their entire national distribution network in one operation. At the same time, they convinced the trade of their professional, business-like approach, and of their confidence in the future.

Some of the many types of sales promotions that can be used are listed in Table 4. Each of these different types are appropriate for different circumstances and each has advantages and disadvantages. For example, case bonusing relates cost to volume, is fast and flexible, effective where the customer is profit conscious, can last as long as required, and is simple to set up, administer and sell. On the other hand, it has no cumulative value to the customer, is unimaginative, and can often be seen as a prelude to a permanent price reduction.

Points schemes (where channel members are allocated points according to quantity purchased in a given time, and receive some reward when adequate points are collected) are flexible, have wide appeal, do not involve the company in holding stocks of gifts and are easy to administer. On the other hand, they offer no advantages in bulk buying, are difficult to budget, and lack the immediacy of dealer loaders which encourage bulk buying by channel members.

Table 4 Various types of sales promotions

Type of promotion		Consumer	Trade	Sales force
Money	Direct	Price reduction	Dealer loaders Loyalty schemes Incentives Full-range buyer schemes	Bonus Commission
Money	Indirect	Coupons Vouchers Money equivalents Competitions	Extended credit Delayed invoicing Sale or return Coupons Vouchers Money equivalents	Coupons Vouchers Points systems Money equivalents Competitions
Goods	Direct	Free goods Premium offers (eg: 13 for 12) Free gifts Trade-in offers	Free gifts Trial offers Trade-in offers	Free gifts
Goods	Indirect	Stamps Coupons Vouchers Money equivalents Competitions	Coupons Vouchers Money equivalents Competitions	Coupons Vouchers Points systems Money equivalents
Services	Direct	Guarantees Group participation events Special exhibitions & displays	Guarantees Group participation events Free services Risk reduction schemes Training Special exhibitions & displays Demonstrations Reciprocal trading schemes	Free services Group participation events
Services	Indirect	Co-operative advertising Stamps, coupons Vouchers for services Events admissions Competitions	Stamps, coupons Vouchers for services Competitions	Coupons Vouchers Points systems for services Events admissions Competitions

Summing up

We have seen that the process of persuading customers to buy a product is complex and involves many factors. The organisation must understand the customer's decision-making process, and the Decision-Making Units which exist. The market itself must be segmented so that the marketing direction can be focused. Within the segments, buyer behaviour and buying patterns must be understood and accounted for.

Having decided on the most appropriate approach to take customers from awareness of the product through to the desire to acquire it, the organisation must set clear objectives. The marketing approach has to be clearly defined in terms of tactical and strategic implementation. Once the approach has been decided and the various elements put into practice, the organisation will have to determine the effectiveness of its campaign. We will examine various methods of doing this in the next chapter.

Application questions
22.1 *How does persuasion work in your markets? What assumptions do you make and on what are they based? How is your 'model of persuasion' reflected in your promotional plan?*

22.2 *How do you identify your customers? Is there a single grouping that you have to reach, or do you need to make a number of groups aware of your product offering? If you are marketing to a number of groups, how do you approach each of these groups? Is there any opportunity to adapt your approach to meet the needs of the different segments? What would you do if your communications budget were reduced by 50%?*
(a) Concentrate on a limited number of market segments?
(b) Adopt a single approach to everyone in the market until the budget was used up?

22.3 *How do potential customers become aware of your product offering? Are there any other ways in which you could create awareness? Once potential customers have become aware of your product offering, how do you ensure that they gain all the information necessary to decide in favour of buying your product in preference to competitors' products?*

22.4 *Within your own organisation, who becomes involved with the persuasion process? What monitoring is done to build up know-*

ledge of the way in which the process works in your market? How could this be improved?

22.5   *How is sales promotion used as a form of communication by your organisation? In what ways does it relate to the other forms of communication used? Are there any other ways in which sales promotion could be used more effectively? How would you justify additional sales promotion of this kind?*

Action points

- *Create* awareness of your products.
- *Develop* customers' positive attitudes towards the products being promoted.
- *Know* the different techniques of sales promotions.
- *Make sure* that sales promotions have clear objectives, so that results can be carefully evaluated.

23 How can we measure the effectiveness of our communications?

Overview

The effectiveness of advertising can only be measured against clearly stated objectives. Once clear objectives have been identified, evaluative research techniques can be used to assess the extent to which they are being achieved. Before an expensive campaign is launched, small-scale research can check whether the advertisement is capable of achieving its objectives. After the campaign, post-evaluation procedures can assess how effective it has been and can indicate what the organisation still has to learn in the successful deployment of advertising.

Advertising objectives must always be clearly distinguished from the marketing objectives of the organisation. Where the objective can be achieved by advertising alone, it can be deemed an advertising objective. Where its achievement is dependent on other aspects of the marketing mix, it is a marketing objective. Achieving advertising objectives cannot guarantee sales success unless all other aspects of the marketing mix are also effectively deployed.

The importance of advertising objectives

Contrary to common belief, the effectiveness of advertising can be measured with some degree of accuracy, provided always that *valid objectives* have been set.

It is important to emphasise at the outset the need for the objectives to be valid. Before we can make any decisions on advertising we have to know precisely what role it is expected to play in the overall marketing effort. Is it expected to explain why the product is more expensive than the customer might otherwise expect it to be? Is it to communicate details about a completely new approach to some task which will require the rethinking of habitual practices by an industrial purchasing officer? Is it intended to emphasise that service is widely and speedily available in the event of a breakdown of machinery, thereby reassuring a client organisation that it can expect few major problems if it buys that particular machinery?

Each of these objectives might be achieved effectively by an advertising campaign but the total marketing operation could still be a failure. The expensive product may not be easily available, or may fail to live up to performance expectations. The quality of service provided may not be as high as the buying organisation had anticipated. In such instances, which are not infrequent, there is little point in laying blame at the door of the advertising. The advertising objectives have been achieved effectively; but the customers' hopes have been dashed by the failure of the rest of the marketing activity. The lesson is to ensure that the advertising objectives are appropriate to the marketing effort overall and that the organisation's communications do not over-claim.

Unless a company is using direct response advertising (where all the available information is conveyed by direct communications and the product is only available direct from the manufacturer or agent offering the product), the role of advertising is to help implement marketing objectives. As we have indicated, it is quite possible to communicate effectively but fail to achieve the marketing objectives of sales, market share, and so on: the successful achievement of marketing objectives depends also on the satisfactory interaction of the other three 'P's – product, price and place. In addition, the successful achievement of advertising objectives will only lead to the fulfilment of marketing objectives if the marketing manager has been correct in his assumptions of how the achievement of the advertising objectives will affect customers' buying decisions.

An example of successful advertising combined with the failure to achieve marketing objectives can be found in RHM's introduction of a pastry mix. The company advertised this new product nationwide but in one area of the country the product was not well received. Research showed that the advertising objectives had been achieved. However, there was a local product on the market and customers preferred to support this. Although the RHM campaign had encouraged the overall use of pastry mixes, in this area a competing product had benefited from the increased interest. In the circumstances, RHM decided to spend no more money on advertising their brand of pastry mix; instead, they used other forms of promotion in order to achieve the marketing objective of selling their product.

A final point to be borne in mind is that since advertising can seldom make sales on its own, it is almost always appropriate to resist the temptation to relate advertising expenditure to levels of sales achieved.

The nature of advertising objectives

Recent studies by the Marketing Communications Research Centre with many of the leading British and European commercial organisations have shown that there are four major objectives which organisations traditionally set. They are as follows:

Branding and image building

Whether the organisation is engaged in industrial products (like the National Coal Board, British Petroleum and Dunlop), in consumer goods (like Cadbury Schweppes, Weetabix and Watney Mann) or services (like the British Tourist Authority and the Midland Bank), it always seeks to communicate an overall image of the organisation and its work to actual and potential customers. Since most organisations believe that a favourably perceived image creates a constructive environment in which to market their outputs, they commonly set the building of such an image as an advertising objective. In markets where there is little product differentiation, branding is frequently used to distinguish a product from its direct competitors.

Education and information

Organisations generally know far better than do their customers what exactly they are trying to achieve in the way of product or service performance. In the well-organised marketing activity, that performance level will have been set on the basis of a very close analysis of customer and consumer needs and wants. The importance of ensuring that customers are aware of, and comprehend, the organisation's offering along with the benefits it can potentially bestow cannot be understated. It is all too easy to assume prematurely that customers are aware and understand. This objective is especially important in market development strategies, when customers are being encouraged to use the product or service in new and different ways. Education and information are also all-important during the early stages of introducing a new product or service to the market.

Affecting attitudes

The initial campaign of education and information must be followed by a campaign to affect potential customers' attitudes in a way favourable to the organisation's output. In Chapter 22, it will be remembered, we discussed the problems involved in seeking to change attitudes and we came to the conclusion that the better course was to build on or develop them.

Influencing potential customers' attitudes was the communications goal set by Plessey when it launched its automatic ignition system for gas installations, especially domestic cookers. Cadbury's faced similar problems when they launched Marvel and Smash. In all three product instances, customers had historical attitudes to products of this type. In the first case, gas ignition systems had a long record of doubtful efficiency. Cadbury's, in their turn, were up against World War II stereotypes of dried milk and powdered potato, as well as being anxious not to damage their image as a manufacturer of chocolate which used real milk. In both cases, the image which the companies had nurtured enabled communications activities to develop attitudes towards the products like, 'If a well established firm like that has produced the product it will be well worth trying, even though I would be extremely doubtful if an unknown firm had attempted it.'

Many assume that the more favourable the attitude held toward the product or service being promoted, the greater the predisposition to purchase. Large budgets are allocated based on this assumption. In some circumstances this relationship does not hold good. Advertisers need to check that the assumption applies to them before they commit their advertising budgets.

Loyalty reinforcement and reminding

The fourth major objective has two dimensions. The first constitutes the *reinforcement of loyalty*. On the one hand, companies wish continually to reinforce their customers' loyalties to their products or services. On the other hand, customers need to be convinced that their pattern of habitual behaviour (in always going to a particular supplier, for example, or always shopping at a specific department store in Paris, London or Rome) is not short-sighted on their part. The advertising objective in such circumtances will be to reinforce the feeling that the habit is correct and sensible and does not need breaking.

The corollary to loyalty reinforcement is, of course, *reminder communication*. Customers can easily forget to keep adequate stock levels of products, or not avail themselves of services often enough. This is especially true in areas of discretionary purchasing or behaviour, where failure to be reminded may well lead to another more recently communicated message having a greater influence on the customer. This point can be illustrated by the example of domestic or office decorations and furnishings. 'Old furniture must go' was a classic campaign by the furniture industry in the mid-sixties, designed to encourage customers to enter a discretionary market. The same style of advertising campaign is used by brewers to remind us to visit their pubs instead of watching television or following other social pursuits.

Finally, the combination of loyalty and reminder communication is intended to ensure that any custom generated does indeed come to the organisation undertaking the campaign rather than to any conveniently available brand. (The case of the RHM pastry mix described earlier in the chapter underlines the importance of this form of communication.)

Clearly, the relative importance of these four major objectives varies according to the state of the market and the life cycle of the particular product. At the introductory stage of a product or service, the generation of awareness and the conveying of information are vitally important. Later in a product's life cycle, branding, image, loyalty and reminding take on much greater significance. The effective marketing operation ensures that appropriate communications goals are set for each of its product ranges or groups of services offered.

Pre-exposure testing of advertising

As was observed at the outset, without valid objectives no real attempt can be made to measure effect. In addition, valid objectives are needed in order to construct appropriate promotional or advertising campaigns to meet these objectives. Different objectives will call for different approaches to communication in the market place. The generation of ideas for campaigns is a specialist task although most managers consider themselves gifted amateurs.

The most appropriate promotion may be a sales presentation using a variety of media to communicate the different points, some form of predominantly visual communication such as a brochure, direct mail circulars and press advertisements, an exhibition presentation with supporting materials and samples, or a television commercial. As far as possible, the ability of the chosen promotion to achieve the objective set for it needs to be ascertained. Pre-testing is one means of doing this.

Pre-testing constitutes sensible insurance against errors in the creative development and execution of ideas. It is a means of checking whether material is technically capable of achieving its objectives. It is not a substitute for other research to identify whether particular advertising objectives are the most appropriate for the product or service being promoted. Available as a standard service, it involves presenting the promotional material to a sample of the correct target audience of customers and measuring their reactions to it.

The customers are presented with the communication in as realistic a context as possible. They may have been questioned beforehand to establish a benchmark for their awareness, interest, attitudes, loyalty, and so forth. After exposure to the communication, these characteristics are measured again. In addition, the opportunity can be taken to allow customers to give verbal reactions to the communications message. Negative aspects of the messages can then be screened out. For many advertisers the major concern is to ensure that negative reactions which could damage the product or service do not occur. It is assumed that if the potential customer holds a negative reaction the likelihood of purchase will be diminished.

A common occurrence in pre-testing is that the customer is found to be confused by the communication. So much information may have been packed into the message that nothing registers clearly with the customer. The customer may be confused too by the use of star personalities in promotional activities: it is often the case that there are inappropriate associations in the mind of the customer. It is also common for the potential customer to pick up a communication not intended by the advertiser. 'You are never alone with a Strand' was interpreted by smokers to mean that people smoking the brand had no friends and therefore had to turn to smoking as a substitute for human company.

Pre-testing procedures can also be used to compare several

alternative approaches to, or mixtures of, communications in order to see which gives the best impact. Yardsticks for comparison with previous advertising campaigns or other promotional activity emerge as data begin to build up. Comparisons can be made with the communications activities of competitors to see how well any particular campaign matches up. Furthermore, pre-exposure tests can be undertaken from the very earliest stages of development when rough formats can be used to test ideas and concepts. The advertiser is well advised to take full account of the results of his pre-testing. If the correct message cannot be conveyed in the artificial test situation, the advertisement stands little chance of communicating effectively in the market context amidst surrounding distractions.

In calculating a budget for pre-testing, it is necessary to consider the cost of *not* carrying out such tests. Unless an advertisement is carefully pre-tested, the advertiser runs the risk of conveying an incorrect message about the product and discouraging people from using it. He may also confuse potential customers about the product being advertised. Where a serious mistake of this nature occurs, the entire campaign may have no impact or, even worse, create negative reactions.

Before any pre-testing is done, the organisation must be very sure about its intentions. Advertising pre-testing must be carried out against stringent advertising objectives. Careful thought should be given to the following factors.

Communications Is the intended message reaching the intended audience? During pre-testing, the respondent is viewing the material being presented in a manner which is completely divorced from reality. The respondent's attention is being focused on the information, thereby increasing the chances of positive reception. If the intended message is not being conveyed during this artificial, contrived situation then there is little likelihood of reception being improved under 'normal' circumstances. When the advertisement is eventually presented it will be competing with the surrounding environment. If the basic communication is not being conveyed, it is unrealistic to assume that the advertisement will achieve its set objectives.

Attitudes Is the attitude most conducive to the product being maintained, created or modified? Many advertising campaigns aim to change an attitude, to 'bring the customer around' to wanting the product. The difficulty in pre-testing for this objective is knowing whether the respondent's attitudes have been modified by the advertisement, were held previously quite independently of the advertisement or were the result of previous experience with the product. This means that pre-testing for attitude must involve a 'before and after' procedure. The respondent's attitudes held before contact with the advertising material must be determined and measured. If the attitudes are measured after exposure to the material, then any shift in attitude can be measured. The accuracy of this is, however, doubtful because any changes are likely to be different in the outside environment when exposure of advertising material is more frequent and (for the respondent) irregular.

Predispositions to behave The organisation will want to judge how an advertisement will change a respondent's behaviour. Will the respondent buy the product, use it and perhaps alter parts of his or her normal routine to accommodate it? This is probably the most difficult advertising objective to pre-test. There are many other influences in the customer's environment besides the advertisement which will determine the customer's behaviour. Pre-testing in this case is only useful to determine which material appears to create a greater predisposition towards the intended behaviour than others. Whether predispositions are directly related to actual behaviour is difficult to determine and therefore must ultimately remain an assumption.

We can see then that pre-testing to see whether advertising objectives can be met is a difficult venture, and any information gained must be accepted cautiously. Extensive research on pre-testing has shown that methodology must be carefully planned and executed. Variables in pre-testing will include demographic factors, the respondent's sex and age and the respondent's socio-economic group. It will be necessary for an organisation to use different advertising formats and to change variables in order to determine more accurate pre-testing results.

Post-exposure evaluation

The execution of the full advertising campaign, including any pre-testing needed, is normally seen as a very expensive affair. In consumer goods industries such as cosmetics, budgets for advertising run as high as 30% of total sales income. For a major company this can mean several million pounds each year. The food industries of Europe have similarly massive advertising campaigns. In industrial markets, communications expense tends to be associated more with personal contact of a technical, advisory and after-sales service nature. Nonetheless, total expenditure on communications for industrial goods can reach very substantial levels.

Accordingly, it is normally only sensible to set aside some of the total communications budget to measure how effective the advertising or other promotional activity was in practice. How much should be expended on evaluative research will depend on the benefits which will accrue from knowing how effective the communication has been. Certainly, any organisation which intends to spend further substantial sums in a subsequent year is extremely unwise if it does not seek to learn carefully from its expensively bought experience. Much of the post-evaluation work undertaken concentrates on measuring the effectiveness of media advertising. Advertising on commercial television, in particular, will account for the major share of the total communications budget.

As in pre-exposure testing, research methods in post-exposure evaluation involve survey work amongst potential and actual customers. Whatever objectives were adopted for the advertising campaign should be checked to see whether they have been achieved. It will be recalled that different levels of effect may have been accomplished. Most customers may well have been aware of the campaign but failed to receive clearly the information it was intended to communicate; or they may have covered both these stages and failed to develop or evolve their attitudes.

Campaigns often have worthwhile effects, but effects that are somewhat at variance with what an organisation hoped to achieve and what pre-tests may have suggested would be achieved. The cause of slippage could be the media which the organisation employed in its major campaign. Pre-testing methods cannot really simulate adequately a television commercial in mid-evening or a colour advertisement in the *Sunday Telegraph*, or a page in *Waterways World*. Any slippage that does occur, however, provides vitally important evidence for the next campaign.

It is both possible and necessary to evaluate the effectiveness of any advertising campaign. How much is spent on evaluating any particular campaign will, of necessity, be determined by what is at stake. What can be at stake is well demonstrated in the instance of a French consumer durable manufacturer based in the electronics industry.

The size of the market was some Fr45–50 million per annum. The manufacturer's was an old established brand with some Fr1 million spent annually on advertising in the media and a further Fr300,000 spent on point-of-sale activities. Private brands by retailers held some 10% of the market while the manufacturer held a more considerable share. There were 10 other branded competitors and the market was highly competitive among them all. The main advertising objectives set were to convey the benefits to be derived from using the product, to develop and convey favourable attitudes towards the product, and to maintain loyalty amongst current purchasers who repurchased relatively infrequently.

For several years, advertising for the product had tried to emphasise a key attribute of the product's performance but had failed to persuade customers of the credibility of the claim. Research showed that certain changes in market conditions had reduced the perceived relevance of the attribute for purchasers. Guided by the research results, the manufacturer proceeded to emphasise other aspects of the product. Customers found the new claims more credible and showed themselves willing to acquire the product.

The organisation can also conduct studies to determine whether attitudes have been successfully developed, altered or maintained. In doing so, it must be careful to ascertain that it has indeed been the attitudes which have changed and therefore contributed to increased sales. An example of this can be taken from milk marketing when a certain company launched a massive campaign to persuade customers to buy milk for its nutritious and health-related qualities. Sales showed a marked increase after the campaign, which initially led the organisation to conclude that it had successfully won over non-milk buyers. However, further studies showed that the most significant new sales were gained from existing customers who increased their consumption of milk. The healthful attributes of milk were not sufficient cause to persuade those people who did not buy milk for other reasons. Many of those people did not like the taste, or calories.

Another illustration of 'insufficient cause' can be taken from the airline industry where a marketing venture must be based on changing attitudes which are relevant to a particular airline. The attitude that flying is safe is fairly well-entrenched, therefore an airline's safety record would not provide sufficient cause for a customer to change airlines. The airline might instead work on the concept of business travel, or comfort.

A manufacturer of motor oil tried to boost its position from second in the market to top. It researched the reasons why customers chose to buy the more popular brand and found three main prevalent attitudes. But when the manufacturer tried to capitalise on those attitudes to increase sales, it found that customers did not respond. The reason was that customers agreed with all the attitudes promoted by the number two brand, but as they were already having those needs met by their current brand they saw no sufficient reason to change.

The organisation which chooses to measure advertising effectiveness through sales must, therefore, be careful of what is actually being measured. Sales increases can result through better distribution, better packaging, a different price, and so on. It is essential that the organisation links any evaluation of advertising effectiveness to the objectives originally set.

Media selection

Clearly, an ineffective message will cause the quality of the communication to deteriorate. However, if media are not properly selected then no one is likely to hear the message, regardless of its effectiveness. Furthermore, media buys that are too diffuse (in other words, have a much larger readership or viewership than is the target market) are not likely to give much return on the pound.

The fundamental principle in media buying is to select those media vehicles that are seen, read and viewed by a large percentage of the target audience. The nature of the message is likely to determine the type of media, depending on whether sight or sound or motion are required: those requirements would frequently correspond to print, radio and television. The amount of media purchased also determines the frequency with which individual customers are exposed to the message.

In other words, media selection is the quantity part of the advertising effectiveness equation. Total advertising effectiveness is a function of both the media and the message, or of quantity (media) and quality (message).

A systematic approach

To measure effectively the success of communications, a systematic approach must be adopted. There are many factors involved in measuring such effectiveness, including the important areas of objective setting, pre-testing and post-exposure evaluation. The stages involved in the process of measuring success are outlined in Figure 29.

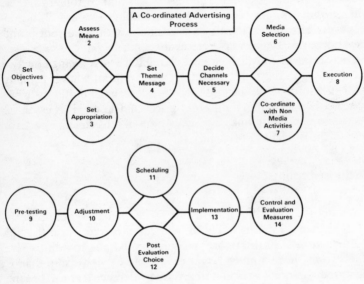

Figure 29

These can be elaborated as follows.

1 *Setting advertising objectives* Advertising objectives become the 'benchmark' against which the effectiveness of the organisation's approach can be measured. As we have discussed previously, these objectives must be clear and must take into account the fact that communications are one part of the marketing mix. They must, therefore, be taken as an integral part of the total marketing strategy. Advertising objectives for products will differ depending on whether the market is static, increasing or declining. Similarly, they may differ according to whether the intention is to change an attitude in order to gain new customers, or to increase the usage of the product by increasing frequency of purchase amongst existing buyers.

2 *Evaluation of ways in which objectives can be implemented* It is not enough simply to state an objective as 'to increase sales'. The objective must be refined in terms of operations, such as increasing revenue or market share, or total sales, by a certain amount in a specified time. It is then necessary to decide and research how such an increase can be achieved.

3 *Appropriation necessary to meet objectives* Assessing the means of achieving objectives must be done alongside calculations of the appropriations thought necessary to carry out the strategy. Previous experience will help here, but if the organisation has no experience in the area then the calculations will help ensure that subsequent activities are carried out according to the overall objective.

4 *Message(s) necessary to fulfil objectives* Once target audiences and objectives have been identified, then an appropriate message or messages can be developed. These must be specific: if the objective is to instil an attitude that the product has health benefits for children aged between three and ten, then this message must be conveyed. The message would be lost if the product was advertised as an all-round family food.

5 *Decision to allocate resources above and below-the-line* This decision will be determined by the historical behaviour of the industry and the task to be accomplished. It is generally agreed that below-the-line expenditure results in short-term sales growth, but does little to build long-term brand loyalty, or increase sales over a long period. Staying above-the-line will commit the company to a longer-term objective where customer response will not be directly attributable to advertising. Therefore, it is important for the organisation to decide which spending activity will meet its objectives. The historical behaviour of the market is important, for those markets which have promotion-dominated sections make it difficult for all brands not to follow suit. It is usually advantageous for a small brand to compete on below-the-line terms, since the cost is the same per item sold as that for a large brand. A small brand cannot usually afford large-scale advertising. Where both above- and below-the-line activities are planned, they must be co-ordinated to complement each other in the achievement of the main objectives.

6   *Choice of above-the-line media*   How the appropriate media can be selected will be discussed in more detail in the next chapter. Suffice it to say here that this choice is often determined by historical practice and by the amount of money available. It is advisable that organisations consider periodically whether their particular choice of media is reaching the target audience and conveying the right message.

7   *Choice of non-media promotional vehicles*   Interest can be created using a wide range of below-the-line activities. The target audience and the objectives will help determine the type of below-the-line activity used. If the objective is to create brand loyalty, for example, it would be appropriate to ask customers to collect a series of packet tops or labels. On the other hand, if an organisation wants to convince the buying public that certain products reflect the organisation's concern for the environment, then a scheme would have to be developed to reflect that. It may include dissemination of information about the organisation's bio-degradable products, or its own involvement in recycling.

8   *Decisions about creativity used in above- and below-the-line activities*   Creativity alone does not sell products. The organisation will do well with an advertising agency which employs great creative flair, but it must ensure that the correct message is still being conveyed. Creativity need not be restrained, but the agency must be aware of its own responsibility to meet the organisation's main objectives.

9   *Pre-testing*   We have discussed in detail some of the strengths and weaknesses of pre-testing. The main point to be made here is that pre-testing, in some form, is often necessary and usually productive, provided that the organisation carefully selects the methodology. Even if testing cannot prove a campaign to be 'right' or show what sales response it can elicit, it can highlight whether or not the intended message has been conveyed.

10   *Any necessary adjustment*   Pre-testing should be done between the concept testing stage and the showing of the final advertisement. All too often pre-testing is done when the advertisement is complete, thus putting the organisation into a 'go/no go' situation. This kind of timing does not take full advantage of the pre-testing opportunity. If pre-testing is to be used effectively, longer time schedules will be necessary.

11 *Scheduling of advertising and promotion* The whole area of media scheduling requires special management. This can either be left to the speciality of an advertising agency, or taken up within the organisation itself. However, because of the complexities involved, the organisation will have to be sure that co-ordinating activities above- and below-the-line is given full care and attention.

12 *Choice of post evaluation methods for both above- and below-the-line activities* The decision on how to measure the effectiveness of a campaign should be made before the campaign is actually launched. This is by no means premature, as it can be argued that a campaign is not complete until it has been evaluated. The importance of post-exposure evaluation has already been discussed in this chapter. It is important to note here that the methods of doing so should form part of the total systematic approach.

Once these 12 stages have been dealt with, the organisation can proceed in confidence that it has done a great deal to minimise the risk of mismanaging the communications effort. Ultimately, this means that some of the risk involved in the total marketing strategy has been reduced.

Other marketing communications

The guidelines contained in this chapter are based on research undertaken by the Marketing Communications Research Centre into the effectiveness of media advertising. The main finding of this research was that valid and measurable objectives are the keystone to the success of any advertising campaign. Associated with this finding were the conclusions that the risks attendant on advertising campaigns can be minimised by the careful construction of a pre-exposure check and by appropriate research into the success or failure of earlier campaigns. Clearly, specific and quantifiable objectives are a prerequisite of all such research.

This framework can also prove useful in the assessment of the other forms of communication (such as sales promotion and personal selling) outlined in the previous chapter. Although a different approach to evaluation may have to be adopted, no organisation should exempt its communications activity from justifying the investment made in it.

Application questions

23.1   *How do your various communications contribute to the achievement of the marketing objectives for each of the products and services you offer? Does everyone in your marketing department agree with your distinction between communications and marketing objectives?*

23.2   *What pre-testing of advertising does your organisation do? What are the advantages and disadvantages of the procedures which you employ? What were the occasions when you changed your communications as a result of the pre-testing undertaken? What would have happened if you had not undertaken any pre-testing on these occasions? If you do not undertake advertising pre-testing, what is the justification for this decision? Under what circumstances would the organisation undertake pre-testing?*

23.3   *How is post-evaluation of your communications carried out in your organisation? How has this contributed to the development of the products monitored? Is there additional post-evaluation research which would help you decide on the allocation of future marketing budgets? On a cost-effective basis, how could such research be justified?*

23.4   *If you work in an organisation where no pre- or post-evaluation is carried out, how do you gain the confidence to promote your products or services? Are there any occasions where you regret not having access to pre- and post-evaluation research? By what means could you persuade your organisation to undertake such research?*

Action points
- *Set* clear, precise objectives for your advertising.
- *Pre-test* your chosen promotion to see whether it can achieve the objectives set.
- *Emphasise* the key aspects of the product.
- *Find out* whether attitudes have been successfully developed.
- *Know* the stages in a systematic measurement of the success of your communications strategy.

How much should we spend on communications with our customers?

Overview

Any organisation which is involved in budgeting for communications will want to know how much of its own financial and human resources to use. Marketing budgets have traditionally been managed by the marketing department or individual concerned, but in recent years more of the responsibility has been extended to other parts of the organisation. The vast amounts of money spent on, for example, television advertising have caused many organisations to take more board-level control. But the organisation still must determine an appropriate budget which should relate clearly to the objectives set and the task at hand.

The choice of spending above- and below-the-line must be carefully considered in light of the targets to be met and the resources available. Some organisations choose sponsorship as a method of promotion, but, like any other method, this must be evaluated in terms of energy, money spent and benefits gained.

Planning the approach

In the preceding section of this unit we considered the nature of communications, the process of persuasion and the importance of evaluating the effectiveness of any promotional campaign. All this may sound like a tall order for any marketer who must also cope with the day-to-day running of a marketing activity. The organisation as a whole does not have boundless resources. Its funds of money, time and human energy must be used carefully to ensure that maximum productivity is combined with maximum efficiency.

   The importance of a planned, integrated approach applies to almost every aspect of communications. A typical mistake would be the case of an organisation which overspends on the marketing activity, only to find itself with insufficient funds to produce the kind of quality point-of-sale literature which the market and product demands. Promotional investments can include many things, most of them related and inter-dependent.

Costing it out

It will be useful here to consider the kinds of costs involved in communications, and some of the criteria which can be applied. In practice, the chief criteria used to determine the ideal vehicle for carrying advertisements are:

– cost of space (as in the print media) or time (as in the electronic media) per 1,000 potential readers or viewers;
– capability of the vehicle to carry the form and content of the message (for example, colour and movement are restricted to certain media);
– appropriateness of the particular vehicle in expressing the message (for example, 'quality' products being advertised in 'quality' newspapers).

Most buying and selling in the media is based on the cost per 1,000 figures. In fact, too much importance is attached to this. Media data only provide an estimate of the potential readers – the number of people who might read or see an advertisement. In making decisions about media advertising, it would be helpful to examine some of the terminology used and the meaning behind it.

Media planning/research terminology

Press
Audited circulation   Number of copies of a newspaper, magazine, etc. sold for an average issue, over a stated period.

Readership   Number of people who claim to have 'read or looked at' an average issue of a newspaper, magazine, etc.

Readers per copy   Average number of people who read an issue of a newspaper, magazine, etc.

Opportunities to see (OTS).

Media surveys measure people's claimed frequency of 'reading or looking at' average issues of newspapers, etc. Suppose Mr A claims to 'read' four out of every six issues of *The Times* and an advertiser has an advertisement in six consecutive issues of *The Times*, then Mr A has four OTS.

Media surveys measure duplication and triplication in people's reading habits, i.e., they determine if Mr A also reads the *Daily Telegraph* and/or the *Daily Express*, etc. If an advertiser puts one advertisement in *The Times* and the *Daily Telegraph* it is possible to calculate the OTS for Mr A.

If an advertiser plans a schedule of advertisements in a series of newspapers, etc., it is possible, from the survey data, to calculate the average OTS for:

– the average person in the target audience, and/or;
– the average person in some specified sub-group of the audience.

Television

Audience   The number of people who had an OTS of watching a programme or an advertisement. *Note:* The BBC calculate audience figures by interviewing a very large (800,000) number of people throughout the year: their audience figures therefore are based on people's memory (or recall) of their viewing (and listening). Commercial television (IBA) calculates audiences from a mechanical method ('set meters') plus diaries. The two sets of figures always differ because they measure different things.

Ratings (measured in television rating points – TVRs)   This is the percentage of homes (capable of receiving commercial stations) which are switched to a commercial station at a particular point in time. Hence for every advertisement it is possible to state a 'rating' that it achieved.

Total campaign ratings (measured in terms of the aggregated TVRs for each individual advertisement)   If an advertiser has a campaign of six television advertisements which achieved respectively 20, 30, 40, 20, 10, 15 ratings, then his total campaign ratings are the sum of these, i.e., 135. This measure is not particularly meaningful but it is used a great deal, as a crude measure of audience. Obviously, the advertiser could also have achieved 135 by 10 advertisements, each achieving 13.5 ratings or any other combination.

General

Coverage   The proportion of the target population having the opportunity to see at least one advertisement.

Frequency   What is usually implied is the frequency distribution of OTS for a campaign, e.g., a campaign of ten advertisements in various press media might be predicted to achieve '40% cover and 30% 2 plus, 15% 4 plus', meaning: 40% will have the OTS the advertisement once or more, 30% twice or more and 15% four times or more.

UK media research sources

National Readership Survey (NRS) Press   Some 40,000 interviews, about 108 publications. Organised by consortium of interested parties (JICTARS). Issued every six months.

JICTAR TVR ratings data   Issued on a weekly basis. For each television area an average of 250 homes monitored for television set use. Currently conducted by market research company, AGB. This data is often referred to as AGB TV ratings (used to be called TAM ratings). Organised/commissioned by consortium of interested parties.

Target Group Index (TGI)   Sample 30,000. Produces single source data on media exposure and product use.

Determining the budget

Advertising, of course, is only one part of the total amount which can be spent in the broad area of communications. In most organisations, these funds will fall into the area of marketing. Ideally, a marketing plan will determine which areas of communications will receive which kind of emphasis. At this stage, the organisation will determine a budget to accommodate those areas in a constructive and integrated fashion.

The process of determining a market budget is common to many organisations, and has changed over recent years. Research conducted by the Marketing Communications Research Centre during the last fifteen years has revealed a changing pattern and the need for more effective marketing budgeting. Traditionally, responsibility for marketing budgets was held solely by those in the marketing function. This has changed, spreading the responsibility to other parts of the organisation. There has been a move to curtail the enthusiasm of the marketer and exert much tighter control. This trend has been demonstrated in a number of ways.

Boardrooms are setting marketing budgets by allocating the residual revenue after deduction of operating costs and profit distribution. They are determining the budget allocated to television advertising (a large expense) and in many cases the marketing director has been replaced by a commercial director. Trade marketing departments now often report to the sales manager rather than the marketing director. Brand performance is increasingly monitored by those in production and accounting, in conjunction with marketing personnel. These trends indicate that organisations may be moving away from marketing orientation and back towards product orientation. They show that fewer people have become involved in the decision-making process, with non-marketing personnel exerting a greater influence.

Marketing budgets are determined at successively more refined stages. The first stage is deciding and agreeing upon the total marketing expenditure. Little detail is included here, sometimes not even the allocation of funds to specific business sectors. The next stage involves allocating the budget to various product groups and then, ultimately, money is allocated above- and below-the-line. These decisions usually occur in organisations in a hierarchy consisting of the marketing director, product group manager and assistant manager. A tight structure such as this means that those contributing to the budgetary process are likely to have been with the company for a number of years and have a perspective about the future of their various businesses.

Their decision is then usually passed up to the board and a negotiating process begins. In the most extreme cases, the budgetary process is retained within non-marketing areas, with decisions being made by senior, non-marketing, executives.

To determine a cost-effective, successful marketing budget certain factors must be considered. An agreed budget will evolve from examining two key issues: what is the communication task and the cost of achieving it; what can be afforded? (For example, what are the forecasts of sales/profits and other expenses?) In addition to considering these prime issues, the budgetary group should also ask the following questions:

– What are competitors spending? Is it important to be seen to be maintaining our exposure?
– What is the industry/market sector norm?
– Are we setting a longer-term objective of building a position in the market place?
– What is expected of us by the trade or middlemen?

– What are the minimum (threshold) levels of cost to enter certain media?

Advertising can have long- or short-term objectives, with its effect spanning, in some cases, several years. Sometimes it will take that long just to achieve a particular result. This means that rolling plans and budgets should exist for those forms of advertising and marketing communications which span several years. In terms of monitoring effectiveness, it is usually difficult and unproductive to try to relate advertising moneys spent to sales gained.

Budgeting criteria

The norm in many organisations today is to try to base budget allocation on sales and revenue forecasts. This expectation, usually emanating from senior executives in the organisation, has had a number of consequences. Often, overly optimistic volume forecasts are made because it is recognised that larger budgets can be justified for greater volumes and associated revenue forecasts. In addition to this, overly optimistic price increases are proposed as a means of legitimately boosting the revenue base against which budgets will be evaluated. The sales group within the organisation often maintains a counter pressure. This group will try to encourage short-term promotional activity in order to boost sales. These methods, such as price discounting, will usually serve to undermine brand strength, thereby giving short-term gain but sometimes long-term loss.

One way in which organisations can be assured of cost-effective and productive budgeting is to adopt a *task-related approach*. This means that no budget is accepted as a right, but must be justified in terms of specific tasks and specific objectives. The relevant manager must challenge assumptions within the sector, be explicit about how the market seems to be working and continually examine information and interpretation of data. If this carefully built up case proves to be wrong, then it will at least be possible to see what went wrong where. The research alone will still be valuable in establishing another set of assumptions and predictions.

Task-related budgeting prevents managers from adopting an unjustified premise and arguing from ignorance. Although at first this approach may seem haphazard and merely based on trial and error, it will allow an organisation to build up knowledge of the relationships operating in a particular market, and will provide an invaluable source of experience from which to proceed.

The difficulty in task-related budgeting is that there does have to be a starting point from which the case can be made to assume a relationship between a marketing activity and purchase behaviour. Another perceived disadvantage is that task-related budgeting assumes stable markets. While it is sometimes difficult for an organisation to react quickly enough to counter activities which undermine basic assumptions, it is also inadvisable to react to all market changes as a matter of course. It is often this instant reaction and response of companies to external variables which threatens the model which the manufacturer has established. Task-related budgeting does involve more effort and time than other systems, but the benefits which come from stringent analysis of assumptions and careful use of funds allocated are well worth the trouble.

Spending above- and below-the-line

Once the sectors of the business have been allocated funds, the details of the marketing mix are to be resolved. The decision now is the relationship between above- and below-the-line expenditure.

As far as above-the-line communications are concerned, the options available to the marketing manager are commonly seen as follows.

Television advertising
– To influence consumer attitudes towards the product, mainly in the long term.
– To maintain brand presence on television in relation to competitors.
– To reach cost-effectively the mass market who are purchasers of the product.
– To combat the growth in own-label products.
– To gain or maintain distribution of products through major outlets.

Although many of the reasons for using television meet longer-term objectives, television is used tactically on occasion.

The press

The press is increasingly being looked at as a viable alternative to television, where budgets are insufficient for television exposure. The reasons for use include:

– a specific socio-demographic target could be reached;
– a specific geographic region could be reached if required;
– the information could be physically retained for current or future use;
– the medium could reinforce and influence attitudes;
– the cost of reaching the target market is relatively low;
– potential purchasers of consumer goods could be reached before shopping trips. Complicated messages could be conveyed.

The cinema

A little-used medium. A number of companies use cinema experimentally because:

– it reaches a particular consumer segment, namely those under 35 years of age;
– geographical targeting is possible;
– a similar type of medium to television, but at much lower cost;
– the cost of reaching the young target market is very attractive.

The radio

Again, this is an experimental medium for many. Reasons for use are:

– a specific geographic region can be reached;
– potential purchasers can be reached before they make shopping trips;
– sponsored programmes may influence consumer attitudes and behaviour;
– consumer segments such as housewives and younger people could be reached effectively.

Posters

The advantages of this medium include:

– a specific region and an individual site can be targeted;
– potential shoppers can be reached whilst out shopping;
– posters can reinforce messages created by other media;
– relatively low cost in terms of opportunity to see.

Direct mail

The allocation of direct mail above- or below-the-line is seen as a function of its purpose. If it is to be used to evoke a sales response such as selling a product off the page, then it is seen as an activity below-the-line. Where objectives are comparable to those employed for other above-the-line media, it is allocated above-the-line. Its attractions are:

- a specific geographic region can be targeted;
- a distinguishable consumer segment can be reached;
- the information can be retained for future use.

Below-the-line: some general points

Activities below-the-line fall into two classifications: consumer promotions and trade promotions. The objective is usually to generate increased sales, both ex-factory and consumer.

Activities in below-the-line communications are used tactically and for short-term impact although, as discussed earlier, tactical use has the disadvantage of eroding brand strength. The dilemma which exists between those activities which ensure short-term success and those which ensure long-term survival has also been discussed earlier in the text. This dilemma will continue, as insufficient is known about these activities in the market place. Decisions are based on incomplete knowledge, assumptions and expectations of how competitors will act or react under different circumstances.

The dilemma can serve a useful purpose, however. It can motivate organisations to stop being defensive, relying on untested but familiar assumptions and become more aggressive in the market place. The role of the marketer in the organisation must, therefore, become more pronounced to ensure that the organisation matches its resources with customer needs.

Sponsorship

A brief word may be said here about another method of spending which some organisations wish to use to their advantage. Sponsorship may seem like an inviting way to promote a product or the organisation itself. The costs involved often seem low in comparison to the high visibility gained. But an organisation considering this form of promotion must weigh the other costs of time and resources.

Any consideration of sponsorship must be made on the same terms as other promotional spending. That is to say, there must be clear objectives set and a method of monitoring the effect of the expenditure. This is particularly difficult with sponsorship, and is one of the reasons organisations may choose not to elect it as a form of promotion. The real cost of sponsorship must be clearly understood. At first, it may seem like a low-cost activity but the real cost in terms of management time spent is very expensive. Many weeks of management time can be used just confirming details and arrangements.

Because of these disadvantages, the organisation should review carefully any plans it may have for sponsorship. It should be clear about whether sponsorship will be used as a clear-cut public relations exercise, or whether in fact the organisation expects to receive a genuine promotional benefit. In the latter case, objectives would have to be confirmed by measurable results in order to justify sponsorship in promotional terms.

Summing up

We have seen, then, the need to plan carefully the total communications approach in order to determine how much to spend. This planning is likely to be most effective on a task-related basis, where managers must constantly assess and re-assess their justifications for funds and the effectiveness of the expenditure. This is necessary no matter what sort of decision-making process occurs within the organisation.

It is also important that decisions about communications spending are felt throughout the organisation. This does not mean that all decisions will be made by committee, but that those decisions should at least be communicated to other sectors. This is particularly important between marketing and sales functions. There must be a feeling of co-operation and liaison between these two groups to prevent situations where the sales team feels it is competing with the marketing function. This can happen when, for example, the sales team feels that an ebb in sales could be counteracted by providing incentives through a special promotion. The marketing function may realise that such a move would be a tactical ploy bringing only short-term results. If the sales function understands the budgets and the rationale behind them, misunderstandings and conflicts can be minimised.

Application questions

24.1 *In your organisation what proportion of sales revenue is spent on communications? Who decides the level of this expenditure? Do you believe that the level of expenditure should be greater or less? What are your reasons for this opinion?*

24.2 *Within the total expenditure for communications in your organisation, how is the money spent on specific elements of the communications mix, such as advertising or public relations? Is it possible to quantify communications expenditure in this way? If this is not done at present, how could such a system be introduced in the future?*

24.3 *Consider a specific advertising campaign, sales promotion activity or other form of particular communications approach undertaken by your organisation. What was the original budgeted expenditure for this activity and what result was anticipated in terms of increased sales and profits? What was the actual expenditure and the actual increase in revenue and profits? If the actual figures were at variance with the budget, what was the reason for this and can such a situation be avoided for the future?*

24.4 *Does your organisation predominantly spend on above-the-line or below-the-line activities? Do you believe your current patterns of spending are the most appropriate ones? Are there better ways in which your communications budget could be spent?*

Action points
• *Consider* both the costs and the criteria of the communications to be chosen.
• *Know* the terminology used in media advertising.
• *Know* the criteria for determining a cost-effective and successful marketing budget.
• *Bear in mind* the relationship between above- and below-the-line expenditure.

25   What role does marketing intelligence play in effective marketing?

Overview

Marketing research provides a flow of data, information and intelligence which enables the organisation to match its resources to the needs of its customers. Companies with marketing planning systems have high levels of actionable marketing intelligence.

The construction of marketing intelligence systems (MIS) is central to the application of marketing information to marketing decisions, so that all information is streamlined rather than uncoordinated. Although the MIS is based on a micro-data bank, the system should be able to provide output at any requested level of aggregation.

Marketing research can take many forms, including both ad hoc *and on-going information gathering. Such research can be either reactive or non-reactive, depending on the information needs of the organisation.*

The role of marketing research

As we have seen, the marketing concept is grounded in the idea that the profitable development of an organisation can only be ensured through a continuing attempt to match the resources of the organisation with the needs of its customers. However, before they can be met, these needs must be identified. When the needs have been identified, a careful assessment must be made of the suitability of the organisation's market offering.

It is the role of marketing research to provide a flow of information which will allow the organisation to make a suitable match between its own resources and the needs of its customers.

Marketing intelligence as a management resource

Research is conducted to provide answers to questions or solutions to problems. Clearly, before answers can be attempted, as much relevant information as possible is needed.

Information is based upon *data*. Facts and figures presented in some specific format – often with the aid of computer-based processing systems – constitute data, but by themselves they do not represent information. *Information* is data combined with direction; it is 'active', whereas data are purely 'passive'. The messages which information contains and which can be revealed by analysis should be the ultimate service sought from marketing research – a service referred to as *intelligence*.

The marketing director is primarily interested in marketing intelligence. He wants to know where the competition is, what the competitors are planning, what they are currently thinking, how he can best grow his business, how he can best attack competitors who are taking business away from him. He needs also to have intelligence about what the customer is thinking.

The marketing director needs to be constantly weighing up the options and possibilities. In order to do this, he will tell the marketing research or data base collector what issues are currently the big challenges in the market place and will ask for information that will help him make better decisions. Making intelligent decisions, therefore, depends critically on a partnership between the marketing director and the marketing researcher.

We can consider the footwear industry, for example. One piece of relevant *data* might be that last year, one million pairs of shoes were sold. Our *information* could include that, of this one million pairs of shoes sold, three-quarters were imported from Italy. Market *intelligence* could explain why this number was imported from Italy, which types of men and women were buying them, what the buyers' preferences were, and why the locally produced shoes were being rejected. Such explanations could then help towards rectifying the failure to capture more of the market.

Companies with complete marketing planning systems have high levels of actionable marketing intelligence. This is consistent with the need for both corporate and individual business units to collect data on an on-going basis so that the system can regularly convert the data into intelligence. Whilst the gathering of marketing intelligence will always pose a problem to most companies, it is far less of a problem for companies with complete marketing planning systems in place. This is because managers are forced to concentrate on the key operational and strategic issues, so that their attention is focused on gathering relevant and timely intelligence. Companies with complete systems tend to have *predetermined* the information which is required at each level in the organisational hierarchy. They use standardised formats for collection and presentation of such intelligence. This is largely achieved through a synthesis of information flows from the bottom up, and the diffusion of valuable experiences from the top downwards.

The differences between data, information and intelligence must be clearly understood if a proper integration between research and marketing management is to be achieved. The marketer must constantly address the problems of how data can be organised and analysed to provide information which will then lead to marketing intelligence. His ability to make successful decisions is clearly enhanced if he is operating under conditions of known risk rather than uncertainty.

If the conversion of uncertainty into risk is the prime marketing management task, the second is undoubtedly the reduction or minimisation of that risk. If the marketing manager is to convert uncertainty into risk and then go on to minimise the risk, he must be assured of a steady supply of relevant information. Good information facilitates successful marketing action; indeed, marketing management can be seen as first and foremost an information processing activity (see Figure 30).

Looked at in this way, marketing research appears as a *systematic and objective search for, and analysis of, information relevant to the identification and solution of any problem in the field of marketing*.

Research as a basis for marketing action

How should marketing managers approach the integration of marketing research with marketing action?

In the first place, it is necessary to view marketing information as a resource. This means that we must be concerned with the problems of producing, storing and distributing it. Marketing information has a limited shelf life – it is perishable. Like other resources, information has a value in use: the less the manager

The Role of Marketing Research

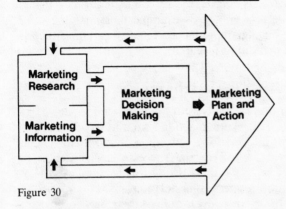

Figure 30

knows about a marketing problem, and the greater the risk attached to a wrong decision, the more valuable the information becomes.

This latter point is an important consideration in assessing marketing research budgets. It implies the need for a cost/benefit appraisal of all sources of marketing information. There is no point in investing more in such information than the return on it would justify. Naturally, it is easier to determine the cost than the benefits. The managerial benefits of marketing research are difficult to pin down. They can be expressed in terms of the additional sales or profits that might be achieved through the spotlighting of marketing opportunities. The benefits can also be calculated in terms of the avoidance of those marketing failures which would have resulted from a lack of relevant information.

One company involved in the development of an industrial application of heat exchangers in Germany believed there was a 20% chance that the product might not succeed, leaving it with a development and marketing bill of DMk2 millions. From this, management inferred that the maximum loss expectation was DMk400,000 (that is, DMk2,000,000 × 20%) and that it was worth paying up to this sum to acquire information that would help them avoid such a loss. However, the company realised that its cost-benefit calculation did not reflect the fact that the information obtained would not be totally reliable; in other words, it would not all form the basis for effective marketing action. The company therefore drew up a reduced budget for research which reflected more accurately the degree of confidence which it had in the results of the research. This example illustrates the need for a careful use of managerial judgement in association with cost-benefit analysis of marketing research.

Management decision and marketing research

Given that the appropriate analysis of marketing information can provide the basis of marketing action, what sort of decisions require what sort of information? This approach to management information needs is central to the successful construction of *marketing intelligence systems* (MIS) for the application of marketing information to marketing decisions.

We can identify three basic levels of marketing decisions where an input of information is essential. The first is marketing information for strategic, long-term decisions; the second is marketing information for tactical, short-term decisions; and the third is marketing information for one-off marketing problems. The first two situations require a continuous, on-going input of marketing information, whereas the last needs an *ad hoc* but speedy response from the marketing research function.

Until the late 1960s, marketing research was largely limited in application to the *ad hoc* and static analysis of marketing problems. Use of techniques such as the retail sales audit and the customer panel would have been of great value to the short- and long-term performance of many organisations, particularly in the field of fast-moving consumer goods, such as breakfast cereals. However, during the 1950s and 1960s, few organisations employed such methods: generally speaking, marketing research was not used to monitor the marketing environment on a continuous basis. In the late 1960s, a major shift in orientation by hitherto largely *ad hoc* users of marketing research, along with the conversion of new organisations and service industries to the use of marketing research, led to substantial interest in the setting up and deployment of integrated marketing intelligence systems.

Today, sophisticated marketing intelligence systems are widely used. International oil companies and airlines with headquarters in Europe, for example, have marketing intelligence systems which enable their executives to know on a weekly basis sales levels for all products in all market areas, levels of inventory at all inter-mediate stations, current production levels and capacity utilis-ation. In addition, their systems can provide trend data, market share estimates, cost information, and data on the comparative profitability of all products or services on a market to market basis. The organisations held all this information previously but, before an MIS was introduced, the information was in a frag-mented and uncoordinated form. The adoption of a 'systems' approach to information requirements and the use of existing computer facilities meant that these companies were able to provide management with a *data bank* orientated to well defined information needs.

Organisations need not limit their MIS to the analysis of current and historical data such as sales statistics and other commonly collected market data. Information on consumer attitudes, advert-ising levels and changes in competitive marketing activity now also forms an input to such systems in many areas of marketing endeavour.

The benefits of an integration of marketing information from all sources, internal to the company and external to it, lie chiefly in the 'direction' that is given to otherwise uncoordinated data. An integration of this kind does not necessarily imply the use of a computer, although the power and flexibility of any MIS can potentially be increased many-fold through such means. What is implied, however, is that management must define clearly its information needs. That is, managers must examine the marketing decisions that they need to make and specify the information, both on-going and *ad hoc* (a distinction to be explored later in the chapter), that they require in order to make those decisions effectively.

Developing a marketing intelligence system

Any organisation wishing to build an MIS faces a number of basic questions. How should we organise? How sophisticated should the system be? Do we build a total system or do we adopt a piecemeal approach? What should be the split between macro-level data and micro-level data? How much should we spend?

Organisation Most companies will have to accommodate existing organisation structures in the construction of the MIS. One team of experts in this field has suggested the appointment of a top-level 'information czar', or coordinator, who is capable of understanding both management information needs and systems problems. They suggest that this person should be the prime contractor who develops MIS plans and specifications and coordinates and reviews the work of the various sub-contractors or suppliers contributing to the programme.

Sophistication The question of sophistication of the system is crucial. Naïve companies may attempt to introduce systems which do not reflect the level of sophistication actually required by managers in making decisions. Recent research in the marketing sphere has shown that many marketing managers, particularly those at the operating level, do not use explicit planning and control systems. The aim of building the MIS should be to strike a balance between the sophistication of the system and that of its users.

Total or piecemeal? It is always tempting when thinking in terms of systems to wish to build a totally integrated MIS from first principles – a system that brings together financial, logistical and marketing information. Experience suggests that such attempts are rarely successful. As a general rule, it is better to think 'total' but to build 'piecemeal'.

One company in the packaging business is currently following this general rule by working within each of its regions across the country to identify in great detail the *local* patterns of competition. It is a national company, but it is frequently in competition with small local companies and, in some regions, the local companies are its major competitors. To be really successful, intelligence in a particular region must be totally local. Nevertheless, decisions made for a particular location must also link in and integrate with the company's own internal marketing and management information system, which is derived from sales invoices and other information held centrally. Further, the local system must also link in with the central analysis of all the aggregate statistics which arise from the industry itself, including import and export data. The system will, therefore, have each region developing its own marketing and sales intelligence pattern, together with a central pattern.

How much micro, how much macro? One of the most frequently encountered problems in marketing management is that data tend to be aggregated: that is to say, the figures relate to total markets rather than to segments, to countries rather than to regions, and so on. On the other hand, the manager can easily be overwhelmed if he is flooded with data. A key requirement of the MIS, therefore, is that, while the system is based on a micro-data bank, the system should be capable of providing output at any requested level of aggregation.

How much to spend? This problem has already been addressed earlier when the notion of information cost/benefit was raised. Building and developing the MIS is normally an expensive task. One major French company has so far spent well over Fr7 million in developing an integrated, real-time system. While this is an extreme example, even the simplest MIS does not come cheaply. Management must specify the benefits that it expects to derive from the MIS and be prepared to put a value on them. In this way, by concentrating on the outputs required from the MIS, a surer basis for setting the information budget is provided.

As a high-level information processor, the marketing manager occupies a vital position in any organisation. He is positioned between a wealth of data and feedback flows from the market place on the one hand, and internal information flows on corporate capabilities and performance on the other. Marketing research has thus the essential role within the organisation of providing an organised means of maintaining and utilising these disparate information flows and ensuring their effective conversion into marketing intelligence.

Guidelines to good planning practice

To summarise, we can consider the following guidelines necessary in planning a complete marketing system:

- widely understood objectives;
- high levels of actionable market information;
- acceptance of the need for continuous change;
- commitment from both the executive and lower levels of management;
- a period of up to three years for the successful introduction of a complete system.

Forms of marketing research

The marketing researcher has different means of gathering the information required, depending on the focus of the questions posed to him. Marketing research can be classified as being either *ad hoc* or on-going. *Ad hoc* research refers to situations where the identification of a research problem leads to a specific information requirement. *On-going* research provides more of a monitoring function, giving a flow of information about the market place and the organisation's performance within it.

A further distinction can be made between external and in-company marketing research. *External* research is conducted within the market or competitive environment in which the firm exists. *In-company* research is based on an analysis of performance gained from data such as sales trends, changes in the marketing mix involving price, advertising levels, and so on.

There is a difference between *reactive* and *non-reactive* marketing research. The reactive approach is based on the assumption that information about the market place and the customers who inhabit it can be gained by 'poking a stick at it and seeing if and how it moves'. Non-reactive methods are based not on reaction but on interpretation of observed phenomena or extant data. Reactive research can involve either asking questions or performing experiments, or both (see Figure 31).

Figure 31

The questionnaire, group discussions and extended interviews and controlled experimentation are all reactive methods available to the researcher.

By contrast, non-reactive research methods do not rely on data derived from respondents. Such methods include observation, where the researcher may join the activity under observation (participant observation) or may stand back recording or using a camera (non-participation); the use of a customer panel; and the conducting of desk surveys using existing information (see Figure 32).

Figure 32

In our next chapter we shall consider the marketing planning process. As we have seen, a marketing intelligence system will work better if there is already in existence a marketing planning process.

The marketing audit puts down on paper everything we can possibly know about a market place and the opportunities that it presents. Marketing information, data and intelligence form an input; when an audit is being done, everything that the data, information and intelligence has revealed is written down, so that the intelligence process is continuous. Out of the audit then come more questions; these in turn generate more information and intelligence gathering for the next part of the cycle.

Application questions

25.1   *What kinds of marketing research are commissioned by your organisation? Which are found to be cost-beneficial? Explain how they contribute to the effectiveness of the marketing effort. Which are not a good investment of time and money? How could the waste be avoided?*

25.2   *How does your organisation identify whether or not it is sensible to collect marketing data to become better informed and to gain marketing intelligence? How does the marketing management link in with decisions about what information to get?*

25.3   *Which external research agencies do you work with? What problems arise in your work with them? Do you give a sufficiently well defined research brief to the agency to be able to gauge its effectiveness? What would be the criteria used in a decision to: (a) change agency; (b) recruit an agency?*

25.4   *If you were asked to establish a marketing information system within your organisation, what would it contain? How would the information be co-ordinated? Who would be responsible for providing input into, and output from, the system? What use would you expect to be made of information provided? Who would you expect to make most use of the information?*

25.5   *If your organisation does not have an MIS, on what grounds is this justified? Is the decision one which you support? Under what circumstances would an MIS be justified for your organisation?*

How can we prepare our marketing plan?

Overview

The marketing audit helps the organisation to understand its true position in the market place and to plan how its performance could be improved. A disciplined method of undertaking a marketing audit is the preparation of a SWOT analysis, which is a framework for identifying the organisation's strengths and weaknesses. The audit and SWOT analysis will help to answer fundamental questions concerning what customers need, what they buy and how competitors are performing. The results of the audit give a basis for setting realistic marketing objectives.

Having prepared a marketing audit, the organisation can then construct a marketing plan which will provide a major contribution to the overall corporate plan. The corporate planning process comprises six steps: a statement of corporate objectives; the preparation of a management audit; objective setting; strategy setting; the production of detailed plans for one year; and the making of plans for following years. The marketing plan itself – beginning with the marketing audit and SWOT analysis – proceeds through the identifying of strategies; the developing of plans appropriate to the strategies; the specifying of programmes of action for the four 'P's; and the monitoring of the plan to give input to the next planning cycle.

The marketing audit

In Chapter 3 we considered the fundamental nature of a marketing plan. Our next step is to consider in some detail one of the most important stages in the marketing planning process – the marketing audit. This audit does not itself appear in the marketing plan, but it provides much of the information on which the plan is based.

Basically, an audit is the means by which an organisation can understand how it relates to the environment in which it operates. It is therefore a way of helping management to make an informed decision on what position it wishes to hold in that environment. A *management audit* is a systematic, critical and unbiased appraisal of the environment and of the company's operations. A *marketing audit* is part of the larger management audit and is concerned with the marketing environment and marketing operations. It addresses the question: where is the company now?

The information gathered during a marketing audit is likely to help an organisation identify many different areas in which business performance could be improved. One company, for example, found that many of its customers would prefer to buy a product range rather than individual products from one manufacturer. Accordingly, the company increased the range of products which its salesmen were offering to include both cut-price and luxury brands in addition to the medium-range brands already carried. The salesmen went on to sell many more products to the same number of customers.

Another manufacturer made use of information gained during its audit to establish exactly how the 80/20 rule or Pareto effect applied to its operations. (The Pareto effect, it will be remembered, was discussed in Chapter 7.) The manufacturer found that it had a good many customers who contributed comparatively little to the total volume of sales. These customers, it was decided, should in future be encouraged to buy from wholesalers rather than direct from the manufacturer.

Often the need for an audit does not manifest itself until things start going wrong for a company, in the form of declining sales, falling margins, lost market share, under-utilised production capacity, and so on. At times like these, management is often driven by a sense of urgency to take immediate action, such as introducing new products, reorganising the sales force or reducing prices. However, such measures are unlikely to be effective if there are more fundamental problems which have not been identified.

Essentially, the argument is that problems have to be properly defined, and the audit is a means of helping to define them before they offer a serious threat to the company's profitability. To summarise, the audit is a structured approach to the collection and analysis of information and data essential to effective problem solving.

The marketing audit, then, involves a thorough evaluation of the company's internal and external operating environments. Internal factors are the company's basic *strengths* and *weaknesses*; whereas external factors are the *opportunities* and *threats* over which the company has no direct control. The identification of strengths, weaknesses, opportunities and threats is usually carried out by means of a SWOT analysis.

A SWOT analysis is a framework; it is not magical and it is not unique to marketing. It is a disciplined way of approaching a marketing audit and eliminates the likelihood of merely random gathering of data. A SWOT analysis structures information so that a coherent statement about the condition of the company can be made.

It is essential that any statement appearing in a SWOT analysis should be completely explicit, because there are cases where an aspect of a company can be both a strength *and* a weakness. For example, to be a dominant brand in a market might be a strength. To have a 65% share of a market means that a lot of energy is being put into that market, with the result that the product has great visibility. The company with such a large share of the market will have, too, better distribution networks than anyone else trying to compete. Such a dominant position, however, can also be a weakness because, with such a large degree of dominance, competitors can chip away and erode small segments of the market for their own purposes. Thus, in a company with, for example, a 65% brand share of the market, and where that product is much larger than any other brand marketed by the company in the same range, the company is vulnerable to competitors taking some of that share and hence eroding a major part of the company.

To avoid ambiguities of this kind, therefore, the SWOT analysis should not use general terms. *Every written statement in the analysis should be completely explicit.* One way of ensuring this precision is to remember that strengths and weaknesses constitute information about those things which are within the control of the company. Opportunities and threats, however, are those things existing in the marketplace *regardless* of the company undertaking the analysis. Such factors include, for example, competitive activity, government legislation or directives, technology, substitute products, and so on. Further, these factors would exist whether or not the company undertaking the analysis went out of business entirely.

The internal factors – strengths and weaknesses – are those factors *within* a particular company's control. The external factors – opportunities and threats – are those factors *outside* a particular company's control.

A SWOT analysis helps to identify the real issues which have to be addressed in the future as a matter of priority; it should summarise what the organisation is trying to do in its various markets; and it should indicate required future actions. It will summarise the key issues emanating from the marketing audit. It will also answer such questions as:

– What do customers need?
– How do customers buy?
– What are the competitors doing?

Figure 33 shows a checklist of areas which should be investigated during the marketing audit. Each one of these headings should be examined with a view to isolating those factors which are considered critical to the company's performance. Initially, the auditor's task is to screen an enormous amount of information and data for validity and relevance. Some data and information will then have to be reorganised into a more easily usable form,

The Marketing Audit

**What are the
Opportunities and Threats, Strengths and Weaknesses
for the**

Business and Economic Environment

Economic
Political/fiscal
Religious
Social
Cultural
Business
Legal
Technological
International

The Market Environment

Size and trends
Supply and demand

Competitive Environment

Market shares and trends
Product range
Pricing
Place
Promotion
Operations and resources

Own Company

Market shares and trends
Product range
Pricing
Place
Promotion
Operations and resources

Figure 33

and the auditor will go on to judge what further data and information is needed to complete the picture.

The auditing process consists of two basic stages:

– the identification, collection, analysis and measurement of all the relevant facts and opinions which impinge on an organisation's problems;
– the application of judgement to areas which remain unclear after this analysis.

It is well advised to carry out a thorough marketing audit at least once a year, prior to the beginning of the planning cycle. In many leading consumer goods companies, the annual self-audit approach is a well tried and tested procedure built into an integrated management process. In drawing up an audit, managers must constantly guard against taking a narrow view of their environment and making easy extrapolations from past trends. One of the great values of the exercise is that it challenges managers to consider in what ways their environment is changing and the implications of such changes for their marketing strategies.

What happens to the result of the audit?

The final, all-important issue, of course, is what happens to the result of the audit. Some organisations consume valuable resources carrying out audits that bring very little by way of actionable results. Indeed, there is always the danger that, at the audit stage, insufficient attention is paid to the need to concentrate on analysis that determines which trends and developments will actually affect the company.

Inclusion of research reports which lead to no action whatever only serves to rob the audit of focus and reduce its relevance. Since the objective of the audit is to indicate what an organisation's marketing objectives and strategies should be, it is clearly desirable that a relevant format should be found for organising the major findings.

To summarise, carrying out a regular and thorough marketing audit in a structured way helps to give the organisation a detailed knowledge of the business, including trends in the market and competitive activity. The marketing audit provides the basis for setting realistic marketing objectives and strategies.

One company in the women's wide-fitting footwear business was suffering a decline in profitability. The audit that was undertaken revealed fundamental weaknesses in terms of fashion styles for the new generation of people with wider feet. The reality was that women's feet were becoming wider at a younger age, due to changed recreation and other behaviour patterns, and styles were out of step with these changes. By redesigning the product range, the company was able to pull itself round, which led to a gradual recovery of its former market position and profitability. Other effects were a transformation in the company's advertising campaign and a re-channelling through slightly different outlets: some of the former outlets had a dowdy image so that the 29–35-year-old woman with wide feet would not patronise them. Since the company rectified the faults indicated by the audit, it has made sure that it carries out a thorough marketing audit at the beginning of each planning cycle.

The corporate planning process

The marketing audit, as we have seen, is one of the most important steps in the marketing planning process. Before turning to the other important steps in this planning process, it is useful to examine how marketing planning relates to the corporate planning process.

The corporate plan aims to answer three questions: where is the company now? Where does the company want to go? How should the company organise its resources to get there? The marketing plan is constructed so as to answer these same questions with regard to the marketing function. In doing so, it makes a major contribution to the overall shape and content of the corporate plan.

There are six steps in the corporate planning process. The starting point is usually a statement of *corporate objectives* for the long-range planning period of the company. These are often expressed in terms of turnover, profit before tax, and return on investment, but may also express intention with regard to growth, market share, and so on. More often than not, this long-range planning horizon is five years, but the precise period should be determined by the nature of the markets in which the organisation operates. For example, five years would not be a sufficiently long period for a glass manufacturer, since it takes that period of time to commission a new furnace. In some fashion industries, on the other hand, five years would be too long a period. A useful guideline in determining the planning horizon is that it should allow a period at least long enough to ensure that sufficient products or services are sold to cancel out the capital investment associated with their introduction.

The next step is the *management audit*, which we have already considered briefly. This kind of thorough situation review – particularly in the area of marketing – should enable the company to determine whether it will be able to meet its long-range targets with its current range of products in its current markets. At this stage, the technique of gap analysis (discussed in Chapter 14) can, if necessary, help the organisation to identify appropriate strategies which will ensure that targets are met.

The most important, and the most difficult, stage in the corporate planning process involves the third and fourth steps, *objective* and *strategy setting*. A clear distinction can be made between these two processes. A company might, for example, agree on a marketing objective of broadening its market by product diversification. It will still find it necessary, however, to decide on the most appropriate means of achieving this objective. A number of choices will immediately present themselves, principal amongst which is likely to be the choice either to acquire an on-going business or to invest in additional capacity to broaden the company's own range. The choice here is between two strategies; the criteria by which one strategy will be chosen in preference to another will relate to the company's overall objectives, resources and position in the market.

If these two steps are not carried out properly, everything that follows will be of little value. Later in this chapter, we shall discuss marketing objectives and strategies in detail. The essential point to be made in the present context is that the setting of objectives and strategies marks the time in the planning cycle when the organisation has to decide how the individual objectives of the different functional areas are to be reconciled into practicable targets. It is often the case that individual functional objectives have to be modified at this stage. A marketing objective of penetrating a new market, for example, is of little use if the organisation does not have the production capacity to cope with the new business and if capital is not available for investment in additional capacity. At this stage, objectives and strategies will be set for the length of the long-term planning period.

The fifth step of the corporate planning process involves

producing *detailed plans for one year*, containing the timing and costs of carrying out the first year's objectives, together with a full description of how responsibilities for the various activities are allocated within the organisation. *Broad plans for the following years* should also be provided at this stage. These plans can then be incorporated into the final corporate plan, which will contain long-range corporate objectives, strategies, plans, profit and loss accounts and balance sheets.

One of the main purposes of a corporate plan is to provide a long-term vision of the organisation's future, taking account of shareholder expectations, environmental trends, market trends, and the distinctive competence of the company as revealed by the management audit. What this means in practice is that the corporate plan will contain the following elements:

– A statement of the desired level of profitability.
– An indication of future developments in each of the functional areas. Guidance will be given, for example, as to the kinds of products to be sold to different markets (marketing); the kinds of facilities to be developed (production and distribution); the size and character of the labour force (personnel); and the sources of funding (finance).
– Other corporate objectives, such as social responsibility, corporate image, stock market image, employee image, etc.

A corporate plan of this kind, which contains projected profit and loss accounts and balance sheets, is likely to provide greater long-term stability than would plans which are based on a more intuitive process and which contain forecasts that are little more than extrapolations from previous business trends.

A major multinational oil company had a planning process of this latter type. The company's headquarters had a sophisticated budgeting system which received 'plans' from all over the world and co-ordinated them in quantitative and cross-functional terms, such as numbers of employees, units of sale, items of plant, square feet of production area, and so on. The financial implications of all this data were carefully calculated. However, this whole complicated edifice was built on initial sales forecasts, which were little more than trend extrapolations. The result was that the whole corporate planning process developed into little more than a time-consuming numbers game and the really key strategic issues relating to products and markets were lost in all the financial activity.

This organisation eventually ran into grave operational difficulties. The main cause of the problem was that the entire planning system, rather than being developed and originated in order to gain a better understanding of the market place, was really put together to give better control procedures for the financial analyst in the organisation. Whilst it is valid to provide such control procedures, it is still essential to go back to the grass roots in the market place in order to know what figures are realistic.

Planning assumptions

Having described the context in which the marketing plan must be drawn up, let us return to the preparation of the plan itself.

We have already discussed the marketing audit and the SWOT analysis. The next step, as outlined in Figure 34, is to formulate some basic assumptions. It is the *systemisation* of this process which is integral to successful marketing planning in practice.

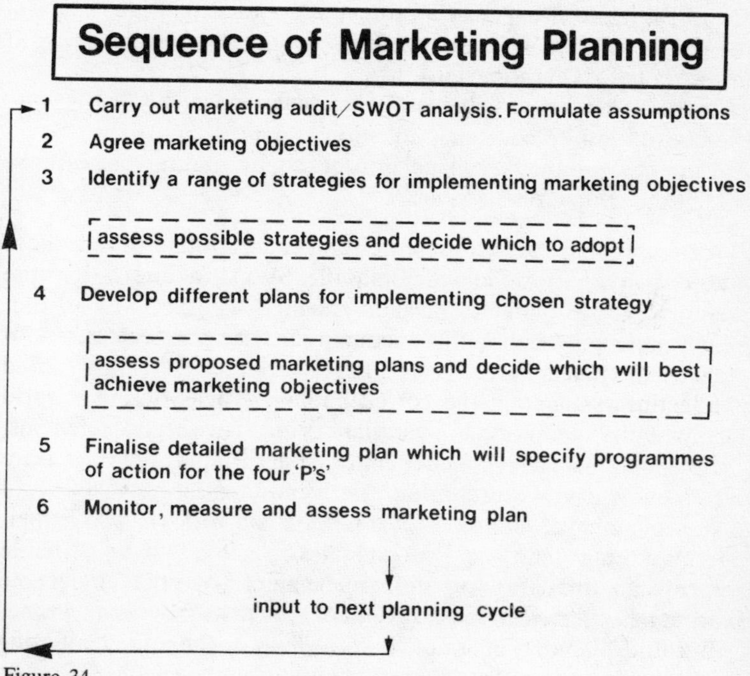

Sequence of Marketing Planning

1 Carry out marketing audit/SWOT analysis. Formulate assumptions

2 Agree marketing objectives

3 Identify a range of strategies for implementing marketing objectives

    assess possible strategies and decide which to adopt

4 Develop different plans for implementing chosen strategy

    assess proposed marketing plans and decide which will best achieve marketing objectives

5 Finalise detailed marketing plan which will specify programmes of action for the four 'P's'

6 Monitor, measure and assess marketing plan

input to next planning cycle

Figure 34

The marketing planning process involves the bringing together of minds at every level of the company. It depends on *interactive communication* up and down the organisation. Without this, the result will be forecasts projected from history rather than the development of genuine objectives based on what is really happening.

There are certain key determinants of success in all organisations about which *assumptions* have to be made before the planning process can proceed. This is basically a question of standardising the planning environment. A sensible plan cannot be evolved from contradictory assumptions, as would be the case, for example, if one product manager asserted that the market was going to decline by 10%, whilst another believed the market was going to increase by 10%.

Examples of assumptions might be:

'With respect to the company's industrial climate, it is assumed that:

1   industrial over-capacity will decrease from 125% to 95% as the economy picks up and as exports boom owing to the decline in the value of the home currency;
2   price competition will force price levels down by 3% across the board, despite continued inflation at 5%;
3   two new products will be introduced by major competitors during the course of the year.'

Assumptions should be few in number and relate only to key issues such as those identified in the SWOT analysis. If it is possible for a plan to be implemented irrespective of the assumptions made, then those assumptions are not necessary and should be deleted.

Each company (and the corresponding business units) should highlight the assumptions which are critical to the fulfilment of the planned *marketing objectives* (which in turn play a critical role in achieving overall corporate objectives).

Key planning assumptions deal in the main with environmental and marketing trends, and anticipated changes which would have a significant influence on the achievement (or not) of agreed marketing objectives.

Because planning assumptions are likely to have a significant impact on the achievement of marketing objectives, the risk of a

particular assumption not being fulfilled needs to be assessed –
this is called *downside risk* assessment. Essentially, it involves
asking what can go wrong with each assumption to change the
expected outcome, and requires a corresponding probability
assessment of such an event occurring. A suggested format for
downside risk assessment is given below:

Key assumption
↓
Basis of assumption
↓
What *event* would have to happen to make the
corresponding objective unobtainable?
↓
What is the risk (or probability) of such an *event* occuring? %
↓
The impact on corresponding objective if *event* occurs
↓
The trigger point for action
↓
Actual contingency action

Marketing objectives

The next step in marketing planning is the writing of marketing
objectives. This, along with the subsequent development of
marketing strategies, is the key step in the planning process.

An *objective* is what you want to achieve. There can be objectives at all levels of marketing. For example, there can be advertising objectives and pricing objectives. However, *marketing objectives* can be distinguished by the fact that they always express the
match between *products* and *markets*. Common sense will confirm
that it is only by selling something to somebody that the organisation can achieve its financial goals; and that advertising, pricing
and service levels are the means (or strategies) by which the
organisation might succeed in doing this. Thus, pricing objectives,
sales promotion objectives, advertising objectives and the like are
subservient to marketing objectives and should not be confused
with them. An example of a marketing objective might be 'to
enter x market with y product and obtain a 10% market share
within one year'.

The simple matrix in Chapter 12 indicates the matching process
which is central to all marketing objectives. Marketing objectives

are always concerned with one or more of the following combinations:

– existing products in existing markets;
– new products in existing markets;
– existing products in new markets;
– new products in new markets.

The objectives should be capable of measurement, otherwise they are not practical objectives. Directional terms such as 'maximise', 'minimise', 'penetrate' and 'increase' are only acceptable if quantitative measurement can be applied to them. Such measurement should be in terms of sales volume, sterling, market share, percentage penetration of outlets, and so on. However, before an organisation undertakes extensive measurement of marketing objectives, it should first ensure that the cost of such measurement is equalled by the benefits to be gained from it.

Marketing strategies

Marketing strategies are the means by which marketing objectives will be achieved. They are generally concerned with the four 'P's, as follows:

Product Product deletions, modifications, additions, design, packaging, etc. For example, the organisation might decide to differentiate the product by adding certain features.

Price Pricing levels for product groups in market segments. For example, the organisation might choose to introduce a penetration pricing policy.

Place Type of channels and customer service levels. In this area, the organisation might think it best to sell only through certain kinds of retailer.

Promotion Means of communicating with customers in the different ways available, such as advertising, sales force, sales promotion, public relations, exhibitions, direct mail, etc. For example, the organisation might decide to employ heavy advertising to create widespread awareness.

Usually, an organisation will identify a range of strategies for achieving marketing objectives. The final choice of strategy will follow a process of assessment and analysis of the firm's particular circumstances, both internal and external. At this juncture, as throughout the marketing planning process, the information gleaned through the SWOT analysis is likely to prove helpful.

The marketing plan

The next stage of the marketing planning process involves the development of different plans for implementing the chosen strategy. Those plans contain detailed sub-objectives, strategies and programmes of action for each of the four 'P's. Thus, an organisation might set as a *sub-objective* for its promotional activities the creation of a 10% awareness level amongst its target audience. The *strategy* chosen to meet this goal might be heavy advertising on television to explain the benefits to be gained from the product. The *programme* devised to implement this strategy might be 20- or 30-second bursts of advertising on television.

The final plan chosen from the range of possible plans identified will be the one which will most effectively achieve marketing objectives.

The acid test of any marketing plan presentation is to ask yourself, 'Would I put my own life's savings into the plan as presented?' If the answer is negative, then further work is needed to refine the ideas.

Measuring progress

The final step in preparing an effective marketing plan is to establish some standards against which actual performance can be measured. These standards should relate to performance in the different activities associated with the four 'P's: product development, pricing, promotion and distribution. The decision as to whether or not to undertake measurement depends, as mentioned earlier, on the results of a cost-benefit analysis.

Actual performance in each area should be monitored. Whenever performance deviates from the standard set, some control action may be necessary. It is clear that if, say, customer service levels were to drop significantly below standard, some action would be taken before demand was damaged seriously. However, control action might also be necessary if customer service levels were to *exceed* by a significant degree the standards set for performance. As we have seen in Chapter 16 there is always a danger of incurring unnecessary additional costs by providing service levels which are well above the level required to meet the market demand.

The identification of deviations between standards and performance allows management to institute effective controls. In this way, progress towards the achievement of the marketing objectives set in the plan can be measured and, if necessary, regulated.

Application questions

26.1   *Who has responsibility for carrying out the annual marketing audit within your organisation? How is the information gained from the audit used? Is there any way in which greater use could be made of the information?*

26.2   *How has the product portfolio of your organisation been affected by the use of information gained from a marketing audit? If the audit had not occurred, how would the product portfolio have been developed?*

26.3   *Identify the marketing planning process adopted in your organisation. Who contributes to the plan and what does each individual contribute? What is the sequence of the planning process? What problems arise during this process? How can they be minimised or eradicated?*

26.4   *What are the marketing objectives set for your organisation's major products or services? Is the achievement of these objectives adequately monitored? Are there additional monitoring procedures which ought to be employed? What prevents their adoption?*

26.5   *How are the sub-objectives for each of the four 'P's related to the major marketing objectives? How is the achievement of these sub-objectives monitored? Does the organisation have sufficient feedback from the market place to enable it to identify where a marketing policy is failing and to help it develop a more effective marketing effort?*

26.6   *For the product or service with which you are most familiar, distinguish between marketing objectives, overall strategy and implementation plans as they relate to the four 'P's. What alternatives could have been adopted and why were they rejected?*

Overview

*Different marketing structures exist in different organisations. The
particular structure used will affect the degree to which marketing
can influence the marketing budget. The structure used – whether
brand management, negotiating or authoritarian – results in either
dominant or less dominant inputs into budget decisions, so that
trends can occur in which marketing loses a significant degree of
its autonomy to the production or account functions.*

*Task-related budgeting argues for funds to be provided for already
well defined objectives, whereas budgeting based on sales forecasts
can fall prey to over-optimistic estimates. Revenue expectations
and estimated costs of implementation are both key factors in the
preparation of the marketing budget.*

*The marketing expense includes all the additional costs – other than
the physical movement of the product – that are incurred once
production is completed. The major areas of cost are related to the
four 'P's. Other costs are incurred in the collection of marketing
intelligence and may deserve a separate treatment in budgetary
terms.*

Changes in marketing structure

In some organisations, the influence of marketing in determining
the marketing budget is becoming less dominant. A reversion to
production orientation is evidenced in such situations as: boardrooms setting marketing budgets by allocating the residual
revenue after deducting operating costs and profit contribution;
the replacing of a marketing director by a commercial director;
the development of trade marketing departments reporting to the
sales, not the marketing, director; and the monitoring of brand
performance by production and accounting management in
conjunction with marketing personnel.

Recent research undertaken by the Marketing Communications Research Centre set out to establish how marketing budgets are set and allocated. The sequence of budget setting, the personnel involved at different stages of the process, and the dominating influences surrounding each activity, were all investigated. Although it is difficult to identify all the operational structures, three quite distinct models emerged from the study:

the traditional structure;
the negotiating structure;
the authoritarian structure.

Marketing budgets are set at a number of levels. First, the total marketing expenditure is agreed. Next, the budget is allocated to the various product groups in the business. Thirdly, moneys will be allocated above- and below-the-line. Only after this will detailed consideration be given to the precise communications mix to be employed for each brand.

The traditional structure
Early in the 1970s it was still customary to find large, hierarchical marketing departments. The traditional structure, as illustrated in Figure 35, shows how a brand management structure of this era operated.

In this traditional structure, there are a number of levels of people. The product or brand managers – who may have assistants – collect together information about their particular brand and have an overall business responsibility for that brand. The underlying concept here is that the brand is treated in isolation; decisions are taken on the basis of wanting growth, so that the particular brand or product is developed to its maximum potential. Each major brand will have someone with particular responsibility for it, who will put forward proposals for the brand to the next level in the organisation.

At the next level, the various proposals will be merged. Very commonly, this produces the reaction that the aggregated proposals are much too expensive for the company to afford. Under such a system, therefore, the budgets are cut back dramatically before being passed further up the structure to the next levels.

One important factor in this process is that in a traditional brand management structure, the people who make the major proposals in the first place are young – perhaps in years, but

The Traditional Structure

Figure 35

certainly in experience – so they do not have a realistic concept of where the total business is going. They work as if their particular brand were the all-important concern of the company. A great deal of work is done at a detailed level and yet no one can realistically expect it all to be implemented. This is the main disadvantage of such a system. A further disadvantage is that budgets derived in this way do not take into account the overall strategic decisions of the company, with their consequent differential implications for each brand or product group.

To overcome problems of this nature, a change of structure and a change in the decision-making process of setting marketing budgets has evolved. This second model involves a *negotiating* structure.

The negotiating structure

Here the marketing hierarchy is reduced and may have as few as three levels of management: marketing director, product group manager and assistant manager. Such changes recognise that it is a waste of resources to have detailed work done, only to have it then emasculated. Further, those who have had their work thus cut will feel their cases were not strong enough or were not well enough presented. Ensuing inter-personal problems can follow.

The negotiating model, as illustrated in Figure 36, suggests that ground rules can be set to show what will be accepted, so that people can work within given parameters. The board may give direction to the marketing director, who in turn will talk with his senior marketing personnel, giving guidelines about what would seem to be a realistic budget. The detail and the precise figure will then be argued for, the marketing director making clear that a budget higher than a given figure will not be accepted. So some constraints are imposed from above and the detailed work takes place below.

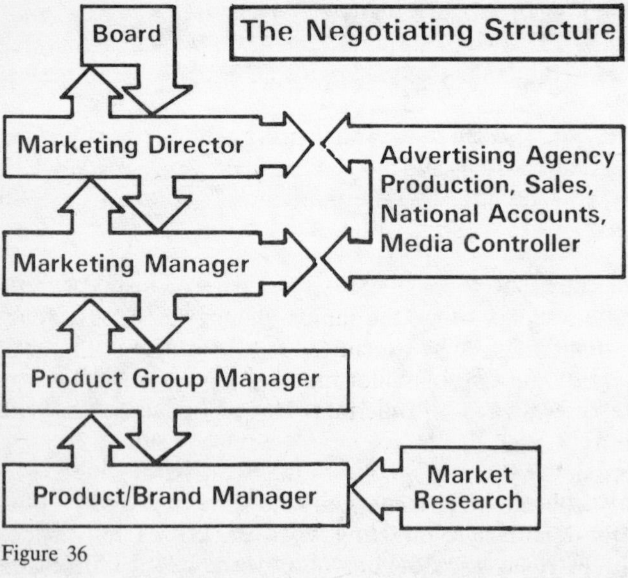

Figure 36

Under the negotiating structure, the brand manager will sort out the detail, but his senior colleagues will point out that, in strategic terms, his product may be expected to decline by 10% or remain at its existing share of the market, or meet whatever other objectives are set by the company. In this way, more direction is given within which to do the detailed work. The advantage here is that the priorities of the company are reflected. Certain sectors of the market may have to be supported because, strategically, they are critical to the company; other sectors, on the other hand, may be withdrawn or allowed to die naturally. It is the marketing director's responsibility to ensure that the board's policy is sensibly reflected.

One consequence of the negotiating model is that there is a reduction of levels of people involved in the marketing structure, so that there is a much wider span of control. In many organisations, the product group manager has become the key person, who runs a well-defined sector of the business against very stringent objectives of profit contribution, product volume and market share. This tightening up of structure means that those making an input to the budgetary process are likely to have been with the company for a number of years and to have gained a perspective of the destination of their various businesses. They assume a major responsibility for their part of the business and have evolved to fulfil the original concept of the marketer as a business custodian.

The individual product or brand manager will think through planning details as directed by the product group manager but will take little initiative in determining the total budget or the major items of expenditure within it.

The authoritarian structure

In the most extreme cases, the major budget decisions may rest with non-marketing senior executives in the company. Here, the product group manager or senior marketing manager will receive specific directives from his superiors. This procedure is illustrated in Figure 37.

This model bypasses the traditional responsibilities of a marketing department. In some companies, the board has become particularly dominant in directing what can and cannot happen; in the most extreme cases, the board will work with the forecasting department, which is quite independent of the marketing department. In such instances, objectives will be set of what volume is to be generated, what the costs of producing it are and the cost of raw materials; there will be a profit contribution that the company will demand, and after all these calculations have been done, there will be a residual sum, out of which the marketing director will be told he must run the marketing of the company.

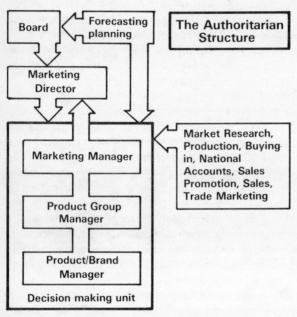

Figure 37

Rather than being in a position to put a case for a budget, the marketing director may well be *given* a budget. As a member of the board, he will play some part in identifying the budget, but many other functions will also become involved in dictating the budget. Under these circumstances, the marketing director will explain to his marketing managers what has to be achieved and they will know that there is no point going beyond the constraints set down. The possibility of putting forward a case for additional funding remains, but the probability of its being accepted is remote.

One of the disadvantages of this sort of structure is that the organisation is likely to become dominated by the production function rather than the marketing function. This would result, for example, in a board stating a budget figure which can be spent on marketing activities, including the cost of running the sales force. The board will further state that a fixed proportion must be spent on television advertising of key brands. Such a decision is not usually expected to be taken at board level, but to come from the marketing department by way of a task-related budget.

Boards dictating budgets in this way are often directing companies in markets where there is fierce competition. All the major manufacturers in the market may well have been competing for brand share and buying their way into the retail outlets, so that gradually it has become apparent to them that they run the real risk of undermining their branding. They have destroyed – or run the risk of destroying – the importance for customers of their particular brand. There may well have been a panic reaction to falling into a rat race with minority brands; the board may feel that it is about to lose a brand franchise, which will mean losing a critical part of the company. Such a reaction will often result in a board deciding that major advertising – on television, for example – will reinstate and sustain major brands. However, this initiative would usually be expected from the marketing personnel rather than from others in the organisation. Where such senior management involvement exists, the marketing department has certainly lost some of its identity and responsibility.

The marketing department can also be seen as losing its authority in those companies which have recognised that much of the business is dependent on trade marketing activities. Among grocery manufacturers, where a huge proportion of revenue is realised from few retailers, it was perhaps inevitable that trade negotiations would be treated on a special basis. The development of the national account salesmen has evolved to a state where some senior sales negotiators now handle the major part of the business. In companies formally appointing trade marketing departments, it is interesting to note that, in structural terms, they report to the sales director and not the marketing director. Inevitably this has led to a jostling of authority over the budget. There are some signs that any trade activity will be taken under the wing of selling, and any direct consumer activity under the wing of marketing. In reality, for the fast-moving consumer goods markets this means that the marketing activity has been significantly reduced. It may have authority over as little as 30% of the volume sold, the rest of the business going via the small number of national accounts.

Another trend militating against the independence of marketing is the development of cross-functional committees monitoring the performance of a brand or group of products.

We are beginning to see the introduction of monthly monitoring meetings where groups of managers discuss the performance of their sector of the business and deliberate on any corrective tactics. Present at those meetings will be the senior marketing man, the marketing services person supplying much of the data on which decisions are based, an accountant allocated to the group who is concerned to see that the financial performance of the brand is acceptable, and the production representative who is concerned to understand how his forecast will need to be monitored to meet changed circumstances.

No changes can occur in the way the brand or product is handled, except on a highly tactical base which has been agreed by all the parties around the table. It is expected that no changes will be implemented without adequate lead time. As an example, no production changes can occur in less than twenty-six weeks. If adhered to too rigidly, such rules might deprive the company of the opportunity to react to changed market circumstances quickly enough to forestall market share decline.

Such a committee structure has the great advantage that it does ensure that marketing sits alongside other functions of the organisation and takes a mature and integrated stand within the company. It has the disadvantage, however, that the concerns and difficulties which can arise in production can overshadow wider considerations. The inherent danger would appear to be that we could be going beyond marketing orientation and back to production orientation. A consequence of this is likely to be missed market opportunities.

These three models show general changes occurring in the identity of those responsible for the budget, in how the budget is negotiated and where the shifts of power occur. Depending on market circumstances, most firms organise the setting of the marketing budget in a manner approximating to one of these three models.

Criteria for establishing the marketing budget

Given the difficulties inherent in setting the marketing budget, what procedures might an organisation adopt to make the most cost-effective use of its resources? Two main approaches are in common use – the first of which, it is argued, is the more effective in the long term.

Task-related budgeting   Budget setting is best undertaken on a task-related basis; that is, arguing the case for the funds required to achieve well-specified objectives. This will challenge all the assumptions on which a manager builds his case, forcing him to be explicit about the way he perceives his market to be working and encouraging him systematically to test his assumptions. Task-related budgeting prevents the manager working from an unjustified basis and stops him arguing his case from unnecessary ignorance.

Budgeting based on sales and revenue forecasts   In practice, many companies have been forced back from attempts at task-related budgeting to the familiar patterns of expenditure in their markets. Many see that the marketing budget allocation will be directly related to the sales and revenue forecasts of the organisation, since this expectation comes from senior executives in the organisation. Some consequences of this are that over-optimistic volume forecasts are made and over-optimistic price increases are proposed. A counter pressure will come from the sales group of the company, who will press for increasing discounts to the trade and subsequent price reductions to the customer.

Developing a dynamic approach to budgeting

In previous chapters, we have discussed in detail the preparation of an organisation's marketing plan. Once this plan has been completed and specific strategies and programmes have been developed, management will have a clearer view of both *revenue expectations* and *estimated costs of implementation*.

These are the two key ingredients in the preparation of any marketing budget. Both should be monitored carefully as the year progresses and, if necessary, corrective action should be taken to ensure a satisfactory outcome. Management control of this kind depends on a thorough understanding of the nature of the revenue flow and of cash incidence.

Most organisations find particular difficulty in assessing the additional revenue likely to accrue from any additional spending on the four 'P's. If an organisation decided to employ an extra salesman, for example, it would find itself faced with such questions as: 'What additional revenue will he generate? Would the money spent on employing him in fact be better spent on media advertising or on reducing the price of the product? How can we make the calculations necessary to answer these questions?'

Since revenue is not directly under the control of the marketing manager, revenue forecasting poses a major problem in the preparation of the budget. In consumer markets, the best laid plans can be thrown off course by a competitive development that catches the imagination of customers. In industrial markets, fluctuating confidence in the economic future can have major effects on the sales of capital equipment as well as stockholding policies. In a service industry such as tourism, a movement in the exchange rate can result in changes in popularity among countries. For reasons such as these, sales forecasting (as described in Chapter 32) must be conducted carefully both for unit volumes and for gross monetary values. At budget preparation time, it is also foolhardy in most circumstances to base all plans on a single point forecast of sales. Anticipated sales outcomes are inevitably imprecise because of factors that are external to the company. In addition, factors within the company may sometimes prevent fulfilment of orders even if the sales have been made. Production or distribution delays, for example, may lead to substantial losses in sales revenue.

Such uncertainty frequently leads companies to adopt a safe approach to sales revenue forecasting: that is, they forecast only what they are *very* confident they can achieve. This approach has the merit of limiting the scope for unpleasant surprises but it can have disadvantages. In their zeal for reliable budgets, organisations adopting this approach will often ignore good opportunities within the market place, simply because they have a high level of risk.

Let us examine more closely the kinds of sales patterns which are commonly encountered in the market place and which are likely to lead organisations to form conclusions about how they should allocate future expenditure. The response curves in Figure 38 illustrate the fortunes of three different products. The point of interest in each case is the interpretation of the relationship of marketing expenditure to sales level.

In the case of Product 'C', sales have increased in direct proportion to marketing expenditure and show no signs of falling off. The conclusion likely to be drawn here is that further expenditure will continue to lead to increased sales. With Product 'A', the curve marks the point at which sales have started to stabilise rather than grow. The likely conclusion to be drawn here is that marketing expenditure is resulting in replacement sales rather than in the attraction of new custom. Accordingly, a reassessment of the marketing budget is called for. It may also prove worthwhile to reconsider the nature of the marketing mix for this product: a different mix may result in a new growth in sales. Product 'B' has followed the pattern described for Product 'A' but has moved beyond this to the point where sales have started to decline. In these circumstances, the likely conclusion would be that all potential customers have been reached and that further marketing expenditure on this product is not worthwhile. Product 'B' is likely to be a very specialised product or service within a very limited market. It could also be one in which the product is in decline, perhaps due to a better alternative becoming available to the market.

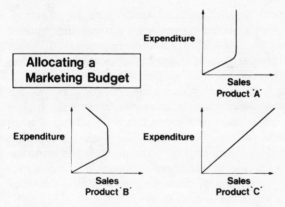

Figure 38

The construction of response curves of this kind for the different products or services within an organisation's portfolio can prove very helpful in the allocation of the marketing budget. The organisation can draw on data and feedback on different products to identify the optimum point of return on expenditure and to ascertain the weight which should be accorded to the different elements of the marketing mix.

Designing a system which takes a truly dynamic approach

towards marketing budgets, as opposed to a static annual view, is a major challenge to the marketing and financial directors of all organisations. Whenever the response to a valid marketing opportunity is that 'the budget has been spent already this year', it is clear that something is coming between the company and its effective prosperity. It is equally the case that matters are none too satisfactory when uneconomic expenditure is continued in an organisation simply 'in order to spend the budget'. This all too frequently occurs when organisations base subsequent years' budgets on previous levels.

The most satisfactory situation for a marketing director is typically that where he is required:

1 to justify each year from a zero base all his marketing expenditure against the tasks he wishes to accomplish and for which he has clearly identified his gross revenue expectations;
2 to review progress continually to ensure that no lapses in interdepartmental communications can hinder good marketing.

This approach is the logical result of tackling the problem of planning the company's marketing activities through the process described in Chapters 3 and 26. If the procedures described in those chapters are followed, a hierarchy of objectives is built up in such a way that every item of budgeted expenditure can be related directly back to the initial corporate financial objectives. This approach, as we have seen, is known as task-related budgeting. Thus, when, say, sales promotion has been identified as a major means of achieving an objective in a particular market, all sales promotional items which appear in the budget can be shown to relate back in a specific way to a major objective.

The essential feature of this system of budgeting is that budgets are set against both the overall marketing objectives and the sub-objectives for each element of the marketing mix. One main advantage of the system is that it allows the organisation to build up an increasingly clear picture of its markets. Whenever the marketing director allocates budgets, he is making assumptions about buyer behaviour in his organisation's markets. By identifying these assumptions and subsequently monitoring market behaviour, he can go on to allocate future budgets with more confidence. Even if his assumptions are proved false, and the budget has been inappropriately allocated, the marketing director can discover exactly where he has gone wrong and can take the necessary corrective steps in the future.

What is the marketing expense?

The marketing expense covers the entire marketing mix. Whether or not the sales force expenditure is considered part of the marketing expense will depend on whether the company has a separate and parallel marketing and sales director or whether both functions occur together. Theoretically, regardless of who has the responsibility, they should be seen as part and parcel of the same budget, because the sales force is simply the sharp end implementation of the whole marketing planning exercise. Even if they are in two people's domains, marketing and sales must still be brought together.

In the last decade, the influence of retailer power has grown, so that much of the budget in many organisations is spent on trade discounts in order to get products into outlets such as major supermarkets. This can be considered either as a distribution expense or as a trade expense, but it is nevertheless an integral part of buying the distribution, since it serves to persuade the retailer to carry the product.

With one notable exception, the marketing expense is made up of all additional costs that are incurred after a product is made available in the factory or after definite resource provision is made to offer a service. Expenses involved in the physical movement of the product or service facility are excluded from this calculation. This latter group of costs is typically called the distribution expense and, while distribution may sensibly be regarded as an integral part of marketing, its costs represent a discrete sub-set.

It is always a difficult matter to draw the line between marketing and distribution costs. The division between production and marketing costs is also sometimes unclear. When, for instance, is packaging a marketing cost, when a distribution and when a production cost? While there can be no universal answer, careful analysis, tempered by the wisdom that continually seeks for simplicity, can normally yield an acceptable solution. Organisations that use all or some of their packaging simply to reduce damage normally call it a distribution cost, whereas those who use their packaging to communicate and to sell (as in most consumer markets) typically regard much or all of it as a marketing cost. In the situation where a free sample is given away with the intention of generating future purchase of the product, the cost of providing the additional amount of product needed to provide the samples would normally be put down as a marketing rather than a production cost.

The major areas of marketing cost incurred by any organisation are related to the four 'P's. We shall examine each of these areas in turn.

Product   The most typical marketing cost associated with product is its packaging (although the considerations mentioned above should be borne in mind here). On occasion, however, there will also be a wastage or obsolescence expense, as in the case of perishable products and services.

In recent years we have seen British Rail devise a variety of schemes to attract customers in order to maintain capacity outside rush hours – schemes such as 'Awayday' fares and Family Railcards – which have certainly increased passenger traffic in off-peak periods.

Many factories also have spare capacity available that could be producing products to sell. The extent to which marketing fails to make use of such capacity, over a medium-term period, is the cost of marketing failure. It constitutes lost opportunities. Few companies look at product or service costs in this way. When they begin to do so, marketing's attention can be constructively focused on the considerable challenges implicit in taking on marginal contribution business or in specific markets or market segments.

However, it should be borne in mind that in certain circumstances it may be more profitable for a company not to operate at full capacity. For example, a sweet manufacturer sold gift presentation tins of the product into Japan in very small volume. The product was sold through exclusive outlets and was seen as a luxury/gift product. An opportunity arose to sell in much larger quantities by introducing the product into the supermarket chains. The manufacturer decided not to take this opportunity. The premium price could not have been charged. The product would have ceased to be exclusive and would have competed with local products. With the additional distribution charges, little would have been gained and an assured market would have been lost.

A further area of product cost that is all too frequently overlooked is related to decisions taken by marketing on the different sizes or capability levels of a product to be offered. The different sizes of product offered are of considerable significance to the retailer in terms of his stockholding capabilities and costs. The manufacturer should consider the benefits to be derived by his customers from different sizes of a brand as carefully as he considers the benefits of different product lines.

Price Three major elements of marketing cost under this heading often escape careful attention. The first is any form of discounting that the organisation may engage in which results in a reduction in its otherwise-to-be-expected gross income yield for each unit sold. Discounting may take the form of quantity discounts, promotional discounts, loyalty rebates, etc. The second element is the amount of customer credit allowed. Unpaid invoices cost money and customer credit is a standard device for gaining business. Its terms will often vary but it will have the effect for a customer of transforming the total real price of the product or service. The third price-related cost is commission, typically paid to salesmen or agents in such a way that it increases in relation to the number of sales made. Such commissions whittle directly away at the gross revenue of the organisation.

Place The present authors include among place-related costs both the direct costs of marketing channel members to the company and the discrete physical movement or distribution costs that create availability. The marketing tasks associated with distribution have been discussed in detail in Chapters 15 to 17, which dealt with place decisions. The channel member's cost is primarily termed the 'margin' or 'mark-up'. The level at which these costs should be set was discussed in Chapter 19. Suffice it to note at this point that the margin or mark-up allowed to or taken by a channel member at one or more levels within a distribution system should be included as a marketing cost. Many companies in fact fail to analyse such margins or mark-ups in the context of their marketing budget. This is a mistake. Without such information, a full view of the marketing activities for a company's products or services cannot be gained.

Distribution costs incurred in the physical movement of goods or in making services available to customers are often a very substantial part of the total expenditure of many organisations; accordingly, they are frequently a dominant element in marketing expense. The main determinant of distribution cost is the level of availability that is deemed appropriate for the organisation's success in the market place. High levels of customer service or availability normally involve substantial investment in inventories and/or rapid transportation and delivery back-up. Distribution cost analysis is a major area of investigation in its own right; it is sufficient in this context to observe that the level of distribution cost is determined by a marketing judgement on the profitable responsiveness of sales to different levels of availability.

Table 5   Examples of marketing budgets

	Consumer product £	%	Industrial product £	%
Gross sales revenue forecast for year	3,000,000	100.00	2,000,000	100.00
less				
Cost of product ex factory	1,000,000	33.33	1,000,000	50.00
	2,000,000	66.67	1,000,000	50.00
less Incremental marketing expenses as follows:				
Packaging for display	50,000	1.67	0	0.00
Returns perished/damaged	5,000	0.17	12,000	0.60
Special discounts	160,000	5.30	0	0.00
Customer credit cost	30,000	1.00	100,000	5.00
Sales commissions	0	0.00	20,000	1.00
Distributors' margins	500,000	16.67	0	0.00
Distribution expense for customer service	348,000	11.60	85,000	4.25
Promotion –				
TV	100,000	3.33	0	0.00
Press	50,000	1.67	12,000	0.60
Technical	0	0.00	12,000	0.60
Catalogues etc	1,000	0.03	8,000	0.40
Sales force expense	50,000	1.67	108,000	5.40
Information costs	45,000	1.50	30,000	1.50
Total incremental marketing expense	1,339,000	44.64	387,000	19.35
Net contribution to company general expense	661,000	22.03	613,000	30.65

Promotion Table 5 illustrates clearly the main differences which are typically found between the expenditures of consumer goods and industrial companies. It is in the area of promotion that these differences are most marked. Industrial concerns spend little on advertising on television or in the national or international press, whereas most consumer advertising appears in those media. The industrial concern is more likely to incur costs on exhibitions; on sales and technical literature for the professional buyer or user of his product or service; on technical representatives making personal calls on clients; and on advisory services on applications in diverse situations.

Organisations offering their products or services through distributors are frequently involved in back-up promotion support. The cost of the major supermarket retailers' weekly press advertising is frequently shared with the manufacturers whose products are featured. In insurance and building society agencies, point-of-sale leaflets are always made available. Distributors of industrial items such as engineering equipment are also kept constantly supplied with sales literature.

Sales force costs have already been mentioned. These are often a substantial expense and are on occasion treated separately. While there can be no objection to a discrete sub-set of sales force costs, it is necessary that they be brought firmly into the total marketing budget of the organisation. At the margin, sales force effort and customer service are marketing costs that can perhaps be better spent elsewhere on the marketing field of action.

The place of information costs

We have already described in Chapter 25 how the collection of marketing information can enhance the effectiveness of marketing activity. We discussed there how the firm can organise its activities so that the benefit derived from use of the information justifies the costs incurred in collecting the information. This gives rise to the obvious inclusion in any marketing budget of an information cost.

What usually happens is that the information cost is budgeted as a fixed item for a twelve-month period and is associated with a long-term forecast of the level of expenditure required. Typically, this gives rise to mistaken levels of information usage. Information is sensibly collected by any organisation at that juncture dictated by the size of the perceived risk it wishes to take and by which it is confronted. New product or service launches, or moves into new international markets, are the situations most

294 Striking the marketing budget

likely to give rise to the need for heavy expenditure on information. Its benefit will, however, be spread over a much longer period than that in which the cost is incurred. Information is an investment in understanding a market situation which could be relevant for one, two, five or even ten years. It is not necessarily a current expense like discounting or sales force commission. It may well deserve a separate treatment in budgetary terms. Once again, the healthiest manner of treatment has been found to be a zero-based dynamic budgeting approach.

In addition to an organisation's individual collection of intelligence, there are also developments in the volume and scope of work undertaken by data collection firms which need to be considered.

In recent years, bar coding has meant that manufacturers now have the means by which they can rapidly tell whether a particular product is selling well in a particular kind of outlet and whether it is generating a greater return than another product in the range. For the retailer, bar coding means that he has a means of sorting out his stock level and identifying the contribution from each line. EPOS – the electronic point of sale – is the point at which the bar code is connected to the computer, which will then adjust stock levels, identify the quantity of product being sold and keep all the records.

Neilson, the data collection firm, have been awarded the contract to collect the data of what products are selling through what outlets, so that a feasibility study can be produced to show how all this information can be brought together. There are disputes about Neilson's audits, but organisations use them because they feel the information given is better than none. Should a national system of this kind be implemented, retailers would have the ability to take in a product, put it through the system and then – at the end of a working week – be in a position to know whether the product was giving as good a return or not as another existing product. At present, a management decision about whether to keep one product rather than another must be made; and with the proliferation of competing brands and sizes of product, the decision must be made on the basis of 'new product in: old product out', simply because shelf space cannot expand indefinitely.

Summing up

In the setting of a marketing budget, therefore, a manager needs to bear in mind the place that his marketing proposals take in relation to the overall strategic decisions of the organisation.

The three most common models of marketing structures – the traditional, negotiating and authoritarian structures – show different levels of input into budget decisions. The criteria a manager will find helpful in his budget setting will ideally be task-related, so that funds requested will be tied to well-specified objectives. In reality there may well be pressure for him to relate his requirements to sales and revenue forecasts. These ought to be monitored carefully throughout the year. Marketing costs are related to the four 'P's, and should also include the costs incurred in collecting marketing intelligence.

Application questions

27.1 *What is the marketing structure within your organisation? Would you describe the structure as traditional, negotiating or authoritarian? What do you believe are the major benefits from this type of structure and what are the major disadvantages?*

27.2 *How is the marketing budget determined in your organisation? How closely related are the various budgets and marketing tasks to be achieved? If a budget is reduced, are the tasks to be achieved similarly reduced?*

27.3 *If you were introducing a budgetary system into your organisation for the first time, what procedures would you introduce? What advantages would you see in your chosen system? How would it differ from existing procedures? Where differences do occur, what prevents the new system from being introduced?*

27.4 *How is the cost-effectiveness of each aspect of the marketing budget monitored? Is this information adequate for you to determine the responsiveness of your budgetary system to the needs of each of your products and services? What additional information do you need to help you set the budgets? How could such information be obtained? How could the cost of collection of the additional information be justified?*

27.5 *What constitutes the marketing expense for your organisation? Are there any elements which are not currently included in this reckoning but in your opinion should be considered part of* the marketing expense? Are there elements which are currently included in this reckoning but which you think should not be considered part of the marketing expense? Justify your opinion in both cases.

28

**How can we structure
our marketing organisation?**

Overview

*The main objective of the marketing function in any organisation
is to acquire a sufficient understanding of customer needs, present
and future, to be able to contribute to the development of overall
corporate objectives. The marketing department seeks to achieve
this objective by generating the right mix of products, at the right
time, in the right place, and with the right promotion. The structure
of the marketing department accordingly must be based on the
allocation of responsibilities both for achieving successful management of the four 'P's and for coordinating the strategies which are
employed in the management of this marketing mix.*

*The marketing department can usefully be seen as just one part
of an integrated pattern of activities which is designed to achieve
corporate goals. Marketing management must work alongside its
colleagues to ensure that the organisation's offering meets present
and future customer needs.*

The coordination of marketing responsibilities

In Chapter 1, we identified marketing's role in any organisation
as ensuring that the four 'P's – product, price, promotion and
place of sale – are successfully managed. Success in this context
means both that the customer is satisfied and that the organisation
makes effective use of its human, physical and financial resources.
We can therefore expect any marketing department to be organised in such a way that these goals are accomplished.

In practice, this is easier said than done. The types of situations
and problems which organisations face vary so widely that
marketing departments operate in very different ways. However,
certain basic marketing tasks are common to all organisations
and are neglected at the organisation's peril. Marketing's main
endeavour is to generate the right mix of sales with customers, at

the right prices, in the right place and with the right promotion. This means that the organisation's structure must be based on the allocation of responsibilities both for achieving each of these objectives *and* for coordinating the strategies which are pursued in order to achieve these various goals. In classical organisation chart terms, this gives rise to a pattern of responsibilities as shown in Figure 39.

Figure 39

Getting the product right involves activities which we discussed in detail in Chapters 12 to 14. If a company has a great many products, it may well wish to group them. If it has a number of important brands, it will often ask a member of the marketing department to take particular care of them. Such a person is frequently known as the Brand or Product Manager.

Getting the promotional activity right was discussed in Chapters 21 to 24. First of all, we saw the need to coordinate all the communications activities. Later, in Chapters 30 and 31, we shall examine in detail how personal selling, often a very important element in marketing, can be successfully developed.

The product or service must also be in the right place at the right time. Strategic decisions have to be made on distribution networks and on levels of availability and customer service. These issues were discussed in Chapters 15 to 17. Finally, as described in Chapters 18 to 20, the product must be sold at a price which is both attractive to the customer and acceptable to the organisation.

The marketing director must manage these operational responsibilities in such a way that the marketing objective of satisfying customer needs and wants is accomplished at the least cost and at the appropriate rate of profit or surplus. It is vitally important that the marketing director should be the focus of the coordination since he will often need to be tough in his attitudes and behaviour with regard to particular elements of the marketing mix. He may well perceive, for example, that a massive increase in distribution service can more than offset the market advantage lost by a reduction in sales and advertising expenditure, thereby providing a better overall marketing outcome. If he is not in coordinative command of those three elements of the mix, however, such calculations are unlikely ever to be made in the first instance, and, even if the calculations are made, their implementation may well be effectively opposed by the sales and advertising managers. The organisation of the marketing department must ensure that all management of individual mix elements is subordinate to marketing direction.

This goal may seem an obvious and straightforward one. However, organisations tend to find that several factors can mediate against effective marketing direction. In some cases, the traditional structure of the company may work against coordination as when, for example, the marketing and sales departments have their own parallel hierarchies. In other cases, companies may appoint fairly senior executives to control advertising or sales budgets; these executives are then likely to rebel against co-ordinative authority.

The difficulties involved in effective marketing coordination can be illustrated with reference to a bank, which may have an upsurge of demand in the market place for particular types of lending. Demand of this kind may well upset the plans of the bank since any bank's aspirations are to have a balanced portfolio of lending across a whole range of industries and a whole range of types of personal risk. Any upsurge in demand can result in an organisation selling far more of a product than the company really wishes to do. Almost any product can be over-sold to such an extent that the additional cost of procuring it at the manufacturing point will be excessive. Effective marketing direction will prevent such situations from occurring.

Marketing posts

We have been careful so far in this text to talk about responsibilities rather than particular posts. We have also failed to introduce into our discussion the need for marketing management to have available to it supporting services, such as those provided by the marketing training officer. Figure 40 shows how a Swiss textile fabric manufacturer assigned roles within its marketing department.

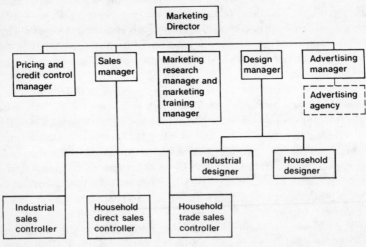

One Marketing Department's Operational Structure

Figure 40

The roles allocated can be seen to be related to the specific nature of the organisation. Its markets include both industrial purchasers and households. The sales manager has three controllers who report to him, two of them dividing household sales between them according to whether the sales are sought direct from customers via direct mail response to advertising or occur through trade sales to wholesalers and retailers. The distinction between household and industrial markets also affects the activities of the design manager, who has overall responsibility for the product. The advertising manager works through an agency which is accustomed to handling industrial, trade and direct response advertising work. Similarly, the pricing and credit control manager handles all areas of activity.

The element missing in the coordination undertaken by the marketing director is distribution, the management function that determines which channels to use for reaching the end customer and, in particular, takes care to ensure that the correct level of logistical support is given. This was a serious bone of contention within the organisation. Because the company was part of a wider grouping of companies in the manmade fibre industry, it was expected to employ the logistics support system used by the other members of the group. There was common warehousing and a common scheduling of deliveries. Direct response sales was the only area where the company had a logistics system tailored to its specific needs.

Compromises of this kind are sometimes necessary even if they appear counter-productive for the particular part of the group concerned. In this case, after careful studies to establish the correct service levels, a change was made in the allocation of responsibility for logistics. Sub-contractors who would meet the required service levels at an economic cost were contracted to carry out the logistics task. The organisation itself then introduced a new member of the marketing team who assumed a similar management role to that exercised by the advertising manager.

Our final comment should perhaps be reserved for the role ascribed to the marketing research manager which, in this case, included the role of training officer. The company was relatively small, with sales of SwFr48 million each year. There were only some 26 staff in the marketing department, including all field sales representatives. Hence, both the information gaining and presenting task and the training roles were not overwhelming. However, the company felt it important that line executives should be provided with this service.

Our illustration of a marketing department's operational structure has deliberately been kept simple. We have emphasised the need, first, to define the responsibilities involved and, secondly, to identify the posts which the organisation needs to establish.

We have seen that the responsibility for several tasks can be assigned to one individual; and that, on occasion, the performance of the tasks can be sub-contracted. What cannot be sacrificed is the marketing director's overriding need to be in a position to coordinate all the posts.

The decision as to whether or not to sub-contract the performance of tasks and, if so, how extensively to use external services, is one which many organisations find difficult. Should the company have a research department or employ a research agency? Should the company rely on a full service advertising agency to provide continuity on a brand or should it undertake this task itself? Should the company with many branded products employ its own media manager to monitor the buying efficiency of the advertising agencies used? The answers to vital questions of this kind will provide another pointer to the kind of operational structure which is most appropriate to the organisation's needs.

Organising marketing within the company

Marketing, as we have stressed, is able only to generate the demand for products or services. The satisfaction of that demand depends on the extent to which all the other functions of a business are working to agreed objectives. These agreed objectives are increasingly defined in terms of performance on *product/market missions*, since organisations frequently coordinate their various lines of business in terms of a matrix structure.

A matrix approach is employed at IMCB for the conduct of its MBA programme, its Continuing Management Development and its research programmes. The vertical inputs to the organisation are teaching inputs and the horizontal outputs are trained managers. (Education is – of course – an example of a non-profit service of the type discussed in Chapter 4.) IMCB has teaching product/market output missions, each of which is co-ordinated by a director. Thus, there is a separate director for the MBA programme. Different professors head the subject groups which work together to make each mission a success. Success comes when all the groups work effectively together to achieve the output; in IMCB's case, this is a well developed and trained manager.

The matrix approach to organisational structure has also proved successful in a commercial context. A specialist book publisher, for example, has established an operational structure which effectively matches products to markets. The vertical inputs to this organisation are the company's finance, marketing, production and management information functions. The horizontal outputs are publishing missions in marketing and logistics, human resources, social economics and managerial law, and information transfer. Each of these missions is responsible for the publication of books and journals in its particular subject area; it is also responsible for developing a pattern of activity which fits in with the overall resources and requirements of the organisation.

In Figure 41 the matrix-based approach is applied to a major Italian concern selling its products into catering establishments, grocery supermarkets and wholesalers.

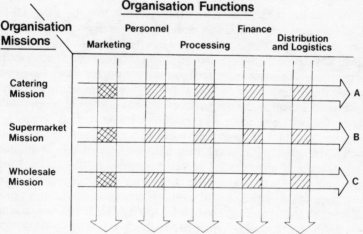

Figure 41

It will be seen that the marketing effort in this company is just one part of an integrated pattern of activity which is designed to take the right processed food products to catering establishments, to national supermarket chains and to wholesalers who supply the smaller retail grocery outlets. At each of the interstices in the matrix shown in darker blocks, marketing will need to coordinate its activities in a different fashion in order to relate effectively with all other company activities.

With its existing plant, the processing function may not be able to make the product mix which is ideally suited to the market. The development engineers may not be able to raise or allocate the desired level of funds to support customer credit policies. Each product/market mission must balance out such competing claims within its total perspective. This allocation of responsibility for achieving an appropriate balance between company resources and customer needs ensures that skills and functions are coordinated in order to have the greatest impact on the market.

The marketing department's role in developing the future

The discussion which has taken place during this chapter can be seen to reaffirm our earlier claim that marketing must plan ahead for more than the immediate period of operational activity. The marketing department's interpretation of emerging customer needs and wants must be taken into account fully by those who take medium- and long-term decisions about the organisation's future direction.

Marketing's colleagues in production, finance, personnel and distribution need and want to know what future viable paths the company can follow in its markets. Marketing must continually explore and display the alternatives. It can only do so by developing an adequate product policy which is based on understanding what customers will need and what they can be persuaded to want. Marketing must give its colleagues their bearings on the market place as they seek to invest in new manufacturing capacity, locate new facilities, develop the skills of the workforce, or analyse cash requirements to fund the business in the years ahead.

We can conclude by demonstrating this role in sharp but realistic relief with the situation affecting the European airlines in 1975. The airlines took delivery of fleets of Tristars and Airbuses in order to meet the levels of business activity forecast three years previously. However, market demand for medium-range air travel dropped drastically in 1975, falling eventually by 25%.

The fleets were not needed, but the product had arrived. The changing patterns of air travel, which had resulted from massive rises in the cost of such travel, could not be accommodated easily by the use of the new type of aircraft. Even though the airlines searched for a wide range of alternative uses, the fleets acquired were not needed and were eventually disposed of, in some cases into military transport. British Airways, for instance, sold five Tristars to the Royal Air Force. Such cases show that forecasting is difficult, so it must be flexible. The European airlines were caught with a crisis as a result of a lack of flexibility in their forecasting and planning, as well as from sheer bad luck. They resolved to include a much deeper marketing involvement in future planning of organisational capability. They may still make the wrong buying decision, but the risk of doing so is thereby considerably reduced.

Application questions

28.1   *Who does the marketing department comprise within your organisation? For each job identified, what are the major responsibilities allocated? Are all aspects of marketing allocated somewhere within the department?*

28.2   *Identify any aspects of marketing management not under the control of members of the marketing department. Where are these responsibilities located if anyone within the organisation assumes them? Is this situation satisfactory, or does it undermine the effectiveness of the marketing department in some way?*

28.3   *How are the many aspects of marketing coordinated? Is logistics and distribution adequately coordinated with the marketing effort? Is the management of the sales force adequately coordinated with the marketing effort? Identify any major problems you believe to exist because of inadequate coordination of the four 'P's. How could these problems be solved?*

28.4   *Has the marketing programme changed in recent years? If so, how has that change been made? Why was it made? Was it made to answer short-term problems or the better to organise in order to capitalise on future opportunities in the market place? If the marketing has not changed, is its present functioning satisfactory in your view?*

28.5   *If you were responsible for your organisation's marketing department, how would you use external resources? How does this recommendation differ from your organisation's present use of such resources? How would you make the change?*

29

**How can we estimate
how much we will sell?**

Overview

*As we have already discussed, the environment in which the
marketing activity takes place is constantly changing and needs
continual monitoring. One result of this is that all estimates of sales
take place against a background of uncertainty. Because of this
uncertainty, therefore, sales estimation must be able to provide a
flexible framework for marketing action and must recognise the
probabilistic nature of sales levels. The central task of sales forecasting is the estimation of market potential and the share of the market
that products might be expected to achieve. This task is influenced
both by the forecasting horizon and by the stability of the markets
in which the organisation is operating.*

Both macro *and* micro *approaches are used in the techniques of
estimation. Macro approaches – which include the use of marketing
models – enable the forecaster to deduce from a broad economic
analysis the implications for a particular product/market. Micro
approaches are based on building up an estimate of sales from an
individual customer level.*

Forecasting future sales

Estimating the level of sales of any product, new or old, is an
ever-present problem. Knowing in advance what level of sales
could be achieved – given a particular marketing programme –
would reduce considerably the complexity of the marketing decision. However, few people can claim the ability to predict the
future both accurately and in detail, so the marketing decision-
maker must fall back on less precise methods.

Before the level of sales can be determined, it is necessary to
decide how sales themselves are to be measured – in terms of
volume, or of value. *Volume* is the number of units sold, whereas
value is the amount of revenue generated. There is a tendency –

perhaps because so much sales data within companies is generated by the accounts department – to calculate in terms of value. The problem with this method is that what is truly happening in the market place can be disguised. With inflation, for example, an apparent increase in sales – measured in value – may not be a true increase in volume. Either the same, or even a smaller, number of units may be sold, yet an increase in revenue is still shown. It is also useful to distinguish between products sold in different packaging sizes. In such cases, the number of units sold should be aggregated into total tonnage. In this way a more accurate measure of sales performance in the market place can be made.

Even some of the most carefully prepared forecasts of future sales can be disproved by events. The wider environment in which the forecast is set changes in ways that are not always foreseen and thus not incorporated in the forecast. Energy crises, crop failures and drought, revolutions – these are just a few of the major events that can upset the forecast. It could be suggested that, if the world is so dynamic, what is the purpose of forecasting anyway?

The answer is quite simply that any attempt to reduce the uncertainty that surrounds the future will, if used as a flexible input to a planning process, make us question the appropriateness of what we are currently doing. It must be recognised, however, that forecasts are useful only if they are indeed used in a flexible way. Sales forecasts can too easily become strait-jackets which inhibit the organisation's activities, as when they are seen as targets, endowed with all the sanctity that numbers tend to assume in a management context.

Forecasts deal with contingencies, not certainties. The head of planning in a large multinational chemical company says, 'We have to have alternative plans that can deal with either/or eventualities.' Establishing the nature of the 'either/or' is the task of the market forecaster. Parallel to the need for flexibility is the need to recognise that the output of the forecast should be expressed in terms of a *range* of possible outcomes. Sales estimates share the imprecision of most forecasting methods. Beyond this, however, it must be recognised that the process whereby any sales level is achieved is essentially *probabilistic*. In other words, chance has a central role in the outcome of any marketing process. Our forecasts can, and should, be made to incorporate the probabilities that are implicit in the marketing environment in which we operate.

The successful use of forecasting can be seen in the case of a manufacturer of household durables. Prior to the start of each fiscal year, he worked out three different forecasts: 'optimistic', 'pessimistic' and 'most likely'. If taxation levels changed, competitive activity became particularly aggressive, or some other phenomenon occurred to alter the market, the manufacturer could adopt an alternative plan without having to repeat the forecasting procedure. This approach enabled the company to react to market conditions with immediate flexibility.

But how do we start to grapple with the sales estimation problem?

Understanding market potential

The distinction between actual and potential customers (discussed in Chapter 7) is vital to successful sales estimation. The forecaster is concerned with establishing what proportion of the total market will be represented in his or her sales estimates. Market potential has been defined as the maximum possible sales opportunities for all sellers of a good or service. As such, it refers to the potential sales that could be achieved at a given time, in a given environment, by all the firms active in a specified product/market area or segment.

Thus, the concept of market potential extends our view of the market for our product in that we see the product as competing against alternative means of satisfying the same need. Successful sales estimation will therefore depend on determining the proportion of the market that can be achieved, given a specific marketing mix and marketing programme. This situation is illustrated in Figure 42.

A presentation of this kind, of course, gives a static picture of actual and potential sales at a given time and in a given environment; it could be influenced both by environmental changes and by changes in marketing effort by any of the firms (including ourselves) in that product/market area.

Looking at the sales estimation problem in this light, we see how it can be possible for estimates to become self-fulfilling prophecies, in that the estimate and the marketing mix/programme are dependent upon each other. In a sense, a given level of market

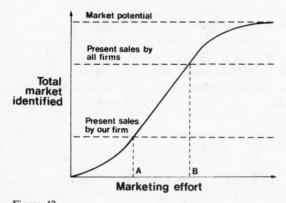

Figure 42

achievement is predicated by what we believe to be potentially achievable.

The forecasting horizon

Clearly, the time period that we select for the forecasting exercise will influence our approach and our choice of estimation techniques. Most managers are accustomed to thinking in terms of short-, medium- and long-term forecasting, the actual length of these periods being determined by the organisation's planning requirements.

As an example, a manufacturer of wine bottles in Spain knows that his short-term forecasting requirements are based on his need to plan production schedules on a weekly basis. His medium-term requirements are determined by the industry demand over the period of time it takes to install and make operational additional production capacity – in this case a year. And the longer term forecasting must take account of changing consumer requirements, such as easy-open bottles, and changing technology in the bottling and packaging fields.

Precise definitions of what constitute the short, medium and long term for any company will clearly vary but should ultimately depend on the reaction-time implicit in a company's activities and its organisation. The reaction-time for firms in ladies' fashion markets must necessarily be much shorter than for those companies engaged in the construction of hydro-electric power projects. Their definition of the forecasting horizon will vary correspondingly.

The firm's definition of that horizon will also be influenced by the variability of demand in their markets. For established products, that variability may not be pronounced, particularly if seasonal variations are allowed for. Even though on a week-by-week basis sales may seem to fluctuate widely, there will often be an underlying steady state or a recognisable upward or downward direction in sales.

The forecasting task for the manufacturers of beef stock cubes, a product in a steady state that has lasted for many years, is quite different from that faced by the Swedish firm Uddeholm, launching on a completely untried market a new grade of stainless steel for use in the processing of fertilisers. The EMI Body Scanner, a high-value, highly complex capital item – which evolved very quickly – initially dominated an entire market, but rapid competitive response meant that it had lost market leadership within a couple of years. Further technical development was allowed to continue at a pace far slower than market developments. The market was itself extremely volatile, in that the medical profession is prepared to accept new product innovation very rapidly; therefore, in such a market, the time constraints become extremely important. In the same way, when someone finds a cancer-curing drug, it will be on the market with the greatest possible speed.

The techniques of estimation

Two broad approaches to market estimation have been employed by market forecasters in their attempts to estimate future sales levels. These may be termed *macro* (or aggregate product-market) estimates and *micro* (or individual product) estimates. These approaches are not alternatives but should complement each other in the information they provide. Both approaches can use qualitative and quantitative methods of estimation, depending on their objectives.

The macro level of estimation

Let us first consider the macro approaches to estimation. Here, the emphasis is on observing the broad picture and, from that, deducing the implications for the product/market in which we are interested. Many business forecasters use leading indicators (that is, indices of related or even non-related activities) as aids in estimating changes in market conditions at a macro level.

For example, in the United Kingdom, the Financial Times Ordinary Share Index has tended in recent years to signal changes in general economic conditions about six months in advance. Similar leading UK indicators, which would be classified as quantitative methods of estimation, are: new housing starts (a lead of about 10 months), net acquisition of financial assets by companies (leading by about 12 months) and interest on three-month bank bills (with a lead of approximately 18 months).

Another leading indicator is generally held to be the CBI surveys of industry, monthly or quarterly figures which survey the whole of British industry all over the country by collecting data from companies on their order books and investment plans, so that a picture of their future economic activity is yielded.

Such indicators will only provide approximate pictures of general business conditions and cannot be guaranteed to offer consistent correlations. On the other hand, the forecaster may discern that there is a close fit between a seemingly unrelated activity and the sales performance of a particular product. One Danish manufacturer of garden furniture has established a satisfactory method of predicting sales on the basis of an apparent correlation between the rise in real wages in Denmark and the sales of his product, with a lag of 18 months. This does not necessarily imply any causal relationship – simply a statistical association – but it did seem to provide a useful aid to sales estimation.

There has been a considerable growth in recent years in the use of *marketing models* to provide a macro-type basis for sales estimation. Generally, these models are based on a number of statistically derived relationships drawn from empirical observations. Some of these can be relatively simple, embodying only a few relationships and requiring nothing more than a calculator to perform the manipulations. On the other hand, one Europe-wide oil company has recently developed a sophisticated energy model to guide it in formulating its strategy on synthetic fuels. The model covers all major energy forms, conversion technologies, transportation modes and demand. It also projects investment, financing and resource depletion to the year 2025 and even attempts to predict prices on the basis of supply and demand. A model of this kind attempts to *explain* the observed market behaviour in terms of marketing trends. This contrasts with the garden furniture example above where the correlation is not explained, only accepted as an observable phenomenon.

The advances that have been made in micro-computer technology mean that these forecasting models are now much more accessible. The question remains as to how many managers actually use them; but whereas in the past they were thought to be highly technical and only within the reach of the large, main frame users, they are now increasingly available.

Not everybody shares this enthusiasm for large-scale models because of the problems of quantifying what are often qualitative and intangible relationships. Such relationships will often change considerably over time, thus making the model obsolete. Another factor weighing against the use of models is the considerable expense involved in collecting the necessary data. In many markets – as in the soup market, for example – it may be more cost-beneficial to employ less sophisticated estimation techniques.

An example of a qualitative macro estimation is the Delphi forecast (named after the Greek oracle which foretold the future). Here, a group of experts discuss a problem, such as 'What will be the major marketing features of the year 2000?', and give their consensus of the answer to this problem.

The micro level of estimation

These macro approaches, it was suggested earlier, are particularly suited to forecasting which is intended, primarily, to depict broad market conditions. In themselves, though, they rarely provide a complete answer to the company's sales estimation problem. The micro level approaches to estimation which tackle the problem from the other direction, from the study of the sales prospects for an individual product, can often provide the missing pieces of the jigsaw.

Micro approaches are based on building up, from an individual customer level, an estimate of what total sales of the product could be in a given period. Quantitative micro methods rely heavily on surveys of actual and/or potential customers. Although the procedures involved may be very sophisticated, these studies basically rely on indications from respondents about their likely purchasing behaviour. For example, a German manufacturer of household electrical goods carries out a regular survey amongst a representative sample of actual and potential customers to ascertain the likelihood of their purchasing particular electrical appliances in the next twelve months. Using this device, he can track the way in which first times sales will move and also the way in which the replacement market is moving.

In the same way, a British manufacturer of cough and cold products will research the incidence of coughs and colds in order to estimate consumer offtake; he can then relate that data back to subsequent movement in retail stocks and hence anticipated ex-factory sales. Here the company is not actually testing with the consumer; the assumption is made that, if people have coughs and colds, they will in due course buy products that alleviate their discomfort. The connection assumed is not between coughs and colds and a specific brand of cough mixture; it is between coughs and colds and a general increase in the sales of coughs and colds products.

At the micro level, many companies rely on forecasts which are based solely on an analysis of past sales. In other words, past sales are charted with a view to identifying patterns and trends and thus enabling projections to be made. The nature of projections must be clearly understood: they are extrapolations from past behaviour and are based upon an assumption that what has happened in the past will be a guide to what will happen in the future. This need not be so.

One striking example is the production of skateboards. Many people were fooled into thinking that the skateboard fashion would go on forever. The boom in skateboards caught out many importers who misread the implications of buoyant sales. Breakfast television is another instance; the British people in the past apparently showed an insatiable appetite for commercial television, which led some to make the assumption that commercial breakfast television would be a winner. The assumption turned out to be misjudged, at least in the short term. Extrapolation was made from past behaviour, because commercial television had always been profitable. In reality, people showed that they were looking for something quite different in their breakfast viewing.

An example of a qualitative micro estimate would be an estimate based on the judgement of members of the sales force concerning future sales.

Successful marketing management must be based upon reliable estimates of market demand. It would probably be true to say that companies pay rather less attention to this crucial input to marketing decisions than they should. Success in the markets of the future will almost certainly require a reversal of this neglect.

Application questions

29.1   *What criteria do you use for assessing the level of sales in your organisation? Is this a value or a volume measure? If you use value measures, what account do you take of inflation in assessing the current year's performance against prior years?*

29.2   *What external considerations do you take into account in arriving at your forecasts? Does your forecasting process include a range of options, e.g., optimistic, pessimistic, most likely? Would such an approach be appropriate for your business and how would you implement it?*

29.3   *How can the market potential for your industry be calculated? Against your estimate for the total market, what is your current market share for all your major products? Does this market share represent satisfactory performance? How could your performance be improved?*

29.4   *Over what period of time do you forecast sales in your organisation? Are all relevant managers aware of the forecasts and do they all work towards them? What is the procedure for monitoring the extent to which forecasts are achieved?*

29.5   *What information in particular do you use to develop your forecasts? How would you categorise this information in terms of macro and micro? Do you use any forecasting models? If not, would you consider such an approach to be appropriate for your business?*

29.6   *Is there any additional information which you would like to help you develop accurate forecasts in your market? In what way could the information help you? How could you obtain the information? What has prevented you from gaining the information in the past?*

30

**Do we need
our own sales force?**

Overview

*The alternatives to a sales force – distributors, agents, contract sales
forces and brokers – are used in many organisations. Nevertheless,
having one's own sales force yields two chief advantages: these are
that employers can retain absolute control and that the sales force
will give complete dedication. The chief disadvantage is expense,
since – apart from salaries – cars and other associated costs must
be added in. Further, a sales force requires appropriate administration and supervision, which adds to its maintenance cost.*

*For many reasons, sales force management and personal selling
often suffer from neglect by marketing management. The solution
to poor sales force management can only be found in the recognition that personal selling is a crucial part of the marketing process
and therefore must be managed as carefully as any other aspect.
The sales force cannot be managed in isolation from broad
corporate and marketing objectives.*

*Personal selling can most usefully be seen as a component element
of the communications mix. Deciding what role personal selling
will have in this mix can only emerge from the organisation's
thorough understanding of the buying process which operates in
its markets. Research into buying decisions offers some help to
organisations in achieving a suitable match between information
required by the customer and given by the company.*

*Particularly in industrial marketing, personal selling has a number
of advantages over other forms of marketing communication; these
should be intelligently exploited.*

Alternatives to a sales force

A manufacturer who does not have his own sales force may decide
to use a *distributor*. This means – in effect – that his product will

be wholesaled in bulk to distributors all over the country. The manufacturer will be using the distributors' sales force to sell his product to their customers. This is the typical beginning of the progression through a spectrum of different selling activities.

Usually, a company starting up will use distributors, mainly for financial reasons. Payment is only made on the basis of results, but this can be a double-edged sword since the distributor will put his effort behind the most rewarding products.

After some time, the manufacturer will move from using distributors to using *agents*. The difference here is that the distributor buys stock, sells it on, and makes a profit on the process; whereas an agent does not necessarily hold stock, but he represents the manufacturer formally in the market place. Enquiries are referred through the agent, who is rewarded by receiving a commission on all sales achieved through that market.

The next logical step after that is to employ a *sales force* directly. This may start as one or two salesmen only but can ultimately build up to a full sales force structure with salesmen, area sales managers, key account salesmen and a sales director.

The progression from distributors to agents and, finally, to a sales force, is typical. There are, however, other alternatives in the spectrum. One is the use of a *contract sales force*, very often used to supplement existing sales activity at particular times; for example, a contract sales force may be used for a product launch.

If a manufacturer of consumer products wants to achieve high distribution for a new type of soup or for a new cosmetic, he might well use a contract sales force who – for two weeks or a month – would go out and sell the product, often in one particular area. This can be a very useful adjunct to sales activity because it is giving additional coverage in the market place. The problem is that the contract force is only handling the product for a limited period, and therefore a good briefing is needed, mainly because the sales force will not have built up any experience of the product and the way it is sold. Contract sales forces are very often associated with regional television companies and are used very frequently in the United Kingdom to supplement the distribution of a product before it is advertised on television.

Another alternative is the use of *brokers*. In this instance, sales responsibility is effectively handed over to a third party. In grocery distribution, for example, control is retained over advertising and all the other elements of the marketing mix, whereas the broker provides the sales input. The advantage here is that brokers will add a manufacturer's product to their portfolios; they will call on supermarkets, groceries, CTNs (confectioner-tobacconist-newsagent) and retail pharmacies. A manufacturer trying to get the same coverage himself would find doing so extremely costly, because he has only a limited range of products to sell. Adding his product to other complementary products means gaining more efficiency from the sales call that is made. At the same time as the broker is selling Brown's jelly beans, he may also be selling Smith's cough drops, so that two products are sold with the one sales call. Several manufacturers thus come together and jointly sell their products through the mechanism of brokerage. Further, brokers will frequently effect delivery for the manufacturer, so they can handle the inventory, but they rarely take title to it.

Advantages and disadvantages of a sales force and its alternatives

The main advantage of having a sales force is that the employer retains absolute control over it and the sales force gives total dedication to the employer. It also gives greater utility and flexibility; for example, if the employer suddenly decides he wants the sales force to call on a different type of outlet, then that option is available to him. There is also the important factor of motivation. By whatever means, an employer retains control of that motivation.

If the employer elects to sell through a brokerage, then he loses the advantage of the salesman's identification with his product. His product will not be the only one being sold by the broker and will be competing with other products to gain the individual commitment of the salesmen. If they are selling three or four different manufacturers' products, then a manufacturer will be wise to be seen to have a presence; for example, attending the sales force briefing meetings. Such a presence will show the manufacturer's support for his product and will help to motivate the salesmen. It is extremely difficult to motivate distributors, mainly because they want to sell things that easily sell themselves. It is equally difficult, at times, to motivate agents, because they will not feel – unless a strong relationship has been purposely encouraged – a commitment to the product.

The disadvantage of having a sales force is that it is expensive to maintain, the expense running at some £30,000 per year, per salesman. The elements that must be costed in here include salary, associated employment costs, a car and its running costs, the salesman's expenses, and a partial cost of management. This last factor leads to another important disadvantage, which is the cost of a sales manager. The employer should not assume that because he has a sales force, the salesmen will necessarily get on and do the job. A system of sales management must be imposed; and a fair measure of this requirement would be to expect a span of control of six; that is, one supervisor for every six salesmen. General company management often assumes that because, for example, a salesman receives commission, he will be efficient and successful; in some companies, sales forces of 15 or 20 report to only one sales manager. It is difficult to see how one sales manager can handle effectively such a broad pyramid. A sales force of thirty-six, for example, will properly need six area managers, together with one manager above them.

An employer with his own sales force must also take into account the other associated overheads. Normally, there must be a sales office through which orders are processed. Using distributors will avoid incurring some of this administrative overhead, simply because the number of customers being serviced is automatically reduced. If there are only six distributors, there will be less administration than if distributors are bypassed and five thousand individual customers must be processed. Equally, as the number of salesmen increases, so too, will the number of administrative staff increase.

Sales force management: some common problems

Most organisations had an organised sales force long before they introduced a formal marketing activity of the kind described throughout this text. In spite of this fact, sales force management has traditionally been a neglected area of marketing management.

There are several possible reasons for this. One is that not all marketing and product managers have had experience in a personal selling or sales management role; consequently, these managers often underestimate the importance of efficient personal selling.

Another reason for neglect of sales force management is that sales personnel themselves sometimes encourage an unhelpful distinction between sales and marketing by depicting themselves as 'the sharp end'. After all, isn't there something slightly daring about dealing with real live customers as opposed to sitting in an office surrounded by marketing surveys, charts and plans? That such reasoning is misleading will be obvious from what was said in Chapter 2 about the difference between selling and marketing. It will be recalled that unless a good deal of careful marketing planning has taken place before the salesman makes his effort to persuade the customer to place an order, the probability of a successful sale is much reduced.

The suggested distinction between marketing 'theory' and sales 'practice' is further invalidated when we consider that profitable sales depend not just on individual customers and individual products but on groups of customers (that is, market segments) and on the supportive relationship of products to each other (that is, a carefully planned product portfolio). Another factor to be taken into account in this context is the constant need for the organisation to think in terms of where future sales will be coming from rather than to concentrate solely on present products, customers and problems.

The authors of this text have investigated scores of European sales forces over the last decade and have found an alarming lack of planning and professionalism. Salesmen frequently have little idea of which products and which groups of customers to concentrate on, have too little knowledge about competitive activity, do not plan presentations well, rarely talk to customers in terms of *benefits*, make too little effort to close the sale, and make many calls without clear objectives. Even worse, marketing management is rarely aware that this important and expensive element of the marketing mix is not being managed effectively. The fact that many organisations have separate departments and directors for the marketing and sales activities increases the likelihood of such failures of communication.

A survey was carried out to examine the effectiveness with which sales representatives made contact with those responsible for influencing purchase decisions. The survey showed that in companies with over one thousand employees, where there were about seven major influencers of the purchasing decision, on average only two contacts per visit were made. A similar proportion of contacts was made in smaller companies. Another survey showed that advertising in the trade and technical press was the major source of information for large companies, while personal visits from sales people constituted the most important source of information for small companies. In both cases, exhibitions and direct mail were also important sources of information. This survey pointed up the fact that any company which uses personal selling as its sole means of communication with customers is unlikely to be fulfilling its communications objectives.

The solution to the problem of poor sales force management can only be found in the recognition that personal selling is indeed a crucial part of the marketing process but that it must be planned and considered as carefully as any other element. Indeed, it is an excellent idea for any manager responsible for marketing to go out into a territory for a few days each year and himself attempt to persuade customers to place orders. It is a good way of finding out what customers really think of the organisation's marketing policies.

The role of personal selling

Although its importance varies according to circumstances, in many businesses the sales force is the most important element in the marketing mix. In industrial goods companies, for example, it is not unusual to find less than £20,000 being spent on other forms of communication and £250,000 or more being spent on the sales force in the form of salaries, cars and associated costs.

Personal selling is also widely used in many service industries where customers are looking for very specific benefits. Insurance companies, for example, do use media advertising but rely for most of their sales on personal selling. Customers for insurance policies almost invariably need to discuss which policy would best fit their particular needs and circumstances; it is the task of the salesman to explain the choices available and to suggest the most appropriate policy.

Personal selling can most usefully be seen as part of the *communications mix* described in Chapter 21, itself an aspect of the 'promotion' element of the total marketing mix. (Other common elements of the communications mix, it will be remembered, are advertising, public relations, direct mail, exhibitions, and so on.) The surveys described earlier show that organisations cannot safely leave the communications task to the sales force. The question remains, however, as to how the organisation is to define the role of personal selling in its communications mix. The answer lies in a clear understanding of the buying process which operates in the company's markets.

Understanding the buying process

It is perfectly feasible to set specific quantifiable objectives to each marketing communication task. But the company can only determine how much relative effort to devote to personal selling and other forms of communication if it has a very clear idea of the buying process in its markets.

We have discussed the decision-making process at some length earlier in the text. Let us here recall some of the main points made. During the past decade, there has been a great deal of similar research into the industrial and consumer buying processes. This process is clearly very important: after all, comparatively few companies sell their goods direct to the end user. In addition, personal selling is a particularly important element in industrial marketing.

The efficiency of any element of communication depends on achieving a match between information required and information given. To achieve this match, the marketer must be aware of the different stages of the buying process. This approach highlights the importance of ensuring that the company's communications reach *all* key points in the buying chain. No company can afford to assume that the actual sale is the only important event.

In order to determine the precise role of personal selling in its communications mix, the company must identify the major influencers in each purchase decision and find out what information they are likely to need at different stages of the buying process. Most institutional buying decisions consist of many separate phases, from the recognition of a problem through to performance evaluation and feedback on the product or service purchased. Furthermore, the importance of each of these phases varies according to whether the buying situation is a first-time purchase or a routine re-purchase. Clearly, the information needs will differ in each case.

Using personal selling effectively

Personal selling has a number of advantages over other elements of the communications mix:

– it is a two-way form of communication, giving the prospective purchaser the opportunity to ask questions of the salesman about the product or service;
– the sales message itself can be made more flexible and therefore can be more closely tailored to the needs of the individual customer;
– the salesman can use in-depth product knowledge to relate his message to the perceived needs of the buyer and to deal with objections as they arise;
– most importantly, the salesman can ask for an order and, perhaps, negotiate on price, delivery or special requirements.

Once an order has been obtained from a customer and there is a high probability of a re-buy occurring, the salesman's task changes from persuasion to reinforcement. All communications at this stage should contribute to underlining the wisdom of the purchase. The salesman may also take the opportunity to encourage consideration of other products or services in the company's range.

Clearly, in different markets different weighting is given to the various forms of communication available. In the grocery business, for example, advertising and sales promotion are extremely important elements in the communications process. However, the food processor must maintain an active sales force which keeps in close contact with the retail buyers. This retail contact ensures vigorous promotional activity in the chain. In the wholesale hardware business frequent and regular face-to-face contact with retail outlets through a sales force is the key determinant of success. In industries where there are few customers (such as capital goods and specialised process materials) an in-depth understanding of the customers' production processes has to be built up; here, again, personal contact is of paramount importance. In contrast, many fast-moving industrial goods are sold into fragmented markets for diverse uses; in this area forms of communication other than personal selling take on added importance.

Many companies in the electronic business use personal selling to good advantage. Word processors, for example, vary enormously in the range of capabilities which they offer. Technical details can be supplied in brochures and other promotional material but the administrative staff likely to be taking the purchase decision often find it difficult to evaluate the alternatives. A good salesman can quickly ascertain the requirements of a particular client and identify to what extent these will be fulfilled by his equipment. For his part, the customer can quickly identify whether the company understands his requirements, whether it appears credible and whether or not it is able to provide the back-up service necessary to install the equipment and establish its use in the organisation. Such considerations are likely to be far more influential than the comparison of technical data sheets in a decision to purchase.

Sales objectives

In the next chapter, we shall be examining the problem of how many salesmen the organisation needs and what they should be asked to do. We shall complete our present discussion of the link between selling and the overall marketing activity by looking at the relationship between corporate objectives and sales objectives.

All companies set themselves overall objectives which in turn imply the development of specific marketing objectives. In this chapter we have discussed personal selling in the context of the overall marketing activity. This approach leads us to the following hierarchy of objectives: *corporate objectives – marketing objectives – sales objectives*.

The benefits to sales force management of following this approach can be summarised as follows:

– coordination of corporate and marketing objectives with actual sales effort;
– establishment of a circular relationship between corporate objectives and customer wants;
– improvement of sales effectiveness through an understanding of the corporate and marketing implications of sales decisions.

The following example illustrates the main point that a sales force cannot be managed in isolation from broad corporate and marketing objectives. The sales force of a company manufacturing cardboard packaging was selling almost any kind of packaging to almost anybody who could buy. This caused severe production planning and distribution problems throughout the business, down to the purchase of raw materials. Eventually, the company's profitability was seriously affected. The sales force was finally instructed to concentrate on certain kinds of products and on certain kinds of user industries. This decision eventually led to economies of scale throughout the whole organisation.

In the following months, the company became successful, profitability improved again, production was more efficient and staff morale rose in line with the company's new-found success.

Application questions

30.1   *Does your organisation have a formalised sales force? What other types of sales activities (e.g., agents, distributors, and so on) has your organisation employed in the past? Are any of these methods still used? Do your present sales arrangements represent the most appropriate means of persuading customers to buy your products or services?*

30.2   *When you are buying products for your organisation, when do you find salesmen particularly useful? Are there any circumstances when you find visits from salesmen a nuisance? Why is this?*

30.3   *How is your own organisation's sales force used? Is this the best possible use of the sales force? In what ways do activities of the sales force complement other forms of marketing communications used? Identify any other ways in which you feel the activities of the sales force could enhance the total marketing communications effort.*

30.4   *How is your sales force managed? Does this arrangement ensure that the sales force is effectively integrated into the marketing activities of the organisation? What problems tend to arise and how could they be overcome? What other management structures might be appropriate for your sales force?*

31   How should our sales force be led and organised?

Overview

Once the decision has been made that a sales force is needed, some basic issues must be resolved satisfactorily if the sales force is to operate efficiently. The first issue concerns the number of salesmen needed; the next, the overall management of the sales force; and the last, the quantitative and qualitative objectives of the salesman's job.

Analysing the salesman's workload involves assessing each element of his job, including the territory he covers. Once this is done, his work can be streamlined in terms of both territory and time. Participation by managers – such as accompanying the salesman on his calls – can further enhance the assessments made of the workload. Territory planning – both by the PIE system and the PETAL system – will help to structure the salesman's time.

The objectives of the salesman's job relate to what he sells, to whom he sells and the cost of his selling activities – as well as the qualitative aspects of how he performs on the job.

The ways in which salesmen are motivated can be described and, therefore, improved. Guidelines are given here for increasing sales force motivation by increasing incentives and decreasing disincentives.

How many salesmen do we need?

In Chapter 30 we discussed the strategic role of personal selling in the marketing mix. We now turn to the basic questions which the organisation must ask, and answer, about the management of its sales force.

– How many salesmen do we need?
– What do we want them to do?
– How should they be managed?

The organisation should begin its consideration of how many salesmen it needs by finding out exactly how work is allocated at the present time. Start by listing all the things the current sales force actually does. These might include opening new accounts; servicing existing accounts; demonstrating new products; taking repeat orders; and collecting debts. This listing should be followed by investigation of alternative ways of carrying out these responsibilities. For example, telephone selling has been shown to be a perfectly acceptable alternative to personal visits, particularly in respect of repeat business. The sales force can thus be freed for missionary work, which is not so susceptible to the telephone approach.

Can debts be collected by mail? Can products be demonstrated at exhibitions or showrooms? It is only by asking these kinds of questions that we can be certain that we have not fallen into the common trap of committing the company to a decision and then seeking data and reasons to justify the decision.

At this stage, the manager should concentrate on collecting relevant, quantified data and then use judgement and experience to help him come to a decision.

Basically, all sales force activities can be categorised under three headings. A salesman:

– talks to customers;
– travels;
– performs administrative functions.

These tasks constitute what can be called his *workload*. If we first decide what constitutes a reasonable workload for a salesman, in hours per month, then we can begin to measure how long his current activities take, hence the exact extent of his current workload.

Organising the sales force

In the selling of any product, there is likely to be a small number of customers who only need calling on with minimal frequency, possibly two to four times per year. The correct way to service them is to appoint a *territory* salesman, who looks after a certain number of counties or regions and on a regular journey can reach these particular customers.

There may well be a rationale for appointing *industry* specialists or *customer-type* specialists; for example, a key accounts manager may have the particular function of handling supermarket chain head offices. In a banking context, a senior corporate account officer would be appointed to call on companies in the aerospace industry, for example. Managers specialising in a particular industry type will become aware of the particular financing problems of those industries. In the aerospace industry there are problems associated with funding the purchase of airliners. Shipping is another industry of this type. A chemical company structures its sales force so that there is one group of salesmen with responsibility for visiting the transport industry, because of the large number of applications for those particular chemical products from motor car companies. Other specialists in the sales force have responsibility for the energy industry.

Sales versus marketing management

In Chapter 30, we considered sales force management as a neglected area of marketing management. It is also worth considering whether sales management and marketing management should be two quite distinct functions. The rationale for integrating them is that selling is a facet of the communications mix and should therefore, perhaps, be logically retained under the control of the marketing management. Against this is the automatic devaluing of the importance of selling.

If a company has decided that a sales force is the right way to promote its product, then the importance of the selling function should, perhaps, be recognised by having a senior manager or director specifically responsible for selling. In this way, the status of the sales force is upgraded. On the other hand, such a move institutionalises the commitment to a sales force, so that if, at a later date, circumstances change and the sales force needs to be disbanded, there is the problem of having to dismiss a director.

Who is responsible?

It is necessary to provide a career progression within the sales force, just as it is provided within marketing. This is particularly important, because very often one of the benefits of having a sales force lies in the personal relationships that are built up over a number of years between salesmen and customers. If a salesman has been successful in his job, he will have built up such relationships, and these should not be abandoned. However, the salesman should not be penalised by being committed to the same job level, in order to maintain his customer contacts. It should be recognised that because of his personal endeavours, he has been able to make and build these relationships, and therefore there should be an opportunity for him to be promoted within the sales organisation.

In banking, for example, an employee may have built up a good relationship with his customers with such success that he merits promotion; but his promotion takes him out of the job he has been doing and thus his customer contacts are lost. The employee taking over the job will have to begin again with the old customers, as well as with new ones.

It needs also to be recognised that different types of customers require different levels of competence. Small customers can often be serviced by a territory salesman but, as customers become more important, it may be necessary to use a key account manager, a senior account manager, or a sales manager, who will retain specific control for those major accounts. This means, effectively, moving away from a system of territory management to a system of account management, or moving from a system of territory selling to one of account selling.

How many salesmen?

Having decided how the sales force is to be structured, what customers are to be seen and how frequently, the next question to be considered is the one originally asked – how many people will be required in the sales force?

The common factor shared by salesmen is the number of their working hours, which is the starting point for a workload analysis. The amount of work per salesman is calculated by assessing the elements of the sales job, which typically include prospecting, travelling, waiting, selling and report-writing. If the number of actual and potential accounts to be visited and the frequency of visiting are already assessed, it is possible to calculate the number of salesmen needed. This can be done by using the following equation:

$$\frac{\text{Number of actual and potential customers} \times \text{Call frequency}}{\text{Average daily call rate} \times \text{Number of working days per year}}$$

$$= \text{Number of salesmen needed}$$

Training the sales force

Training is part of organising and motivating a sales force. Typically, training is seen as a separate function, but it is an integral function of sales force management, and constitutes a continuing need, despite the experience a sales force may already have. No salesman is so good that he will not receive benefit from some refresher training, and the best place to train is in the field. Formal classroom training has a part to play, but should not be seen as the end of the process. The trainer should take the ideas out of the classroom and demonstrate them by example.

Another function of management is to accompany salesmen, rather than to come in as the senior person in an organisation and therefore the one to take over a sales call. When the manager accompanies the salesman, he sees at first hand exactly how the salesman is handling the customer. Having observed this, he can make assessments based on the salesman's actual performance. Training can then be applied to rectify any bad habits which have been observed. Selling is a lonely occupation with very little feedback, so a sales force needs to be encouraged to accept participation by managers and to respond to constructive feedback following such participation.

Territory planning

Some managers resent the time spent by salesmen outside the call – driving between calls, waiting, and so on – because they employ the salesman for his customer contact skills. Territory planning helps to rationalise this time spent outside the call, so that it is used more efficiently. There are two basic ways of doing this: the *Pie System* and the *Petal System*.

Both the Pie System and the Petal System are designed to give the salesman a framework around which to structure his calls and time to allow him flexibility. This helps overcome the salesman's common response, which is to rush towards the customer who shouts the loudest or who has the biggest problem. The danger in this response is that the salesman ends up zigzagging all over his territory. Good management of time, as well as helping towards greater efficiency, will also contribute towards the salesman's need for a framework.

The Pie System   Two major causes of increased travel time are the retracing of routes to pick up previously abortive calls, and the making of detours to deal with urgent enquiries and complaints. Both these problems can be lessened by organising the week according to the territory to be covered.

The salesman's territory is divided into five segments, each one representing a day of the working week. It is assumed that the salesman lives near the centre of his territory and travels to and from his home each day. Each segment is then divided into a number of parts equivalent to the number of weeks in the journey cycle and containing one day's work. If the journey cycle – or call frequency – is every four weeks for all customers, then each segment is divided into four portions. By working to this system, the salesman will visit each segment of his territory each week.

In this way, a call missed on Wednesday of week 4 can be picked up by a short detour only seven days later on Thursday of week 1 without making a special journey or waiting four weeks until the next journey cycle visit. Equally, if an enquiry comes from any part of the territory, it can be handled within a week of its arrival.

The Petal System   Further time can be saved by logical organisation of each day's work. The Petal System minimises mileage covered by making the mid-point of the calls the midpoint of the journey. The petal-shaped route is derived by taking the shortest distance between each point of call, in contrast to the traditional routes: either driving out to the furthest point and working back, or working out to the furthest point and driving back home at the end of the day. Both these traditional routes will lead to longer travel time than the adoption of the Petal System route.

A workload analysis sometimes produces surprising results, as when the company's 'star' salesman is found to have a smaller workload than the one with the worst results, who may be having to work much longer hours to achieve his sales because of the nature of his territory.

There are, of course, other ways of measuring workloads. One major consumer goods company used its Work Study Department to measure sales force effectiveness. The results of this study are summarised in Table 6.

This table showed the company how a salesman's time was spent and approximately how much of his time was actually available for selling. One immediate action taken by the company was to initiate a training programme which enabled more time to be spent on selling as a result of better planning.

What do we want our salesmen to do?

Whatever the method used to organise the salesman's day, there is always comparatively little time available for selling. In these circumstances, it is vital that a company should know as precisely as possible what it wants its sales force to do. Sales force objectives can be either *quantitative* or *qualitative*.

Table 6   Breakdown of a salesman's total daily activity

		Per cent of day		Minutes per day	
	Drive to and from route	15.9		81	
Outside	Drive on route	16.1		83	
call	Walk	4.6		24	
time	Rest and breaks	6.3		32	
	Pre-call administration	1.4		7	
	Post-call administration	5.3		27	
			49.6		254
	Business talks	11.5		60	
	Sell	5.9		30	
Inside	Chat	3.4		17	
call	Receipts	1.2		6	
time	Miscellaneous	1.1		6	
	Drink	1.7		8	
	Waiting	7.1		36	
			31.9		163
Evening	Depot work	9.8		50	
work	Entering pinks	3.9		20	
	Pre-plan route	4.8		25	
			18.5		95
			100.0		8hrs 32 min

Quantitative objectives

Principal quantitative objectives are concerned with the following measures:

- how much to sell (the value of unit sales volume);
- what to sell (the mix of product lines to sell);
- where to sell (the markets and the individual customers that will take the company towards its marketing objectives);
- the desired profit contribution (where relevant and where the company is organised to compute this);

– selling costs (in compensation, expenses, supervision, and so on).

The first three types of objectives are derived directly from the marketing objectives.

There are, of course, many other kinds of quantitative objectives which can be set for the sales force, including tasks to do with point-of-sale literature, reports, trade meetings and customer complaints.

Salesmen may also be required to fulfil a coordinating role between a team of specialists and the client organisation. A company selling mining machinery, for example, employs a number of 'good general salesmen' who establish contacts and identify which contacts are likely to lead to sales. Before entering into negotiations with any client organisation, the company selling the machinery may feel that it needs to call in a team of highly specialised engineers and financial experts for consultation and advice. It is the task of the salesman in this company to identify when specialist help is needed and to coordinate the people who become involved in the negotiation. However, most objectives are subservient to the major objectives outlined above which are associated directly with what is sold and to whom.

Qualitative objectives

Qualitative objectives can be a potential source of problems if sales managers try to assess the performance of the sales force along dimensions which include abstract terms such as 'loyalty', 'enthusiasm', 'cooperation', and so on, since such terms are difficult to measure objectively. In seeking qualitative measurements of performance, managers often resort to highly subjective interpretations which cause resentment and frustration amongst those being assessed.

However, managers can set and measure qualitative objectives which actually relate to the performance of the sales force on the job. It is possible, for example, to assess the skill with which a person applies his product knowledge on the job, or the skill with which he plans his work, or the skill with which he overcomes objections during a sales interview. While still qualitative in nature, these measures relate to standards of performance understood and accepted by the sales force.

Given such standards, it is not too difficult for a competent field sales manager to identify deficiencies, to get agreement on them,

to coach in skills and techniques, to build attitudes of professionalism, to show how to self train, to determine which training
requirements cannot be tackled in the field, and to evaluate
improvements in performance and the effect of any past training.

One consumer goods company with thirty field sales managers
discovered that most of them were spending much of the day in
their offices engaged in administrative work, most of which was
self made. The company proceeded to take the offices away and
insisted that the sales managers spend most of their time in the
field, not necessarily training their salesmen, but accompanying
them, in addition to looking after major accounts themselves.
There was a dramatic increase in sales and, consequently, in
the sales managers' own earnings. This rapidly overcame their
resentment at losing their offices.

Such instances show that, because of the necessary administration surrounding a sales force, there is a danger of converting
sales managers into administrators, which is not, after all, the
company's objective. To administer a sales force properly there
should be a sales office and sales administrators.

How should we motivate our sales force?

Sales force motivation has received a great deal of attention in
recent times, largely as a result of the work done by psychologists
in other fields of management. There is now widespread appreciation of the fact that it is not sufficient merely to give someone a
title and an office and expect to get good results. Effective leadership, it is acknowledged, is as much 'follower-determined' as it
is determined by management. Whilst for the purposes of this
discussion it is not necessary to enter into a detailed discussion of
sales force motivation, it is worth mentioning briefly some
important factors contributing to effective sales force
management.

If a sales manager's job is to improve the performance of his
sales force, and if performance is a function of incentives minus
disincentives, then the more he can increase incentives and reduce
disincentives, the better will be performance.

Research has shown that an important element of sales force
motivation is a sense of doing a worthwhile job. In other words,
desire for praise and recognition, the avoidance of boredom and
monotony, the enhancement of self image, freedom from fear and

worry, and the desire to belong to something believed to be worthwhile, all contribute to enhanced performance. One well known piece of research carried out in the USA examined the reasons for the results of the twenty highest producing sales units in one company compared with the twenty lowest producing sales units. The research showed all the above factors to be major determinants of success.

However, remuneration will always be a most important determinant of motivation. This does not necessarily mean paying the most money, although clearly unless there are significant financial motivations within a company, it is unlikely that people will stay. In drawing up a remuneration plan, which would normally include a basic salary plus some element for special effort, such as bonus or commission, the following objectives should be considered:

– to attract and keep effective salesmen;
– to remain competitive;
– to reward salesmen in accordance with their individual performance;
– to provide a guaranteed income plus an orderly individual growth rate;
– to generate individual sales initiative;
– to encourage teamwork;
– to encourage the performance of essential non-selling tasks;
– to ensure that management can fairly administer and adjust compensation levels as a means of achieving sales objectives.

The theory of motivation that is most useful is known as the *path-goal approach*. We start from the position that each individual has a set of needs and of desired results; these range from fairly straightforward physiological needs – food, clothing and shelter – to more complex ones, such as friendship, belonging needs and the desire for achievement and recognition. The individual decides how much energy or effort to expend on any particular activity or set of activities on the basis of the following considerations:

– the strength of the need;
– the expectation that expending the effort will lead to a particular result;
– the potential of that result to satisfy the need.

For example, a man who has a strong need for power, if given a task to do and promised promotion at the end of it, will expend energy on that task to the degree of his belief that good performance will lead to promotion and that promotion will satisfy his needs for power.

Individuals are continually making calculations of this nature, although such calculations range from the instinctive and largely unconscious to the totally conscious and deliberate. However, the more information the individual has at his disposal, the more satisfactorily he can make the calculation. If the required results are clearly understood and believed to be attainable, then the individual is motivated to expend the effort. Obviously, if he is involved in deciding the desired results, he will be able to complete his personal calculation. In addition, the more feedback he receives on results, the more likely he is to remain motivated. This means, basically, that the effort put into a job is very firmly linked with the employee's personal expectations of what he will get out of the job, having once expended that input.

To summarise, the sales force is a vital but very expensive element of the marketing mix and as much care should be devoted to its motivation and management as to any other area of marketing management. This is most likely to be achieved if intuitive sense, which is associated with experience, can be combined with the kind of logical framework we have outlined here.

Application questions

31.1   *What are the key functions of salesmen in your organisation? How is their work coordinated?*

31.2   *How is the sales force deployed: by geographical territory; by product range; by type of customer? Is this deployment optimal? What other patterns of deployment should be considered by your organisation?*

31.3   *Who is responsible for the sales force in your organisation? What is the relationship between this post of responsibility and other marketing responsibilities in the organisation? Does this cause any problems? Where problems arise, how could they be solved?*

31.4   *How does your organisation ensure that the sales force receives adequate training? How are training needs assessed? Who is responsible for providing training for the sales force?*

31.5   *What objectives do you set for your salesmen? Are these quantitative or qualitative? How do you assess whether these objectives have been achieved? Is your assessment totally objective or is it coloured by some subjectivity?*

31.6   *What methods do you use to motivate your sales force? How significant is commission or other bonus payments in the total remuneration package? Are commission and/or bonus payments an appropriate method of remunerating your salesmen? Do you feel there are other methods by which your sales force could and should be motivated?*

Overview

*This chapter looks at some techniques which can help to ensure
that sales targets are met. A simple reporting system will encourage
the salesman to structure his working day well.*

*Targets must be both realistic and flexible, or they can act as
demotivators. Participation by the salesman in negotiating an
acceptable target will help to enlist his commitment. Once set,
targets must be monitored – preferably monthly, or even weekly.*

*Tracking sales results can be done simply, by using a moving
annual total (MAT) or in a more detailed way, by using a Z chart.*

*If progress towards sales targets is going off track, the use of
discounts and promotions may help to remedy the decline. Both
methods, however, have the in-built disadvantages which come with
using short-term measures.*

Reporting systems

In previous chapters, we considered how to lead and organise a
sales force and how to estimate how much product we can sell.
We have seen that forecasts must remain flexible; otherwise they
become straitjackets which inhibit the organisation's activities.
Nevertheless, it is important to ensure, as much as is possible,
that our sales forecasts are converted into practicable targets for
our sales force. In this chapter we shall look at some of the
techniques which can enable us to reach our targets.

The most important factor about the reporting system used is
that it should be simple. Far too frequently, salesmen are just let
loose and, as long as they bring in business, nobody bothers
unduly about what they are doing. This attitude makes little business sense. It is important that salesmen report not only what
orders they have received, but also what calls they have made

and how they have spent their time. If a salesman knows that he must submit a daily report, he is more likely to structure his working day sensibly and efficiently.

Converting sales forecasts into targets

It is basic to the success of a sales target that the target is itself realistic. If the target is set at an unrealistic level, one result will be lack of commitment from the salesman expected to fulfil it. An unrealistic target can even be a positive demotivator. In converting the sales forecast into individual targets for the salesman, there should be an element of participation by the salesman, in order for him to develop a commitment to achieving the target. This does not mean asking him to set his own targets; but it does mean not imposing a figure on him. The most successful method is to go through a process of iteration with the salesman in order to *negotiate* an acceptable target.

Having agreed a target, it must then be *monitored*. There is no point, having once set a target, in sitting back for eleven months only to wonder, in the twelfth month, why the sales target figure shows no sign of being met. There is a tendency in some companies to argue that there is little point in monitoring targets too closely, because of the necessary administrative burden created by doing so. Such companies may, therefore, settle for quarterly monitoring. However, quarterly monitoring can produce the following, fairly typical, scenario.

A company is dealing with a product where there is no seasonality; the product has a steady rate of offtake throughout the year. The sales target set is 120 units for the year. Therefore, the reasonable expectation is that 30 units are achieved per quarter. In the event, the sales for the first quarter reach only 25. That may not seem too dreadful to management, who may decide to wait and see what the position is at the end of the second quarter. By July, it emerges that only 15 units have been sold in the second quarter, so the sales achievement is already one third down on the target. That in itself is bad news, but what is even worse is that the target for the second half of the year is now the original of 60 with a further 20 added. This may not appear enormous, but that is only so if the new need is compared to the old one. The reality is that 80 units must be sold in the coming six months, where the actual achievement of the first six months is only 40. This means that the sales force must achieve twice as much as it did in the first half of the year. Furthermore, only five months of the year are left in which something can be done to motivate the sales force.

Such a picture shows that as soon as targets begin to be missed, it is time to put more effort and energy into selling. This means having a very simple system of *management by exception*. As soon as progress towards a target goes off line, extra attention is provided. Rather than reviewing targets on a quarterly basis, it is best to look at them monthly, or even weekly. Similarly, if an individual goes off target, his performance should be monitored regularly and frequently.

Tracking sales results

We have just considered quarterly reviewing of a non-seasonal product. If we turn to seasonal products, we find a new set of problems. If a sales peak is expected during the summer months, how can a company know how well it is doing in the winter months, when traditionally there is a low level of sales?

One method of analysing this problem is to use a moving annual total (MAT), which is a summation of the previous twelve months' figures. To find the MAT for the end of a current January, for example, management can simply subtract the figure for the old January and add the figure for the new January. In this way, the total for the previous twelve months is always accessible. Given that seasonality is normally associated with a twelve-month cycle, the use of the MAT will eliminate the peaks and troughs of seasons. As long as the line moves up, then sales are progressing. This is a simple method of ˙assessing whether this year's bad January is worse than last year's bad January.

Another tracking method, giving more detailed information, is a Z chart (see Figure 43). This combines the MAT with an aggregate and with an individual monthly total and enables three comparisons to be made on a single diagram: monthly performance against target, cumulative performance against target and, via the MAT, the present year compared with the previous year.

The Z Chart

	Previous year	This year budget			This year actual		
	Actual	Month	Cum	Mat	Month	Cum	Mat
Jan	3	3	3	108	3	3	108
Feb	4	5	8	109	4	7	108
Mar	3	4	12	110	4	11	109
Apr	6	7	19	111	6	17	109
May	8	8	27	111	9	26	110
Jun	15	16	43	112	13	39	108
Jul	17	19	62	114			
Aug	20	22	84	116			
Sep	15	16	100	117			
Oct	10	10	110	117			
Nov	5	7	117	119			
Dec	2	3	120	120			
Total	108	120					

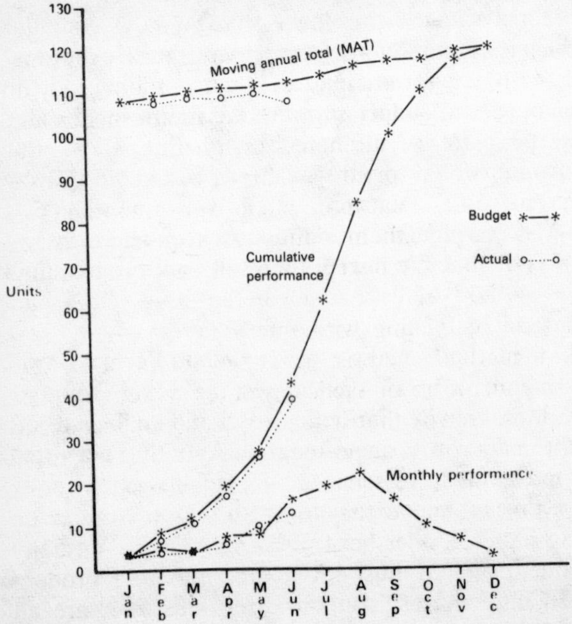

Figure 43

Using discounts and promotions

There are two methods of dealing with the situation where sales targets are not being met. One is to provide, very rapidly, a *discount* to existing customers. This can be effected with a quick communication to the sales force, offering an additional 5 per cent discount, for example, to customers. The problem with offering a discount is the danger of bringing forward the next month's sales, especially if the discount is particularly attractive.

In an industry where sales take place through a variety of stages – for example, selling to a manufacturer, who sells to a wholesaler, who sells to a retailer, who sells to a consumer – there is no guarantee that the discount will be passed down the chain of sales. It may, for instance, be taken by the wholesaler as additional profit. If the discount is given to a retailer, there is no guarantee that it will be passed on to the consumer, so that all that may happen is filling the distribution pipeline. Similarly, in the area of industrial consumables – such products as nuts and bolts, or office stationery – the giving of discounts may not increase the use of the product; what may happen instead is merely pushing more of the product down the line.

Discounts are very often only a short-term expedient for bringing sales back up to the level anticipated. Fundamentally, they do not increase the use of the product unless there is some mechanism for affecting the price at the ultimate consumer interface. For example, 2p discount off the price of a tin of baked beans may encourage people to buy and eat more baked beans. However, it may, conversely, encourage them simply to store more baked beans, with the result that the next six months' sales potential is threatened.

The other method of dealing with the situation where sales targets are not being achieved is *sales promotion*. Like the discount, this is a short-term or tactical marketing activity. The essence of sales promotion is that it features an offer to defined customers or consumers within a specific time limit. To be termed a sales promotion, as we have seen earlier in the text, an offer must be made over and above the normal terms of trade, the objective being to increase sales beyond what would be normally expected. The benefit offered must not be inherent in the product or service itself. Competitions, coupons, free gifts, etc. are all familiar devices in this area.

Sales promotions will probably form part of the original strategy for selling a product, but additional gimmicks can be thrown in at the last minute if sales targets are being missed. A specialist book publisher, for example, uses devices every year as an integral part of its marketing plan, but the publisher also uses them as a gimmick. If renewals are down, then it will send in extra support; instead of sending out one renewal reminder, or five, it will send out perhaps ten, and will offer a free book if a renewal is taken out by the end of the month.

The problem with promotional devices, as we saw in Chapter 22, is that they are all too often introduced at the last minute as a panic measure, without due consideration of the long-term effects.

Analysis of sales

Up to this point we have been discussing the overall sales performance. However, if the organisation has a complex product range, although the total sales might look all right, the picture may change when the performance of each is considered separately.

For example, the organisation may have budgeted to sell 100 items of one product and 100 items of another; it may then discover that it has sold 150 of the first and only 10 of the second. It is essential that information of this kind is fed back to the salesmen, so they then can ensure that all individual sales targets are met.

Application questions

32.1   *How do you set sales targets for the members of your sales force? Are the salesmen always aware of the targets set for them? Do they participate in the target setting process?*

32.2   *Looking back over the last three years, how close to the target have actual sales been? How were those targets set? How frequently was performance reviewed against those targets? In retrospect, would it have been desirable and possible to set more realistic targets? Would it have been desirable to review performance more frequently?*

32.3   *In situations where performance has been out of line with the targets set for the sales force, what steps have you been able to take to remedy the situation? Have the actions taken by you been essentially of a short-term nature? What long-term effect have they had on the organisation's sales performance?*

Robert G. Maxwell
Marketing £2.95
a fresh approach

This book pinpoints the role and application of marketing in commerce,
explaining and illustrating all key aspects for business readers and for use
by students on professional training syllabuses – BEC National and Higher
level marketing courses, Institute of Marketing Certificate of Marketing,
Communication Advertising and Marketing Education Foundation, and
foundation courses in Overseas Trade – Marketing.

A Pan Breakthrough book, published in collaboration with the National
Extension College. NEC FlexiStudy recommended text.

John Fenton
How to Double your Profits Within the Year £2.50

A programme of improvements, applicable to all types of business, to help
you at least double your profits within twelve months. Fictional but highly
practical, the book is an extended memorandum, an action plan, written by
the MD of an imaginary company to his top managers. It shows, for example,
how you can choose which customers contribute most to your profitability;
recruit the right people; improve production efficiency; price for maximum
profit; control your sales force. In the few hours it takes to read the book,
you will be convinced that the title's claim is a modest understatement.

The A-Z of Sales Management £2.50

A book for the sales manager determined to succeed. This humorous yet
highly practical book covers the ins and outs of managing a sales force
from Advertising to Zest, taking in all the vital aspects: credit control,
meetings and conferences, decision-making, sales forecasting,
remuneration schemes, job specifications, motivation, planning and control,
leadership, expense accounts and – last but not least – how to achieve
consistently good sales results.

John Winkler
Bargaining for Results £2.50

Skilful bargaining is crucial to business success, especially when money is tight. John Winkler, one of Britain's leading marketing experts, presents the key to effective negotiation – the methods to adopt and when to employ them. The approach is highly practical, using case histories, illustrations and helpful maxims in a book specially designed for business managers.

John Adair
Effective Leadership £2.50
a modern guide to developing leadership skills

The art of leadership demands a keen ability to appraise, understand and inspire both colleagues and subordinates. In this unique guide, John Adair, Britain's foremost expert on leadership training, shows how every manager can learn to lead. He draws upon numerous illustrations of leadership in action – commercial, historical and military – to pinpoint the essential requirements.

Graham Mott
Investment Appraisal for Managers £1.95
a guide to profit planning for all managers

Every responsible manager wants a say in how his company uses its resources. This text provides non-accountants with sufficient financial knowledge to evaluate profit opportunities and contribute effectively when investment decisions are made. The clear and uncomplicated treatment is also geared to the requirements of students on the relevant professional courses. The author identifies the main assessment techniques, and looks in detail at yearly cash flows, taxation and effects of inflation, with examples and case studies.

Rosemary Stewart
The Reality of Management £1.95

'Not just another manual for executives, it is rather more like a set of compass bearings to help the manager plot his course in his career and his social life'
NEW SOCIETY

The Reality of Organizations £1.95

'Addressed to managers whether in industry, commerce, hospitals, public administration or elsewhere and includes examples from these latter fields . . . its style is excellent, concise and free of jargon'
PUBLIC ADMINISTRATION

Terry Rowan
Managing with Computers £2.95

A book to dispel the myth that computers are special and that they deserve special treatment. *Managing with Computers* helps managers recognize the powerful capabilities of computers and how they can be usefully exploited; what systems are available and the tasks they can perform; how managers can select the source of computing power most suitable for their needs; the essential steps in implementing and developing a computer system; and how a business may need to adapt itself to the presence of a computer. An invaluable guide to an indispensable management skill.

Peter Drucker
Managing in Turbulent Times £1.95

This is Peter Drucker's latest and probably most searching analysis of the
problems and opportunities facing us as managers and individuals. This timely
and important book considers how to manage the fundamentals of business
– inflation, liquidity, productivity and profit – going on to demonstrate how
tomorrow's manager must concentrate his skills on managing innovation and
change – production sharing, new markets, redundancy planning, the
developing countries, transforming businesses to take account of changes in
the world economy.

Management £3.95

Peter Drucker's aim in this major book is 'to prepare today's and tomorrow's
managers for performance'. He presents his philosophy of management,
refined as a craft with specific skills: decision making, communication, control
and measurement, analysis – skills essential for effective and responsible
management in the late twentieth century.

'Crisp, often arresting . . . A host of stories and case histories from Sears
Roebuck, Marks and Spencer, IBM, Siemens, Mitsubishi and other modern
giants lend colour and credibility to the points he makes' ECONOMIST

The Effective Executive £1.95

'A specific and practical book about how to be an executive who *contributes*
. . . The purpose of this book is to induce the executive to concentrate on his
own contribution and performance, with his attention directed to improving
the organization by serving outsiders better. I believe Mr Drucker achieves
this purpose simply and brilliantly – and in the course of doing so offers many
insights into executive work and suggestions for improving executive
performance. I can conscientiously recommend that this book be given the
very highest priority for executive reading and even rereading' THE DIRECTOR

Chris Brewster
Understanding Industrial Relations £2.95

Emphasizes the importance of management's role before explaining the
involvement of unions and the state. The legal framework is shown in detail
and later chapters examine industrial relations in practice, at the workplace
and during negotiations. Ideal for use on Institute of Industrial Management,
Institute of Personnel Management and NEBSS courses and for practising
managers.

A Pan Breakthrough book, published in collaboration with the National
Extension College.

Rita Harris
Understanding Office Practice £2.95

Explains and illustrates the structure and working methods of the modern
office, covering all the traditional skills and devoting close attention to the
impact of new technology. The book caters for many syllabuses and training
courses: BEC General level World of Work, Office Machines and Equipment,
Clerical Services; MSC Youth Training Schemes; SCOTBEC, RSA and LCCI
Office Practice.

A Pan Breakthrough book, published in collaboration with the National
Extension College.

Geoffrey Knott
Practical Cost and Management Accounting £2.95

The principles of costing in business are explained, showing how to assess
and apply information provided by management accountants. Coverage is
geared to relevant parts of many courses: BEC National and Higher National,
BEC Post Experience Certificates, Diploma in Management Studies, Institute
of Chartered Accountants, Institute of Cost and Management Accountants,
Association of Certified Accountants, etc.

A Pan Breakthrough book, published in collaboration with the National
Extension College. NEC FlexiStudy recommended text.

Michael Herbert
Practical Accounts 1 £2.95

Covers the book-keeping elements of all major business and professional syllabuses, complements and should be used in conjunction with *Practical Accounts 2*. To encompass the following courses: GCE O level Principles of Accounts, B/TEC National level Accounting 2, RSA Book-keeping I and II, LCCI Book-keeping, Institute of Bankers I and II, Association of Certified Accountants 1, Institute of Cost and Management Accounts Foundation A, Institute of Chartered Secretaries 2.

A Pan Breakthrough book, published in collaboration with the National Extension College.

George Bright
Practical Accounts 2 £2.95

Explains the key principles of financial and cost/management accounting, with coverage which complements that of *Practical Accounts 1*. Especially relevant to GCE O level Principles of Accounts, BEC National level Accounting 2, RSA Book-keeping stages I and II, LCCL Elementary and Intermediate Book-keeping, Institute of Bankers, Institute of Cost and Management Accountants, Institute of Chartered Secretaries and Association of Certified Accountants courses.

A Pan Breakthrough book, published in collaboration with the National Extension College.

David Floyd
Making Numbers Work £2.95
an introduction to business numeracy

A book to introduce the basic skills of business numeracy and explain how to apply them. An ideal text for the BEC General Module on Business Calculations, it also meets requirements of BEC National Module on Numeracy and Accounting, RSA Arithmetic Stages I, II and III and relevant parts of RSA Stage I Mathematics.

A Pan Breakthrough book, published in collaboration with the National Extension College.

Peter Clark
Using Statistics in Business 1 £2.95

Volume 1 shows how to acquire, judge and apply statistical information.
Especially suitable for statistics courses at BEC National level in Numeracy
and Accounting, RSA Stage II and LCCI Intermediate, it will also serve
students of professional syllabuses: Institute of Chartered Accountants,
Institute of Cost and Management Accountants, Institute of Chartered
Secretaries, and Association of Certified Accountants.

A Pan Breakthrough book, published in collaboration with the National
Extension College.

Using Statistics in Business 2 £2.95

Volume 2 shows how to present and draw conclusions from statistical
information. It develops the ideas explained in volume 1, and is especially
suitable for statistics courses at BEC National level in Numeracy and
Accounting, RSA Stage II and LCCI Intermediate. It will also serve students of
professional syllabuses: Institute of Marketing, Institute of Personnel
Management, Institute of Chartered Accountants, Institute of Cost and
Management Accountants, Institute of Chartered Secretaries and Association
of Certified Accountants.

A Pan Breakthrough book, published in collaboration with the National
Extension College.

Terry Price
Practical Business Law £2.95

Pinpoints and explains the key areas of law which govern commercial life. The
book is designed for use over a wide range of syllabuses: BEC General level
Law and the Individual, BEC National level Organization in its Environment,
RSA Stages II and III Commercial Law, LCCI Commercial Law syllabus higher
stage, AEB O and A level Law, Oxford Local Examinations Board O and A
level Law.

A Pan Breakthrough book, published in collaboration with the National
Extension College.

Roger Carter
The Business of Data Processing £2.95

A comprehensive guide for managers, small businesses and students. It explains data processing systems and computer applications, with exercises for practical illustration. The book covers syllabus requirements of BEC National level Data Processing, BTEC Computer Studies, SCOTBEC Computer Studies, RSA Computers in Data Processing, LCCI Business Computing, also the data processing elements of the Institute of Cost and Management Accountants, Association of Certified Accountants and Institute of Administrative Management courses.

A Pan Breakthrough book, published in collaboration with the National Extension College.

W. J. Brown
Practical Company Law £2.95

A complete guide to the modern law, incorporating key statutory provisions and leading cases. Ideal for use as a reference handbook by company secretaries, businesses and financial advisers, the book is geared to the major college and professional courses: Institute of Chartered Secretaries and Administrators, Institute of Chartered Accountants, Association of Certified Accountants, Institute of Cost and Management Accountants, Association of Accounting Technicians.

A Pan Breakthrough book, published in collaboration with the National Extension College.

Roger Oldcorn
Management £3.50
A fresh approach

A fresh introduction to the role of the modern manager. Coverage is geared to various syllabus requirements including the CNAA Diploma in Management Studies and those of the Institute of Industrial Management, Institute of Personnel Management, Institute of Purchasing and Supply and BEC Certificate in Management Studies courses.

A Pan Breakthrough book, published in collaboration with the National Extension College.

Nicki Stanton
What Do You Mean, 'Communication'? £2.95
An introduction to communication in business

Describes the scope, skills and techniques of business communication.
Coverage is geared especially to communications courses at BEC National
and Higher levels whilst serving various other syllabus requirements: RSA
Stage II, LCCI Intermediate, City & Guilds Communication Skills, and
foundation courses for professional examinations.

A Pan Breakthrough book, published in collaboration with the National
Extension College.

The Business of Communicating £2.95
Improving your communicating skills

Advice on the key elements of communication: writing letters, using the
phone, interviewing, speaking in public. This book develops the principles
explained in *What Do You Mean, 'Communication'?*. Coverage is geared to
communication courses at BEC National and Higher levels whilst serving
various other syllabus requirements: RSA Stage II, LCCI Intermediate, City &
Guilds Communication Skills, foundation courses for professional
examinations.

A Pan Breakthrough book, published in collaboration with the National
Extension College.

All these books are available at your local bookshop or newsagent, or
can be ordered direct from the publisher. Indicate the number of copies
required and fill in the form below   12

....

Name _____
(Block letters please)

Address _____

_____

Send to CS Department, Pan Books Ltd, PO Box 40, Basingstoke, Hants
Please enclose remittance to the value of the cover price plus:
35p for the first book plus 15p per copy for each additional book ordered
to a maximum charge of £1.25 to cover postage and packing
Applicable only in the UK

While every effort is made to keep prices low, it is sometimes
necessary to increase prices at short notice. Pan Books reserve
the right to show on covers and charge new retail prices which
may differ from those advertised in the text or elsewhere